|酒店及旅游业管理系列教材|

主编 邱汉琴

Hospitality and Tourism in Chinese Mainland

中国内地酒店及旅游业

邱汉琴（Hanqin Qiu） 任连萍（Lianping Ren）/著

ZHEJIANG UNIVERSITY PRESS

浙江大学出版社

图书在版编目(CIP)数据

中国内地酒店及旅游业＝Hospitality and Tourism
in Chinese Mainland：英汉对照/ 邱汉琴，任连萍著.—
杭州：浙江大学出版社，2019.6
ISBN 978-7-308-19274-3

Ⅰ.①中… Ⅱ.①邱…②任… Ⅲ.①饭店业—经济
发展—研究—中国—英文②旅游业发展—研究—中国—英
文 Ⅳ.①F719.3②F592.3

中国版本图书馆 CIP 数据核字（2019）第 129672 号

中国内地酒店及旅游业

Hospitality and Tourism in Chinese Mainland

邱汉琴（Hanqin Qiu）　　任连萍（Lianping Ren）　　著

责任编辑	樊晓燕	
责任校对	袁菁鸿	
封面设计	春天书装	
出版发行	浙江大学出版社	
	（杭州市天目山路 148 号　邮政编码 310007）	
	（网址：http://www.zjupress.com）	
排　　版	杭州林智广告有限公司	
印　　刷	杭州杭新印务有限公司	
开　　本	787mm×1092mm　1/16	
印　　张	13.5	
字　　数	352 千	
版 印 次	2019 年 6 月第 1 版　2019 年 6 月第 1 次印刷	
书　　号	ISBN 978-7-308-19274-3	
定　　价	52.00 元	

总 序

香港理工大学酒店及旅游业管理学院已经有 40 多年的历史。学院致力于引领全球酒店及旅游教育的发展，无论在科研还是教学等方面，都在全球享有较高知名度，尤其是在发表学术研究文献方面，在全球位列第二，在教与学方面，亦处于国际领先地位。学院 65 位教职人员来自 22 个国家和地区，着重教学创新与研究。学员能够在多元文化环境下追随国际知名的学者学习有着良好职业前景的学科。2011 年，香港理工大学的教学及研究酒店——唯港荟正式启用，强化了学院的人才培育工作，以满足香港地区内以至全球酒店及旅游业界对专业人才的殷切需求。

"酒店及旅游业管理硕士学位课程"是引进了国内外最前沿的教育理念，为从事旅游业研究与实践的业界人士而开设的学历教育课程。该课程自 2000 年与浙江大学合办以来，依托世界一流的香港理工大学和浙江大学的教学资源，已经培养了 600 多位政府各级官员、业界管理人才以及学术界科研精英。课程通过综合的、先进的知识为学生提供了宏观的视野，让学生在具有扎实的工作经验的基础上，提高经营管理的深度，建立超前的意识，发展系统地解决问题的能力。

虽然香港理工大学酒店及旅游业管理学院的酒店及旅游业管理硕士学位课程取得了一定的成功，为业界培养了优秀人才，但是在办学的过程中，我们深刻地意识到教材资源的缺乏。因此，香港理工大学具有优秀双语能力的教授等师资人员专门为"酒店及旅游业管理硕士学位课程"设计

Prelude

With more than 40 years' history, the School of Hotel and Tourism Management (SHTM) at The Hong Kong Polytechnic University (PolyU) is positioned to lead the world's hospitality and tourism education in the years to come. It has high reputation in both academic research and teaching. Especially, the School is ranked No. 2 in the world among academic institutions in hospitality and tourism based on research and scholarly activities. In terms of teaching and learning, it is also in a leading position. With a faculty of 65 academic staff members from 22 countries and regions, the School offers innovative teaching and research in a creative learning environment. Students are able to study in a multicultural context and to learn from an internationally renowned faculty whose programmes provide outstanding career opportunities. The official opening of the teaching and research hotel—Hotel ICON in 2011 has further strengthened the School's efforts in nurturing hospitality graduates to address the growing demands of the hospitality and tourism industry in Hong Kong, the region, and around the world.

The MSc in Hotel and Tourism Management is a programme designed for hotel and tourism practitioners, with the aim of introducing latest education concept in Hong Kong and internationally. Since 2000, the programme has been offered collaboratively by the Hong Kong Polytechnic University and Zhejiang University, which has cultivated more than 600 government officials, industry managers, and academic talents. The programme provides students with a macro perspective from the comprehensive and advanced knowledge, improves the ability of management, and establishes advanced awareness, as well as develops systematic problem-solving skills based on solid work experience.

了一套中英文对照双语教材——"酒店及旅游业管理系列教材"。本系列教材包括《中国内地酒店及旅游业》《酒店及旅游业人力资源管理》《酒店及旅游业财务管理》《酒店及旅游业研究方法》以及《酒店及旅游业市场营销》。这种双语式的硕士学位课程教材在酒店及旅游业管理专业的研究生教育历史上是具有开创性的，充分体现了我们开办该课程的特色与进一步构建更好的教学交流平台的愿望。该系列教材的开发和推出，将有力地促进香港理工大学与浙江大学的双语课程的持续发展。同时，我们也期待该系列教材可以有助于中国内地日益成熟的旅游管理学硕士（MTA）市场的发展。中国的各行各业已逐渐趋向于国际化，旅游教育更是如此，我们希望这套双语教材的问世将会对内地的旅游教育起到促进作用。

最后，作者要特别感谢舒小佩慈善基金的全力资助，该基金的慷慨资助使得本系列教材得以面世。舒小佩女士寄语并祝福每位读者都能在书中找到自己的"黄金屋"，并为响应国家的"一带一路"倡议做出最好的准备。

丛书总编

邱汉琴教授

香港理工大学酒店及旅游业管理学院

Although the programme of MSc in Hotel and Tourism Management offered by SHTM-PolyU has been highly successful and has cultivated many talents for the industry, we are fully aware of the lack of bilingual teaching and learning resources during the process of delivering these courses. Therefore, professors, who have excellent bilingual competencies from The Hong Kong Polytechnic University, have designed and developed this bilingual book series for this programme, including *Hospitality and Tourism in Chinese Mainland*, *Hospitality and Tourism Human Resource Management*, *Hospitality and Tourism Financial Management*, *Hospitality and Tourism Research Methods*, and *Hospitality and Tourism Marketing Management*. The uniqueness of this bilingual book series is that it is the first time that such book series were created for a bilingual master degree in hotel and tourism education history, which fully represents the characteristics of this programme and also acts as an interaction platform for students and teachers to interact in order to enhance the teaching and learning experiences. The development and introduction of the bilingual book series is not only to promote the sustainable development of bilingual programme offered by The Hong Kong Polytechnic University and Zhejiang University, but also to look forward to facilitating the development of the increasingly mature market of Master of Tourism Administration (MTA) in Chinese Mainland. Nowadays, various industries in China have been gradually internationalized and we hope that the introduction of the bilingual book series will play a significant role in enhancing tourism education in the Mainland.

Last but not least, the authors wish to express their sincere gratitude to the Katie Shu Sui Pui Charitable Trust for its financial support in making the project of publishing of the Bilingual Hotel and Tourism Management Book Series a reality. They also hereby acknowledge Ms. Shu's wish for each reader to find his/her own dream career by making the best use of the material in the book series in preparation for China's "Belt and Road" Initiative as a result.

Managing Editor

Hanqin Qiu

Professor

School of Hotel and Tourism Management

The Hong Kong Polytechnic University

目 录

Part Ⅲ　Hotel Development in Chinese Mainland—Past and Present

Part Ⅳ　International Hotels

第五篇　经济型酒店

Part V   Budget Hotels

中国内地入境旅游
Inbound Tourism to Chinese Mainland

第1章　中国内地入境旅游概况

 学习目标

- 了解中国内地入境旅游市场的特征
- 了解中国内地入境旅游市场的结构
- 能够比较不同区域客源地的特点

1.1　概　述

在政府的政策引导和经济发展的带动下,中国在短短 40 年间便已经成为世界上主要的旅游出入境国家(联合国世界旅游组织(UNWTO),2015)。尽管中国的改革开放政策直到 1978 年才由邓小平提出,但中华人民共和国成立伊始,政府便决心发展旅游业。然而在中华人民共和国成立初期,国家满目疮痍,百废待兴,政府不得不将工作重心放在基本的经济和社会问题上。在过去的几十年里,尽管一些政治家对旅游业持有怀疑态度,但现在旅游业已被政府确认为经济发展的支柱产业之一。本章概述了这一演变的历史进程,并阐释了旅游业如何完成了从"旅游为政治服务"到"旅游服务经济"的角色转变。近 40 年来,中国内地入境旅游市场已从最初的小规模逐渐发展成为全球主要的入境旅游目的地国家(见图 1-1)。从发展初期以接待国际友人作为建立外交关系的一种方式开始,旅游业现已成为经济发展的重要组成部分,为国内生产总值(GDP)的提高做出了贡献(见图 1-2)。这一章旨在阐述中国内地旅游业从一个阶段发展到另一个阶段的过程中所产生的主要变化。

Chapter 1　Overall Inbound Tourism to Chinese Mainland

 Learning Outcomes

- Understanding the features of the inbound market of Chinese Mainland
- Having a clear map of the structure of the inbound market of Chinese Mainland
- Comparing the features of the source markets in different regions

1.1　Introduction

China is now recognized as being the main tourist generating and receiving country in the world (The World Tourism Organization (UNWTO), 2015). It has reached this pinnacle as the result of government foresight, policies and plans in a relatively short period of approximately 40 years. Although China's reform and opening up policy was not proposed by Deng Xiaoping until 1978, there is evidence of earlier government initiatives to develop the tourism industry before this date. The dire state of the economy at the founding of the Republic in 1949 required the nascent government to address fundamental economic and social problems. Over the years, despite some political skepticism towards both the concept and understanding of tourism, it is now recognized as being one of the pillar industries in the economy. This chapter outlines the historical stages of this evolution and considers how moving from the initial stage of "tourism serving politics" to the current position where "tourism serves the economy". For the past almost 40 years, the inbound tourism of Chinese Mainland has gradually grown from a very small volume to what is today as the leading country in inbound tourism (see Figure 1 – 1). Started with a small scale of receiving tourists as a way for foreign relationship building, it has grown to a scale where the modern economy is partially depending on it as reflected by tourism's contribution to the national GDP (see Figure 1 – 2). The chapter will seek to explain the transition from one phase to another.

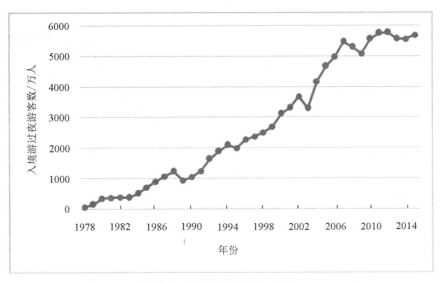

图 1-1　中国内地入境游过夜游客数量（1978—2014）

（资料来源：国家旅游局，2016）

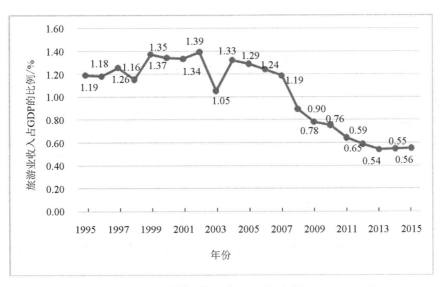

图 1-2　中国内地旅游业收入占 GDP 的比例（1995—2015）

（资料来源：国家旅游局，2016）

1.2　中国内地入境旅游发展的五个主要阶段

自 1978 年改革开放以来，中国内地旅游业的发展经历了五个阶段。每个阶段都有其独特的社会、政治和经济发展背景及发展过程。

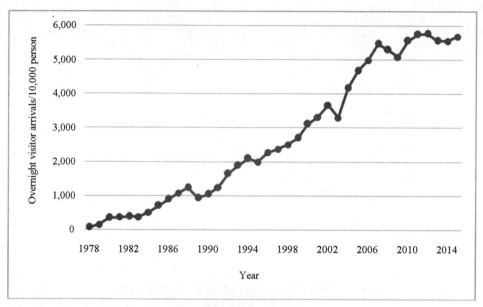

Figure 1 - 1　Tourist arrivals in Chinese Mainland by overnight stay（1978—2014）

（Data source：China National Tourism Administration，2016）

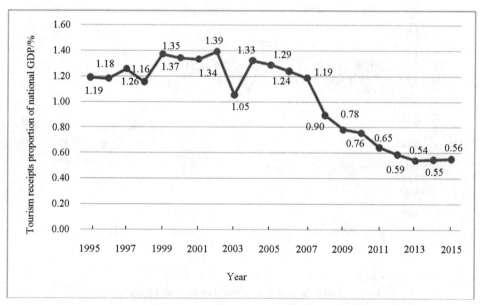

Figure 1 - 2　Tourism receipts proportion of national GDP（1995—2015）

（Data source：China National Tourism Administration，2016）

1.2　Five Major Phases of Chinese Mainland Inbound Tourism Development

Since the reform and opening up in 1978，China's tourism industry has experienced five stages of development which will be discussed one by one. Each stage has its unique social，political，and economic development background and its development process.

第一阶段(1978—1985 年)的发展是在邓小平鼓励发展入境旅游的推动下开启的。在这一时期,入境旅游经历了前所未有的快速发展。由于这个古老而又神秘的东方国度长期与世隔绝,大批境外旅游者借此机会前来游览(见图 1-3)。然而,由于基础设施、相关服务设施和符合条件的服务人员严重短缺,中国内地当时无法接待如此多的国际游客,因此限制了来旅游的国际游客数量。或许是出于建立和强化与某些国家的关系的需要,中国在这一早期阶段有选择性地向外国游客开放,这些游客往往来自支持新中国的那些国家。总体来说中国内地的旅游业在这一阶段发展的方式就是尝试从错误中学习,积累经验。当国内国际环境安全时,就加大开放的力度;当不确定性因素增强时,就收紧开放的程度。中国内地在这一阶段从未尝试向更多的国家和地区开放入境旅游,对于许多潜在的外国游客来说中国内地仍然是隔在"竹帘"后不可企及的神秘国度。

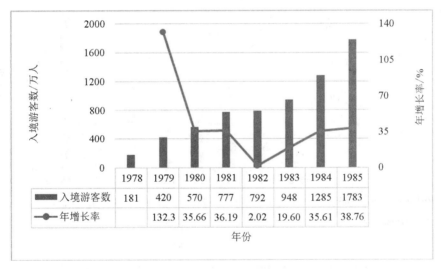

图 1-3　第一阶段(1978—1985 年)入境游客数量及年增长率
(资料来源:国家旅游局,2016)

在第二阶段(1986—1991 年),旅游被列入了社会及经济发展的国家计划之内。《国家旅游发展规划 1986—2000》的目标是通过提高服务质量及发展旅游基础设施,使中国跻身国际旅游接待国的前列。经过不懈努力,当中国内地旅游业的服务质量及基础设施大幅改进后,入境游进入了快速发展的时期。然而,1989 年的政治风波阻碍了旅游业的发展,使得入境游客数量较前一年锐减 22.70%。直至 1991 年,入境游客数量才恢复到 1989 年前的水平(见图 1-4)。

The first phase (1978—1985) of international tourism development was initiated and encouraged by Mr. Deng Xiaoping, started with a small base, but developed rapidly. Attracted by this mysterious oriental country which had been closed to the outside world for a long period, there was a sudden influx of visitors from abroad (see Figure 1 – 3). However, the serious shortage of necessary infrastructure, service facilities and capable personnel meant that Chinese Mainland was unable to properly deal with so many visitors, so limits on intended visitor numbers were imposed. In this early stage of opening the country to selected foreign visitors was perhaps indicative of the need to establish and reinforce links with countries supportive of the new Republic. The overall approach adopted was one of trial and error when it is safe to open whereas it can be less open when uncertainty was experienced. No attempt was made to establish a broader visitor base and for many potential visitors Chinese Mainland remained inaccessible behind a "bamboo" curtain.

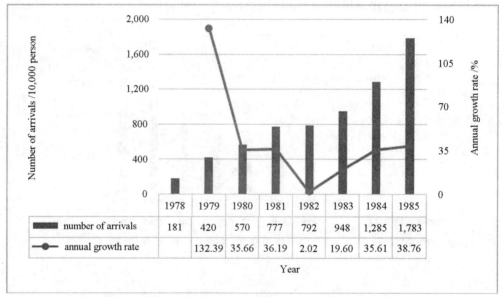

Figure 1 – 3   Phase 1 (1978—1985): Number of arrivals and growth rate
(Data source: China National Tourism Administration, 2016)

In the second phase (1986—1991), tourism became incorporated into the national plan for social and economic development. The goal of "National Tourism Plan 1986—2000" was to enable China to enter the ranks of more advanced tourist receiving countries in terms of service quality and infrastructure development. While inbound tourism began to enjoy a fast pace of development after hard efforts to improve services, infrastructure and quality, it experienced an unexpected impediment in 1989 and inbound tourist arrivals suddenly decreased 22.7% from the previous year. It took until 1991 for inbound tourist arrivals to recover to the level before 1989 (see Figure 1 – 4).

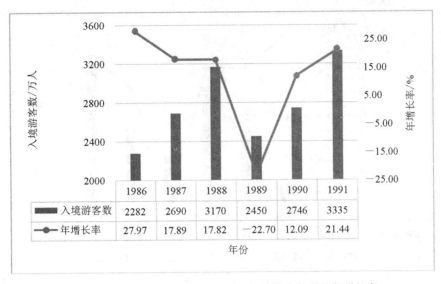

图 1-4　第二阶段(1986—1991 年)入境游客数量及年增长率
(资料来源：国家旅游局,2016)

　　在第三阶段(1992—1998 年)，随着经济改革步伐的加快和经济增长速度的提高,中国进一步打开国门,吸引了更多的国外投资者。虽然国际旅游发展稳定,但是巨大的供给投入和内地游客的实际增长远超过了国际游客对中国的旅游需求。中国内地的国际旅游地位从接待市场逐渐转变成为客源市场。由于周边竞争者日益增多,传统意义上的长线客源市场优势不再。中国内地的旅游业进入了一个调整时期,以迎接日益激烈的市场竞争,并积极开拓新兴的客源市场(见图 1-5)。

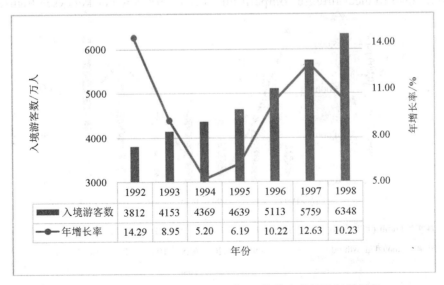

图 1-5　第三阶段(1992—1998 年)入境游客数量及年增长率
(资料来源：国家旅游局,2016)

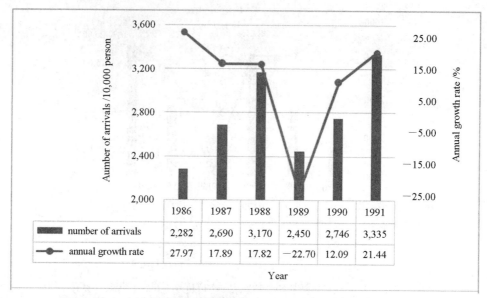

Figure 1 - 4   Phase 2 (1986—1991): Number of arrivals and growth rate

(Data source: China National Tourism Administration, 2016)

In the third phase (1992—1998), with the increased pace of economic reform and fast economic growth, Chinese Mainland opened its door even wider and attracted more foreign investment than ever. Though international tourism developed steadily, the huge input and actual increase of domestic tourists far exceeded the increase of international tourism demand. Chinese Mainland's international tourism turned from a sellers's market to a buyers's market. The traditional long-haul market gave up its prominence to the fast expanding peripheral market. The tourism industry of Chinese Mainland entered an adjustment stage to meet intense competition and explore new markets (see Figure 1 - 5).

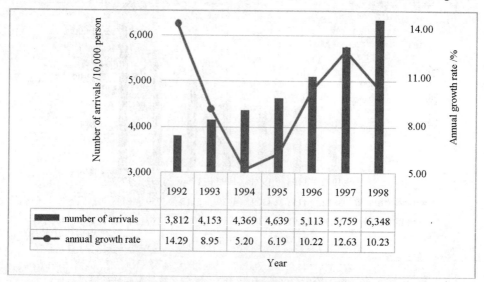

Figure 1 - 5   Phase 3 (1992—1998): Number of arrivals and growth rate

(Data source: China National Tourism Administration, 2016)

　　这或许是政府第一次意识到若想发掘国家的潜在旅游资源,需要拓展更广阔的客源市场,而不仅仅是"同胞和朋友"。世界上大部分的旅游客源国都位于西欧和北美,但吸引这些国家的游客来中国内地旅游仍存在着诸如签证和其他限制旅游的障碍,同时中国内地也缺少符合国际标准的接待设施。所以政府需要转变自己的策略,加强基础设施的投资,强化对从业人员的培训,培养一批专业的涉外人才,从而打造国际一流旅游产业。

　　第四阶段(1999—2008 年)开始于亚太金融危机之后。虽然全球经济衰退,国际竞争白热化,但中国内地的国际旅游业正逐步走向成熟,并保持稳定的增长。随着中国国际影响力的增强以及服务质量及基础设施的进一步完善,国际游客的旅游需求持续上涨。旅游业已经成为国家以及区域经济中不可或缺的产业之一(见图 1-6)。

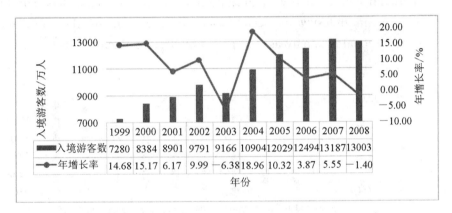

图 1-6　第四阶段(1999—2008 年)入境游客数量及年增长率
(资料来源:国家旅游局,2016)

　　2001 年,中国内地入境游客人数达到 8901 万人次,其中过夜游客3317 万人次,比 1990 年增长了 3 倍,位居世界第五大入境目的地国(联合国世界旅游组织 UNWTO,2001)。中国内地入境旅游总收入在 2001年是 178 亿美元,分别较 1990 年和 1980 年增长了 7 倍和 26 倍,并首次在世界上排名第五(联合国世界旅游组织 UNWTO,2001)。入境旅游收入已经成为国民经济中主要的外汇来源之一。

　　与此同时,涉外旅行社也得到了迅猛的发展。在 20 世纪 80 年代,涉外接待任务主要由中国国际旅行社(CITS)、中国旅行社(CTS)及中国青年旅行社(CYTS)三大旅行社垄断。虽然三大旅行的年接待游客量不断提升,但它们的市场份额却在不断下降。这三家旅行社在 1978 年包揽了 38% 的市场份

Perhaps for the first time the government appreciated that to develop the potential of the country's tourism resources it had to attract a much wider market, not just "compatriots and friends". Most of the world's main tourist generating countries were located in Western Europe and North America. There were many barriers to attracting tourists from these countries to Chinese Mainland, including visa and other travel restrictions and a lack of tourist facilities in line with international standard. It would require a major change in the government's political perspective and substantial investment in infrastructure, training and also foreign expertise to create an international class tourism sector.

The fourth phase (1999—2008) survived the impact of the Asia-Pacific Financial Crisis. Despite global economic regression and fierce international competition, the international tourism industry of Chinese Mainland became more mature and maintained steady growth. With the rise of China's international reputation and the improvement of service infrastructure and quality, international tourism demand has continued to increase. The tourism industry has established itself as one of the most important industries in the national economy as well as regionally(see Figure 1 - 6).

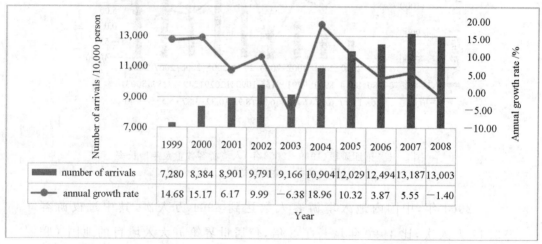

Figure 1 - 6   Phase 4 (1999—2008): Number of arrivals and annual growth rate
(Data source:China National Tourism Administration, 2016)

In 2001, inbound tourist arrivals to Chinese Mainland reached 89.01 million with 33.17 million staying overnight, a threefold increase from 1990, and ranked 5th in the world (UNWTO, 2001).Total inbound tourism receipts in Chinese Mainland in 2001 was $17.8 billion, a sevenfold and twenty-six fold increase from 1990 and 1980, respectively, and ranked 5th in the world for the first time (UNWTO, 2001). Inbound tourism has become one of the largest sources of foreign exchange in the national economy.

In addition, international travel service companies also grew quickly. In the 1980s, international travel services were dominated by three main organizations: China International Travel Service (CITS), China Travel Service (CTS) and China Youth Travel Service (CYTS).

额,而 1984 年的市场份额则下降至 10% 左右,到 1999 年,其市场份额仅为 3%。到 2001 年,在中国内地共有 1310 个涉外旅行社,接待入境游客超过 1450 万人。

在第五阶段 (2009—2015 年),由于受到各种因素的影响,外国游客数量保持稳定或略有下降。2008 年,由于美国金融危机对世界经济的影响,中国内地的入境旅游也受到影响,经历了金融危机和各种突发事件。在 2008 年和 2009 年,外国游客的数量有不同程度的下降。2009 年入境外国游客数为 1.26 亿人次,较前一年减少 2.73%(见图 1-7)。

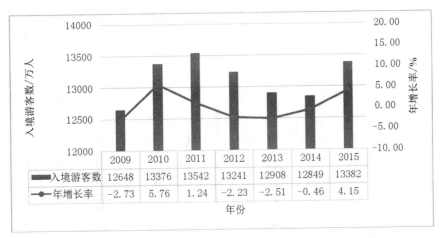

图 1-7　第五阶段(2009—2015 年)入境游客数量及年增长率
(资料来源:国家旅游局,2016)

2011 年是中国"十二五"计划的第一年,中国政府表示要"把旅游业变成中国经济战略性支柱产业和现代服务业,提高公众满意度"。在 2011 年,中国内地接待入境游客 1.35 亿人次,较 2010 年增加了 1.24%,旅游外汇收入 485 亿美元,增长 5.78%。

在政府持续的鼓励和支持下,中国内地旅游业,包括入境游、出境游和国内游都实现了与经济的同步发展。2009 年至 2015 年期间,随着中国内地旅游业的发展,中国内地已成为世界上吸引国际游客最多的目的地之一。而且,随着国内生活水平的上升和可支配收入的增加,以休闲为目的的出境和国内旅游也得以蓬勃发展。

Though the tourists received by these three main travel companies is still increasing, their market share has decreased significantly. These three travel companies took 38% of the market share in 1978 and more than 10% of the market share before 1984, 1999 their market share is only 3%. In 2001, there was a total of 1,310 international travel service companies in Chinese Mainland, receiving more than 14.5 million inbound tourists.

The fifth phase (2009—2015) was influenced by various factors, foreign tourist arrivals was kept stable or slightly decreased. In 2008, because of the effects of the US financial crisis on the world economy, Chinese Mainland's inbound tourism was also affected and had suffered a financial crisis as well as various emergencies. In the years of 2008 and 2009, the number of foreign tourists from each continent had different rate of decline compared to the previous year. The total number of foreign tourist arrivals was 126.48 million in 2009, decreasing 2.73% from the preceding year (see Figure 1 – 7).

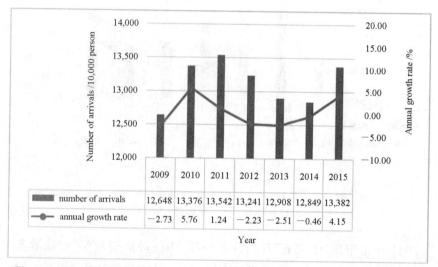

Figure 1 – 7   Phase 5 (2009—2015): Number of arrivals and annual growth rate
(Data source: China National Tourism Administration, 2016)

2011 is the first year of Chinese Mainland's "12th Five-Year Plan" period, Chinese government indicated "Turning tourism into a strategic pillar industry of the Chinese economy and a modern service industry with improved public satisfaction". In 2011, compared with 2010, Chinese Mainland recorded 135 million of inbound tourist arrivals, up by 1.24%, $ 48.5 billion in foreign exchange tourism revenue, up by 5.78%.

With the encouragement and support from government, tourism industry in Chinese Mainland, including inbound and outbound, as well as domestic trourism, developed at a similar pace with the economic development in China. The period from 2009 to 2015 was essentially one of growth in the tourism industry with the country becoming the top world destination for international tourists and with rising domestic living standards and increasing disposable incomes facilitating greater demand for both international and domestic leisure travel.

1.3　中国内地主要入境客源市场

图 1-8 显示了 1995 年、2005 年和 2015 年中国内地接待来自不同客源地游客所占的市场份额。亚洲仍然是主要的旅游客源地，紧随其后的是欧洲和美洲。大洋洲和非洲的市场份额相对较小。市场份额的特征表明地理距离和经济地位是影响国际旅游市场的重要因素。

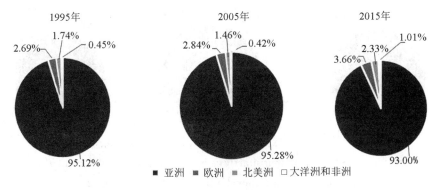

图 1-8　1995 年、2005 年和 2015 年中国内地入境游客来源
（资料来源：国家旅游局，2016）

在 2015 年，有 1.245 亿名亚洲游客到访中国内地，所占入境游客的市场份额最大，为 93.00%。欧洲作为第二大份额贡献了 489 万名游客，占总数的 3.66%。紧随其后的是北美洲，有 311 万名游客，占整个市场份额的 2.33%。第四大市场是大洋洲，有 78 万名游客来到中国内地，占 0.58%。排在最后一名的是非洲，有 58 万游客，占全部游客数量的 0.43%。

图 1-9 到图 1-11 显示了 1995 年、2005 年和 2015 年中国内地排名前 15 位的主要入境游客源国。20 多年来，日本、韩国、俄罗斯和美国一直排在前四位，被认为是中国内地最重要的入境游客源市场。

1.3 Major Inbound Tourism Markets for Chinese Mainland

Figure 1 – 8 shows the number of inbound tourists to Chinese Mainland from different continents in 1995，2005，and 2015. Asia is still the number one tourist generating continent，followed by Europe and the Americas. The Pacific and Africa remain insignificant market shares compared to other markets. The situation indicates that geographic proximity and economic status were important factors influencing the international travel market.

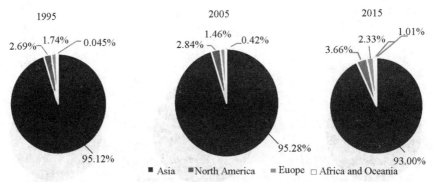

Figure 1 – 8   Inbound tourist arrivals by region in 1995，2005 and 2015

（Data source：China National Tourism Administration，2016）

In 2015，at 93.00%，Asian tourists were still the largest share of inbound visitors. There was a total of 124.50 million visitors from Asia. The second largest share was from Europe which contributed a total of 4.89 million visitors，accounting for 3.66% of the total. Next was the North American market. With a total of 3.11 million visitors，it occupied 2.33% of the whole market share. The fourth largest market was Oceania，with 0.78 million tourists to Chinese Mainland，accounting for 0.58%. Finally，there were 0.58 million visitors from Africa，comprising a market share of 0.43%.

Figure 1 – 9 to Figure 1 – 11 show the top 15 foreign inbound tourist generating countries in 1995，2005 and 2015. Japan，R.O. Korea，Russia and the United States has been ranked as the top 5 for over twenty years，and they are regarded as the most important inbound tourism markets for Chinese Mainland.

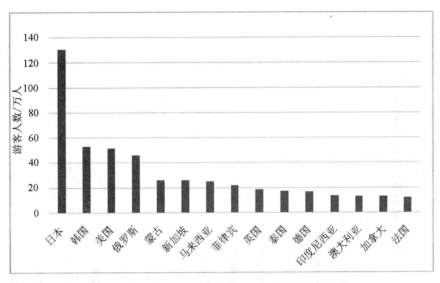

图 1-9　1995 年中国内地前 15 个入境游客源市场
（资料来源：国家旅游局，2016）

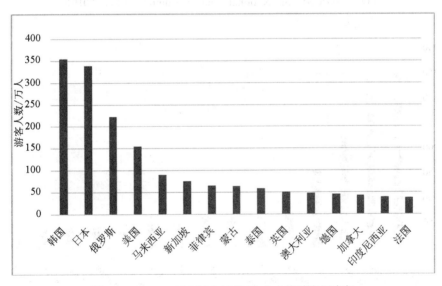

图 1-10　2005 年中国内地前 15 个入境游客源市场
（资料来源：国家旅游局，2016）

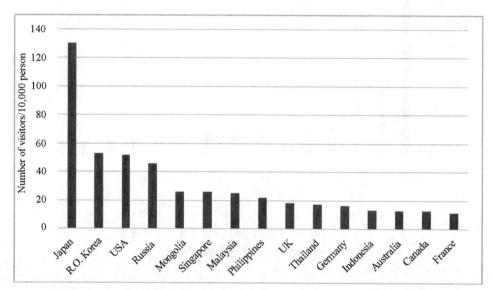

Figure 1 – 9　Top 15 markets of foreign visitors to Chinese Mainland in 1995

（Data source：China National Tourism Administration，2016）

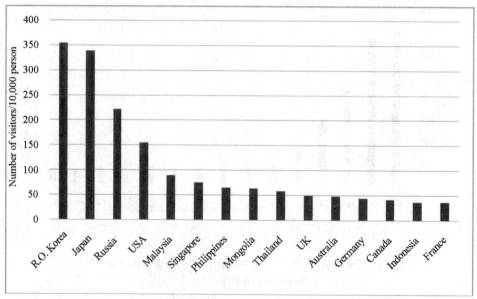

Figure 1 – 10　Top 15 markets of foreign visitors to Chinese Mainland in 2005

（Data source：China National Tourism Administration，2016）

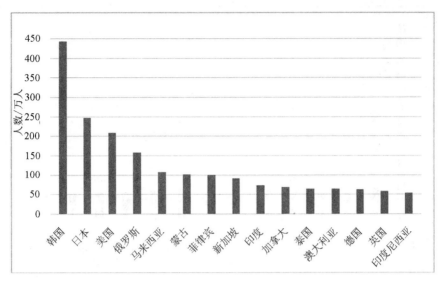

图 1－11　2015 年中国内地前 15 个入境游客源市场
(资料来源：国家旅游局,2016)

2015 年,共有 1662 万名外国游客来自亚洲,而其中大多数是来自韩国。从图中可以发现,韩国现在已取代 20 世纪 90 年代的日本,成为中国内地最大的旅游客源国家。此外,与 2005 年相比,印度进入了前 15 大客源国。

来自其他地区的游客也飞速增长。作为中国内地第二大的客源区域,从 1995 年到 2015 年,欧洲赴中国内地旅游的游客主要来自俄罗斯、德国、英国和法国。

1.4　亚洲市场

2015 年,亚洲市场占中国内地入境外国游客市场的 63.96%,从 1995 年到 2015 年间,亚洲市场的增长速度远远超过其他市场。其中,韩国游客的数量在 2015 年达到 440 万人次,年增幅为 6.3%;而日本游客为 240 万人次。韩国和日本来华旅游市场的规模主要受政治、经济和社会文化因素的影响。

经济因素：日本是亚洲为数不多的发达国家,而且其收入水平也排在世界前列。这使得日本成为世界上一个重要的游客输出国家,并使中国内地获益于此。直到 2000 年,日本经济才摆脱亚洲金融危机的影响并开始复苏。而在第五阶段,随着韩国经济的发展,其超越日本成为中国内地最大的入境外国游客市场。

政治因素：中国稳定的政治环境使得商业和旅游文化交流有了显著增长。

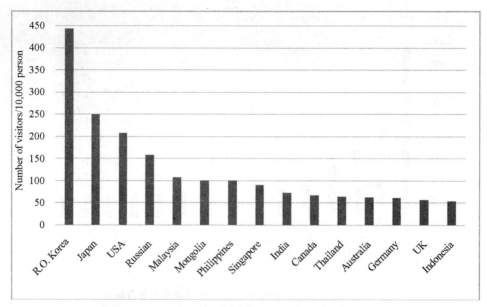

Figure 1 – 11　Top 15 markets of foreign visitors to Chinese Mainland in 2015

（Data source：China National Tourism Administration，2016）

In 2015，there was a total of 16.62 million foreign visitors from Asia and most of them were from R.O. Korea. It has been reported that R.O. Korea is now the largest tourist source country for Chinese Mainland and in the 1990s Japan was the largest tourist source country for Chinese Mainland. In addition，compared with 2005，India joined the top 15 tourist source countries in 2015.

There were also surges in tourism coming from other areas. As the second largest region of source markets，the number of travelers from Europe are mainly from Russia，Germany，United Kingdom，and France from 1995 to 2015.

1.4　The Asian Market

The Asian market accounted for 63.96% of foreign inbound tourists，and its growth rate far exceeded the other markets in the 20 years from 1995 to 2015. The number of R.O. Korean tourists reached 4.4 million with a 6.3% annual increase，and Japan sent 2.4 million. Factors contributing to the significance of the R. O. Korean and Japanese markets，include economic，political and sociocultural factors.

Economic factor：Japan is one of the few developed countries in Asia and the income of the Japanese is among the highest in the world. This makes Japan an important tourist generating country for the whole world，and Chinese Mainland benefits from this general trend. In 2000，the economy in Japan revived after the impact of the Asian Financial Crisis. In the fifth stage，with its economic development，R.O. Korea overtook Japan as Chinese Mainland's largest market for inbound foreign tourists.

Political factor：With the stable political environment，business and cultural exchanges have increased significantly.

社会文化因素：中国文化在日本和韩国的历史上发挥了重要作用。即使在今天，中国文化仍对日本社会和生活的许多方面有显著的影响。所以怀旧情感和文化相通性也是许多日本人到中国内地旅行的原因。

韩国市场的快速增长归因于在亚洲金融危机之后韩国经济的快速复苏，以及两国之间不断增加的相互交流。为了实现其经济复苏，韩国政府颁布了鼓励消费的政策，从而激发了旅游活动的增加。2015 年，每周往返于中韩两国的航班达到 1209 架次，占韩国国际进出港航班的 30.9%，所以两国之间的旅游变得非常便利。

东南亚是中国内地入境旅游的传统市场，包括马来西亚、新加坡、菲律宾、泰国和印度尼西亚。这 5 个国家都属于中国内地 15 个主要的入境游客源市场。在 2015 年，有超过 417 万人次的游客来自这 5 个国家。地理邻近、文化相似和高重游率是主要的原因。

马来西亚经济的快速增长刺激了更多的游客来中国内地旅游。新加坡是众所周知的高收入国家，每年为中国内地带来近 100 万人次的游客，使中国内地成为继澳大利亚、新西兰和日本后新加坡的第四大出境目的地。

1.5 洲际市场

在亚洲市场快速增长的同时，洲际旅游市场的发展也同样令人瞩目。2015 年，欧洲市场的访华游客为 489.14 万人次，占入境外国游客总数的 18.82%。接下来是美洲市场，共有 311.53 万人次游客，占入境外国游客总数的 11.99%。第四大市场是大洋洲，有 77.64 万人次游客到中国内地参观游览，占 2.99%。最后，有 2.23% 的游客来自非洲，约有 58.02 万人次游客。

美洲是中国内地入境游市场的重要组成部分，2015 年美国成为中国内地第四大外国游客客源国，紧随中国的邻国日本、韩国和越南。2015 年，约有 209 万人次的美国游客参观访问中国内地。2015 年，加拿大也位列中国内地 15 大外国游客客源国。

1.6 港澳台市场

中国内地入境旅游市场通常划分为四个：（1）香港和澳门同胞；

Socio-cultural factor: Chinese culture has played an important role in both Japanese and R.O. Korean history. Even today, the influence of Chinese culture is still significant in many aspects of Japanese life and society. So nostalgia and cultural similarities might contribute to the motivations of many Japanese traveling to Chinese Mainland.

The fast growth of the South Korean market might be attributed to the revival of R. O. Korea's economy after the Asian Financial Crisis, plus the increased communication between the two countries. In order to achieve its economic recovery, the R.O. Korean government developed a policy to encourage consumerism, which in turn contributed to an increase of tourism activities. In 2015, there were 1,209 scheduled flights per week between R.O. Korea and Chinese Mainland, accounting for 30.9% of the international flights from R.O. Korea, so traveling has become very convenient between the two countries.

Southeast Asia is a traditional market for Chinese Mainland, including Malaysia, Singapore, the Philippines, Thailand and Indonesia. These five countries are all among the top fifteen inbound tourist generating countries to Chinese Mainland. In 2015, there were more than 4.17 million arrivals from these five countries. Several factors may be identified as stimulating the development of this market. They are geographic proximity, cultural similarity and also the high revisit rate.

The fast economic growth in Malaysia has stimulated more international travel to Chinese Mainland. The high income of Singaporeans is well known, and this helps it generate around one million tourists to Chinese Mainland every year, making Chinese Mainland the fourth tourist destination of Singaporeans following Australia, New Zealand and Japan.

1.5   Inter-Continental Market

In line with the fast growth of the Asia market, the development of inter-continental tourism is also remarkable. In 2015, Europe contributed a total of 4.89 million visitors, accounting for 18.82% of the total. Next was the America market. With a total of 3.11 million visitors, it occupied 11.99% of the whole market share. The fourth largest market was Oceania, with 0.78 million tourists to Chinese Mainland, accounting for 2.99%. Finally, there were 0.58 million visitors from Africa, composing 2.23%.

America is an important tourist source market for Chinese Mainland. In 2015, the United States was the fourth tourist generating country of Chinese Mainland, after Chinese Mainland's neighboring countries Japan, R.O. Korea and Vietnam. In 2015, the United States generated 2.09 million tourists to Chinese Mainland. Canada is among the top 15 tourist generating countries to Chinese Mainland in 2015.

1.6   Compatriots Inbound Markets

Chinese Mainland's inbound tourism market is usually divided into (1) Compatriots

（2）台湾同胞；（3）居住在其他国家的华侨、华人；（4）其他国家持有外国护照的游客。

来自香港、澳门、台湾地区的同胞是中国内地入境旅游市场的主要力量。2015 年，香港游客的数量为 7944 万人次，比上年增长了 4.14%。来自澳门的游客数量为 2288 万人次，比上年增长 10.9%。在同一时期，来自台湾的游客数量为 550 万人次，同比增加了 2.5%。

海外侨胞及港澳台同胞的重要性有两方面：一方面他们常常入境来拜访家人和朋友；另一方面，他们通过汇款和投资来补充国家的外汇储备。

from Hong Kong and Macao; (2) Compatriots from Taiwan; (3) Overseas Chinese—Chinese who reside in other countries; (4) Foreigners—foreign travelers with other countries' passports.

Compatriots from Hong Kong, Macao and Taiwan are the major force of inbound tourism market in Chinese Mainland. In 2015, the number of inbound visitors from Hong Kong was over 79.44 million, representing 4.14 % increase over the previous year. Throughout 2015, 22.88 million people from Macao visited the Chinese Mainland, with an increase of 10.9%. Also in the same period, there were 5.5 million visitors from Taiwan, increased of 2.5%.

The importance of the overseas Chinese and compatriots was two-fold: to facilitate travel to the home country for expatriates to visit family and friends; and also, through remittances and possible investment, to ameliorate the paucity of foreign exchange reserves.

第 2 章　香港市场

 学习目标

- 了解香港到内地的入境旅游需求
- 了解香港游客的特征
- 学习如何分析某个入境旅游市场

在第 1 章中我们介绍了中国内地的入境旅游市场主要由来自香港和澳门的同胞构成。而香港无疑是内地入境旅游最大的客源地。为了对中国内地的入境旅游市场有更全面和深刻的认识,本章主要介绍香港市场的旅游需求和特征。

2.1　香港市场简介

数据显示,香港居民离港总人次数近年来呈稳定上升的趋势。2015年,香港居民赴内地旅游总人数达到 7944 万人次(见图 2-1)。这一数字显示香港居民的外游意愿强烈,外游市场极具潜力。

在内地入境游客中,香港游客占比约 60%。即每 10 个入境内地的游客,就大概有 6 个人是香港客人。这一比例在 2013 年至 2015 年间保持在59.4%～61.9%,相对稳定。这一数字显示了中国内地的主要客源是香港居民。这一趋势,与两地之间长期稳定的政治、经济合作,民间的相互往来,以及便捷的交通网络密不可分。

由国家旅游局的统计结果可以看出,香港人赴内地的各个省份过夜游的人次分布呈现如下规律:广东省所占比重最大(高达 75.88%),比其他地区过夜人次数总和还要多;广东之外的其他地区则是,福建、湖南和广西

Chapter 2　The Hong Kong Market

 Learning Outcomes

- Understanding the tourism demand from Hong Kong to the mainland
- Understanding the characteristics of Hong Kong tourists
- Learning how to analyze a specific inbound tourism market

As discussed in the last chapter, the inbound market of Chinese Mainland is dominanted and by the compatriots, the residents from Hong Kong and Macao. Particularly, Hong Kong is the dominant source market of the mainland. To have a deep and comprehensive understanding of the international tourism of Chinese Mainland, this chapter focuses on the introduction of the Hong Kong market.

2.1　Introduction of the Hong Kong Market

Data shows that the total number of Hong Kong residents' departures in recent years is dramatic. There were 79.44 million Hong Kong residents traveling to the mainland in 2015 (see Figure 2 - 1). The number shows that the traveling motivation of Hong Kong residents are strong and the outbound tourism market has a great potential.

In inbound tourists to the mainland, the percentage of Hong Kong residents accounted for about 60%. That means there are at least six Hong Kong residents out of ten inbound tourists. The proportion from 2013 to 2015 remained relatively stable at 59.4% ~ 61.9%. This figure shows the main source of inbound tourists are Hong Kong residents. This trend is inseparable from the long-term stability of politics, economic cooperation, civil connection, and convenient transportation network.

From the statistics of CNTA it can be seen that the regional distribution of Hong Kong residents traveling to the mainland is as following: the nights in Guangdong accounted for the largest proportion (75.88%), which is much more than the sum of the number of other regions; apart from Guangdong, Fujian, Hunan and Guangxi were the top three. Overall, for Hong Kong residents traveling to the mainland the distribution is from the near to the distant, from the south to the north, from the eastern coastal areas

位列前三名。总体而言,香港人赴内地旅游的分布格局遵循由近及远,由南
到北,由东部沿海到西北部内陆地区,由发达地区到不发达地区依次递减的
空间规律。东部沿海地区占 86.71%,中部地区占 8.75%,西北部内陆地
区占 4.54%。

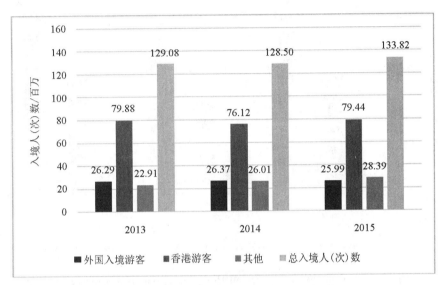

图 2-1　外国以及香港居民入境总人(次)数
(资料来源:国家旅游局,2016)

2.2　总消费规模

从图 2-2 中可以看出,香港居民赴内地因私旅游的消费总额在各种
形式的旅游中都有不同程度的上升。在所有形式的私人旅游中,消费总额
从 2011 年的 344.9 亿美元上升至 2013 年的 377 亿美元,平均年增幅为
6.11%。

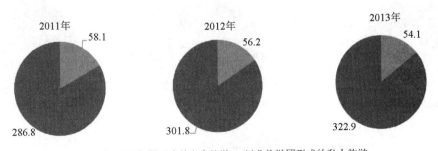

图 2-2　2011—2013 年香港居民前往内地因私旅游总消费规模(单位:亿美元)
(资料来源:香港特别行政区政府,2014)

to the northwestern inland areas and from developed areas to underdeveloped areas. The eastern coastal areas accounted for 86.71%, the central regions contributed 8.75%, and the northwestern inland regions occupied 4.54%.

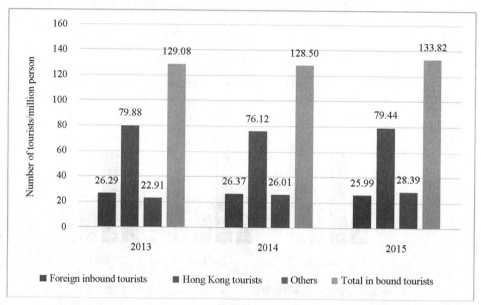

Figure 2 – 1   International tourists and Hong Kong tourists to Chinese Mainland
（Data source：China National Tourism Administration，2016）

2.2 *Total Consumption Scale*

As it can be seen from Figure 2 – 2, the total consumption of Hong Kong residents to Chinese Mainland in all forms of tourism has a different increasing trend. In all forms of personal traveling, the total consumption increased from ＄34.49 billion in 2011 to ＄37.7 billion in 2013, which showed an increasing rate at 6.11%.

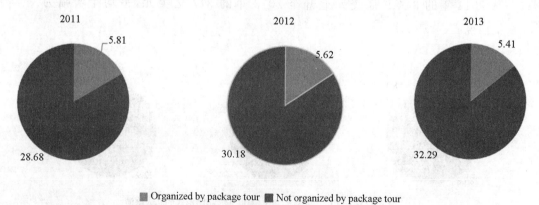

Figure 2 – 2   Hong Kong resident travel expenditure in Chinese Mainland in 2011—2013（Billion USD）
（Data source：Hong Kong SAR，2014）

以旅行团形式进行旅游的消费占所有出游形式总消费的 16% 左右。这一形式的消费在 2011 年至 2013 年间略微下降,平均下降幅度为 3%。

非旅行团形式的私人旅行开支是赴内地旅游总开支的主要部分,约占所有出游形式总消费的 84% 左右。从 2011 年到 2013 年,非旅行团形式的消费金额不断上涨,从 2011 年的 286 亿美元上升至 2013 年的 322 亿美元,平均涨幅为 7.72%。

2.3　人均消费情况

从人均出游的消费水平来看(见图 2 - 3),以旅行团形式出游的人均消费远远大于以非旅行团形式出游的人均消费。整体来说,所有形式的出游人均开支从 2011 年的 780 元人民币增长为 2013 年的 860 元人民币,其中涨幅最大的年份为 2013 年,涨幅为 7.69%。团队旅游的人均消费在 2011 年至 2013 年间主要呈下降趋势,由 2011 年的 1220 元人民币下降到 2013 年的 1100 元人民币,平均跌幅为每年 3% 左右。非团队旅游的人均消费虽然明显低于团队旅游,但其一直保持良好的上升趋势,与所有形式的出游人均开支的增长趋势基本相同,由 2011 年的 730 元人民币升至 2013 年的 830 元人民币,平均年增长率近 8%。

图 2 - 3　香港居民前往内地因私旅游人均消费(单位:元)
(资料来源:香港特别行政区政府,2014)

2.4　人均消费量

如图 2 - 4 所示,人均过夜消费都明显高于在每个区域内的人均消费。按地区划分,2011 年至 2013 年香港居民在深圳旅行的过夜人均消费金额有所上升,至 610 元人民币。香港居民在广东旅行的过夜人均消费在 2013 年经历了明显的增长,从 2010 年的 760 元到 2013 年的 800 元人民币。相比之下,香港居民赴广东旅行的总人均消费低于过夜的人均消费,三年均值为

The consumption of group tours accounted for 16% in all forms of traveling. It declined slightly between 2011 and 2013, which showed an average decreasing rate at 3%.

The expenditure of non-package tourists was the major part, which contributed about 84% to the total consumption of mainland traveling. From 2011 to 2013, non-package tours were growing constantly, increasing from $US 28.6 billion in 2011 to $US 32.2 billion in 2013, which showed an average increasing rate at 7.72%.

2.3 Average Travel Expenditure

From the average travel expenditure (see Figure 2 – 3), the average consumption of group tours is much higher than the non-package tourists. Overall, the average expenditure of all forms traveling increased from ¥780 in 2011 to ¥860 in 2013 with the largest increasing rate (7.69%) in 2013. There is a decreasing trend among package tourists between 2011 and 2013, declining from ¥1,220 in 2011 to ¥1,100 in 2013 with an average declining rate at 3%. Although the average expenditure of non-package tour was lower than the group tour, it remained a stable growing trend, which is similar with the increasing rate of all forms of traveling, showing an average increasing rate at 8% from ¥730 in 2011 to ¥830 in 2013.

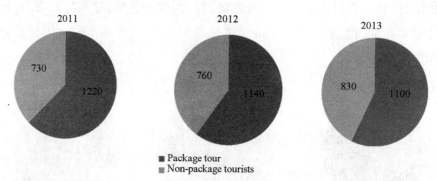

Figure 2 – 3   Average travel expenditure in Chinese Mainland (¥CNY)

(Data source: Hong Kong SAR, 2014)

2.4 Average Expenditure

It can be seen from Figure 2 – 4, the average expenditure of overnight visitors was significantly higher than average visitor expendture in all the destination regions. By regions, the average expenditure of Hong Kong residents to Shenzhen for overnight trips increased to ¥610 between 2011 and 2013. Also, it had an obvious increase in Guangdong in 2013, growing from ¥760 in 2010 to ¥800 in 2013. Comparatively, the total average expenditure of Hong Kong residents in Guangdong was lower with an average expenditure at ¥590 in three years. The average consumption of Hong Kong residents to other areas for overnight trips remained a continuous increase after 2011.

590 元人民币。香港居民赴中国内地其他地区的过夜人均消费也在 2011 年
之后连续 3 年保持增长。

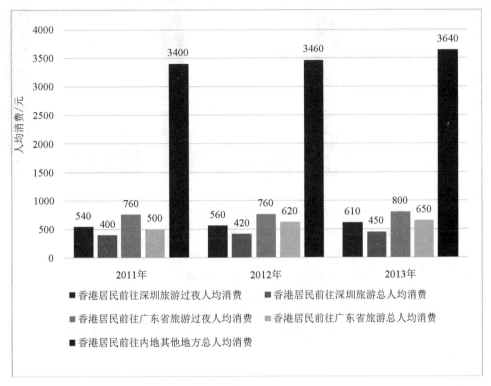

图 2-4　香港居民前往内地因私旅游人均消费规模（单位：元）
（资料来源：香港特别行政区政府，2014）

2.5　2011—2013 年香港居民以非旅行团方式赴广东省因私旅游消费结构

　　在非旅行团形式赴广东省旅游中，住宿与餐饮在消费中占有重要的位
置。其次是娱乐交通及其他，例如交通费、保健按摩、卡拉 OK 及高尔夫费用
占总体消费的近三成。购物类消费仅占整体消费的一成左右。这与客源地
香港本身就是世界性的"购物天堂"有很大关系。按年份来看，2011 年的消
费分布为：58% 用于住宿和餐饮（过夜消费占比较大）；31.5% 用于娱乐交通
（若去较远的地方，交通费用占比较大）；10% 用于购物（香港本地具有较大的
购物优势，香港居民前往中国内地进行购物的欲望不高，实际购买行为也不
多）。此后两年的比例与 2013 年基本相当，但是住宿餐饮的支出略微有所上
升，而娱乐交通及其他消费的支出比重有所下降，购物支出则基本保持不变
（见图 2-5）。

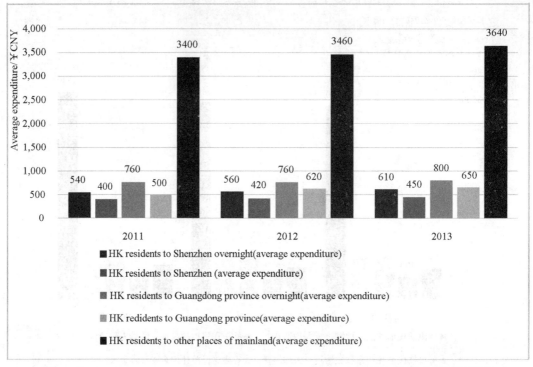

Figure 2 - 4　Average expenditure of Hong Kong residents to Chinese Mainland（￥CNY）

（Data source：Hong Kong SAR，2014）

2.5　Non-package Hong Kong Tourists' Expenditure to Guangdong Province between 2011 and 2013

In non-package tour to Guangdong province，accommodation and catering occupied an important portion. Followed by transport and entertainment，etc., for example，travel expenses，massage，Karaoke and golf accounted for 30% in total consumption. Shopping accounted for 10%. This has a great relationship with the source market，Hong Kong which is a "shopping paradise". By year，the distribution of consumption in 2011 was：58% for accommodation and catering（overnight consumption accounted for a large proportion）；31.5% for entertainment and transportation（when traveling to remote destinations，transportation costs accounted for a large proportion）；10% for shopping（shopping in Hong Kong has a large advantage，so that the shopping motivations of Hong Kong residents to Chinese Mainland is not high and they purchase less）. The proportion of the following two years were similar with the one of 2013，but the expenditure of accomodation and catering had an increase，while the percentage of transportation，entertainment and others decreased，and the expenditure for shopping remained stable（see Figure 2 - 5）.

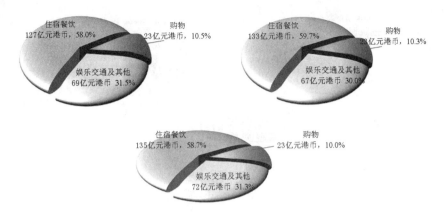

图 2 - 5　2011—2013 年香港居民以非旅行团的方式赴广东省因私旅游消费结构
（资料来源：香港特别行政区政府，2014）

2.6　香港居民赴内地旅游的信息来源

以下内容均引自香港理工大学于 2014 年和 2015 年撰写的研究报告：《港澳年轻上班族赴中国内地旅游研究报告》和《港澳中老年人赴中国内地旅游研究报告》。报告研究发现互联网仍然是现代人获取日常信息的主要渠道，在了解旅游目的地具体情况方面，搜索引擎、旅游者评价网站或论坛和目的地政府旅游网站都是较为常见的旅游信息获取平台和网络工具。网络预订的使用也和自由行的流行有着紧密关系。根据访问中收集的信息，网络并不是部分受访者第一时间选择的旅游信息获取渠道。他们表示通常情况下是已经大致选好出游目的地，或者是在已和同伴商量的情况下，再使用网络进行进一步的信息获取，来帮助决策。受访者表示，相比于家用电脑，他们更倾向于使用手机去查找相关信息。这也从侧面显示，社交媒体平台，比如脸书、微信，也开始成为人们了解旅游目的地和与出行相关的信息的渠道。

调查显示，在旅游计划的不同阶段，被访者使用的信息来源存在差异。在旅游计划的初期，多数被访者表示会去网络搜索引擎（如谷歌、雅虎、百度等）搜索有关目的地的一般信息。除互联网外，传统的信息媒介仍会起到一定的作用。一些被访者表示会先去旅行社收集宣传手册，根据宣传手册的项目决定出游目的地及景点。此外，电视节目、旅游书籍、电视广告以及平面广告都会在被访者制订出游计划的初期起到提供信息的作用（见表 2 - 1）。

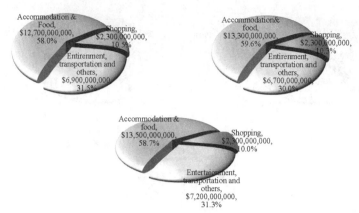

Figure 2 – 5　Non-package Hong Kong tourists' expenditure to Guangdong province（2011—2013）

（Data source：Hong Kong SAR，2014）

2.6　*Information Source of Hong Kong Residents to the Mainland*

The following discussions are based on *Survey on Hong Kong and Macao Young Working Residents Traveling to Mainland China*（2014）and *Survey on Hong Kong and Macao Senior Residents Traveling to Mainland China*（2015），two reports issued by the Hong Kong Polytechnic University. It is found that internet is still the main channel for the Hong Kong residents to access the daily information. In terms of understanding the specific circumstances of tourism destinations，the search engine，tourist review websites or forums，and government tourism websites are common tourism information platform and network tools. The use of online booking has a close relationship with the popularity of independent travel. According to the information collected in the interviews，network is not the first choice of some respondents to acquire information. They said that in most cases they had selected most travel destinations，or consulted with partners，before they used the network to obtain further information for decision-making. Respondents said that compared with mobile phones or computer，they also tend to use the phone to find relevant information，which shows that social media network，such as Facebook，Wechat have started to become a tourism channel for people to understand tourism destinations and relevant information.

According to the survey，at different stages of travelling plans，there are differences in information source used by the respondents. In the early travelling plans，the majority of respondents said that they would use search engines（such as Google，Yahoo，Baidu，etc.）to get general information about tourism destinations. In addition to the Internet，traditional information media still plays a role. Some respondents said they would collect travel brochures from travel agencies and decide destinations and attractions according to the promotion projects. Besides，TV shows，travel books，television advertisements，and print advertisements also play a role in initial traveling plans（see Table 2 – 1）.

表 2-1　香港居民赴内地旅行信息来源

来源	代表性实例
互联网媒体	一般我们会上网找一些旅游信息。
搜索引擎	我们主要会通过网上搜索,例如百度、雅虎、谷歌等。
网络预订商	会通过网络预订商来订房,订机票,了解当地情况等。
旅游者评价网站或论坛	会去看一些论坛,在论坛里找一些旅游经验等。
目的地政府旅游网站	通常会去政府旅游网站上看。
亲友介绍	会向朋友了解一些当地的情况。 朋友的介绍感觉比较可靠。
报纸、杂志、图书	会看旅游书、报纸等与旅游相关的内容。
旅行社	会去一些自己熟悉的旅行社了解旅游信息。 会去旅行社找一些旅游资料等。
电视节目	电视里的旅游特辑,可以吸引人。 对于旅游,电视宣传很重要。

决定出游目的地后,被访者表示会去旅游者评价网站或论坛查阅有关目的地的游记,看一些去过的人的一些旅游经历,并咨询去过的亲友以获取更加详细的信息。许多被访者都表示,口碑或者网络口碑对其出游的决策有非常大的影响。而在旅游产品购买阶段,被访者表示会使用网络预订平台来预订酒店及机票。

也各有超总人数三成或以上的被访者认为,其他主要的旅游信息来源,包括亲友介绍,报纸、杂志的广告和专栏介绍,对于激发他们的旅游兴趣和获取相关信息十分重要。

2.7　香港居民赴内地旅游的出游动机

结合调查信息发现香港居民前往内地旅游的出游动机主要有以下六个方面:增长见识、娱乐、放松、人际交往、享受家庭时光和购物(见表 2-2)。

Table 2 – 1   Information sources used by Hong Kong residents when traveling in Chinese Mainland

Source	Typical examples
Online social media	Normally we can surf the Internet to find related travel information.
Search engine	We mainly use online search, such as baidu, yahoo, Google, etc.
Online travel agency	We will book a flight, hotel, understand the local information by online booking, etc.
Online review website; Bulletin board system (BBS)	Find tourist experience by BBS.
Destination government office website	Normally go to the government tourism website to see.
Relatives and friends recommendation	To collect information from the local friend. The recommendation of friends are more trustable.
Newspaper, magazine	We will read travel book, newspaper, or magazine.
Travel agency	To know travel information by some familiar travel agency. To get some travel resource by travel agency.
TV program	TV programs are attractive. For travel, TV promotion is very important.

After deciding on tourism destinations, respondents said they would go to review websites or forums to see travelling journals and travelling experiences from other tourists, and enquire with relatives and friends who have been to the destinations to obtaining detailed information. Many respondents also suggested that good reputation or good reputation from network plays an important role in decision-making. In the later stage of tourism products purchasing, respondents said they would use an online platform to book hotels and flights.

Other major information resources, included friends and relatives, newspapers, advertisements and column presentation of magazines and books. In addition, there was over thirty percent or more respondents who believed that it could stimulate their interest to travel and access relevant information.

2.7   *Motivations of Hong Kong Residents Traveling to the Mainland*

Based on the survey, there are several motivations of Hong Kong residents traveling to the mainland: enriching knowledge and experience, enjoyment, relaxation, social communication, family time enjoyment and shopping (see Table 2 – 2).

表 2 - 2　香港居民赴内地旅行出游意愿和动机

内容	代表性实例
增长见识	增长见识,感受一下当地特色。 看一下祖国的大好河山和祖国的文化。 看一下其他省(区、市)的环境和香港有什么不一样。 到其他省(区、市),可以看到另外一种文化,一些平常自己没有的东西,看不到的东西。 获得一些你平时看不到的新知识。
享受	喜欢去享受,可能去泡温泉啊,或者按摩啊,或者是去看一些自然的风景,到一个地方,可以看看书,吃吃饭,享受美食。
放松	可以放松心情,放松工作上的压力。 喜欢阳光沙滩,很放松,很自由,似乎不用思考任何问题,还有趁自己能逛、能走时就多去旅行。 只要不在香港,不要工作,到内地哪里我都愿意,就是想放松。
人际交往	多认识一些朋友,可以和朋友交流。 聊聊大家的文化,交交朋友,会认识不同的人,你的知识就会增长。
享受家庭时光	因为你是和家里人一起去的,大家心情都会放松一点,也可以改善大家的关系,关系会融洽一点。
购物	旅行就是要花一下钱,买一些小礼物,我比较喜欢购物和放松,有购物的冲动,容易花一些钱。

有一半的被访者提到出外旅游能"增长见识""开阔视野",了解"新鲜的"事物,见识到和香港不一样的世界。许多香港居民也说,内地的历史文化、风土人情非常吸引他们。许多被访者表示去内地旅游主要是为了游览历史名胜如故宫、兵马俑、长城,还有欣赏风景,了解其他地方的人的生活方式及习俗。

此外,旅游一直是香港人生活方式中很重要的组成部分,不少被访者表示"享受"和"放松"是他们出外旅行的主要因素,加上香港的工作十分忙碌,生活节奏很快,他们希望通过出外旅行来"放松心情""享受舒适""品尝美食",并感受当地不一样的特色,可以"自由,不用想问题"。其中一位被访者还着重强调,"只要不在香港,不要工作,到内地哪里我都愿意,就是想放松……"

其次,"人际交往""享受家庭时光"和"探望亲戚"也是相对较多提到的动机因素。部分被访者提到,他们到内地旅游也是为了和亲戚重聚,和旧朋友见面,以及和家人享受天伦之乐,说明他们也认为旅游是社交活动的一种,能够享受亲友的陪伴和满足人际交流的需求。一位受访的香港居民说道:"因

Table 2 - 2   Hong Kong residents' travel motivation to the mainland

Content	Typical examples
Enrich knowledge and experience	Enrich knowledge and experience, to better understand the local culture. To know the mother country's scenery, and mother country's culture. To know the different environment. To experience Chinese culture and history, which we cannot easily experience in daily life.
Enjoyment	To enjoy life, like hot spring or massage, or enjoy the natured scenery. To read books or just have dinner, enjoy food at somewhere.
Relaxation	To relax from work. It seems nothing to think, and just enjoy sunshine, sand. I can relax and feel freedom. To relax when I can travel to visit more destinations. I just want to relax and escape from HK, and no matter where in the mainland.
Social/interpersonalization	To make more friends and communicate with friends. To interact with various culture, and make different friends, and then your knowledge and experience could be enhanced.
Enjoy family time	To enjoy the travel moment with family and improve the relationship.
Shopping	To spend a bit money and buy some gifts. Enjoy shopping and traveling.

Half of respondents mentioned that traveling can be "informative", "horizon-broadening", "getting new things", gain an insight into a different world. Many Hong Kong residents also mentioned history and culture of the mainland were very attractive to them. Many respondents said that they mainly went to the mainland to visit the historic tourism attractions such as the Imperial Palace, Terra-cotta Warriors and the Great Wall. Also, they wanted to see the sceneries, learn more about other lifestyles and customs.

In addition, travelling has been an important part of Hong Kong residents' life. Many respondents said "enjoyment" and "relaxation" were the main factors for travelling outside. Besides, because of high pace of life and work in Hong Kong, they desired to relax, feel comfortable, taste food and experience different characteristics for "free and thinking nothing". One of respondents also emphasised "he/she wants to relax no matter where he/she goes in the mainland as long as he/she is not in Hong Kong…"

Secondly, interpersonal interaction, family time enjoyment, visiting to relatives are also relatively more mentioned motivations. Part of respondents mentioned that traveling

为你是和家里人一起去的,大家心情都会放松一点,也可以改善大家的关系,关系会融洽一点。"

虽然被访者在内地旅游时用于购物的花销比例较低,很多人仍然表示购物是他们赴内地旅游的一个重要动机。一方面是为了给亲朋好友准备礼物,另一方面是在旅游地购物可以带来愉悦感。有被访者表示"就算买同一样东西,在别的地方更喜欢花钱……有购物的冲动,花一点钱,这些我都比较喜欢"。

2.8　香港居民赴内地旅游满意度

关于香港居民赴内地旅游的满意度调查,在总体框架上,使用深入访谈法收集数据体现出以下几个显著优势:一是可以深入挖掘出导致旅游者满意或不满意的具体细节。比如针对旅游景点的满意度调查,旅游者对有关景点不同方面的满意度表现出极大的差异,有时甚至呈现完全对立的观点。多数旅游者对游览项目十分满意,但对景点的价格、安全和舒适度/拥挤程度十分不满,特别是对残疾人通道和景区厕所等方面的旅游设施的欠缺多有微词。这些内容在传统的旅游者对景点满意指数的笼统表述中无法得到准确体现。二是从旅游者对自己以往旅游经历的详细描述中,可以整理出关于满意度方面的新的主题和分类。例如本项研究中发现,"不安全""不卫生""不方便"是引发香港游客对购物、景点、交通、住宿等各个方面不满意的一个共同因素。这个发现为充分了解旅游者的消费心理,进而采取针对性的营销措施提供了有价值的信息。三是被访者对于和满意度相关的内容都提供了更为生动的描述。他们都讲述了自己在内地旅游时遭遇的各种令人印象深刻的故事(见表 2-3)。

表 2-3　香港居民游客赴内地旅游满意度

内容	表示满意的实例	表示不满意的实例
景点	景点很美,很多地方真的很漂亮。 很多景点有历史感,有的还是世界文化遗产,很值得看。 内地景点类型很多,到处都可以看看,有历史的,有山水的,有温泉的,还有的是世界遗产,令人叹为观止。	有些景点卫生间太脏,不敢去。 景点商业化太严重,景点人工化的东西太多。 有些景点、商铺会骗游客钱,强迫消费,景区里的东西特别贵。 有些景点人很多,很拥挤,特别是节假日。如果你在旺季的旅游季节去,人多得不得了。 有些景点的门票太贵了。

to mainland is for gathering with relatives and old friends, enjoying with family members, which shows that they regard traveling as a social activity that are able to accompany with friends and relatives and meet interpersonal interaction needs. One Hong Kong resident said that when traveling with family members, they could relax better, which could improve and harmonize their relationships.

Although the shopping proportion of respondents in the mainland is low, many respondents said that shopping is still an important motivation to travel to the mainland. One is to prepare gifts for friends and family, the other is to gain a sense of pleasure in shopping tourism. Some respondents demonstrated that "even if you buy the same thing, you are likely to spend on elsewhere that it seems to have some... shopping motivation, spending a little money, which is what I prefer."

2.8 Satisfaction of Hong Kong Residents to the Mainland

This section aims to assess Hong Kong residents' satisfaction with the mainland using an in-depth interview. Firstly, in-depth interviews are useful when you want detailed information about a tourist's satisfaction or dissatisfaction. For example, in terms of tourist satisfaction with a destination, there's a great deal of different views, sometimes even the point-of-view is exactly the opposite. Most tourists are very satisfied with the destination, but for the price of the scenic spot, safety and comfort/congestion, especially the disabled path and other tourist facilities such as toilets are dissatisfied. Traditional tourist index about influences of tourist satisfaction cannot indicate the above factors. Secondly, from the description of their travel experience we can attempt to sort out the various ways of classification and subjects of tourist satisfaction. In this study, for example, "unsafe" "unhealthy" "inconvenient" are the common reasons of causing HK tourists in dissatisfaction towards shopping, transportation, accommodation, which provides valuable information to understand consumer behavior. Thirdly, interviewees provides a more vivid description about satisfaction by describing their experience and impressive stories (see Table 2 – 3).

Table 2 – 3 Hong Kong residents's travel satisfaction in the mainland

Content	Satisfaction examples	Dissatisfaction examples
Attractions	Lots of attractions are very good. Some attractions are full of history. It's worth to visit the world nature and culture heritage. The mainland has various types of attractions, including historical, nature, hot spring, and world nature and culture heritage.	Toilets in some attractions are dirty. Some attractions are too artificial and commercial. Shops in some attractions cheat customers. Some attractions are very crowded, especially during holiday or peak seasons. Tickets of some attractions are too expensive.

续　表

内容	表示满意的实例	表示不满意的实例
酒店住宿	酒店价格便宜,性价比高。 酒店接待比较好,还有住宿、饮食、交通也很好。 酒店很大,服务、环境都挺好,很漂亮。	酒店卫生没有达标,有些被子很臭,有烟味,不太干净。 服务人员的服务质量没有达标,服务意识不够。 酒店有些设施设备还不够完善,例如有些房间里的灯的开关的设计。
交通	很多城市交通系统很好,有公交、的士、专车、地铁等,很方便,有些地方规划得比香港还要好。 交通很方便,可以坐高铁,不用那么拥挤了。	公共交通设施还是差一点,社会公德行为有所欠缺。有的的士司机会拒载,或是不按照计程器收钱。 飞机延误太厉害了。有时还不如乘高铁。
食品及餐厅	好想到中国内地去,地方大,吃的东西便宜。总体上也比较安全,有的环境比香港还好。 喜欢吃内地的小吃,物美价廉。 现在餐厅很干净,卫生都不错,吃得很放心,有些餐厅比香港还漂亮,理念更加先进。 餐厅接待没问题,服务很好。	东西很好吃,但是对食品安全有些担心。 服务员的态度有待改善。这个需要系统的管理和培训。 有些地方卫生条件不好,吃的东西很一般。
购物及其场所	内地的购物体验不错,可以买到小礼物,有很多选择。 内地的东西其实不贵的,买来送给朋友,他们都很喜欢,很满意。	假的东西太多,品质差,没有多少特色,而且不便宜。 我不喜欢花太多时间在购物上。
出入境	出入境还好啊,香港过去很方便吧,从内地回来也很不错。	过关有时会很拥挤,很麻烦。
当地城市形象	大城市,如北京、上海等比较好,很现代,很吸引人。 很多城市相较从前,卫生要好很多,干净多了。 内地景点类型很多,到处都可以看看,有历史的,有山水的,有温泉的,还有的是世界遗产,令人叹为观止。	有些城市的卫生条件很差,例如厕所。有些景点的商铺会骗游客钱,强迫消费。景区里的东西特别贵。有些景点对内地和境外的游客使用不同的票价。

Continued

Content	Satisfaction examples	Dissatisfaction examples
Accommodation	Hotel price is cheap value for money. Accommodation, dinner and transportation are good. The hotel is very big, service and environment are both very good.	Sanitation in the hotel is not up to the standard. The guilts have strong smells, and there is smoking smells. It is not clean. The hotel service quality is not good. Some hotel facilities are not standardable, for example, the design of room light.
Transportation	Transportations in many cities are very good and convenient. Some cities are even better than HK. It's very convenient to take high-speed train.	The public facilities still need improvement. Social responsibility should be further improved, for example, some taxi drivers may refuse to take passengers. Some drivers do not follow rules. Flights are often delayed It's better to take high-speed train.
Food and restaurant	The mainland has more choices for food and the price is cheaper than HK. The restaurant environment is better than HK. I like the snacks in the mainland, which are good and cheap. The restaurant is clean and some restaurants are more advanced than HK. Service is good	The food is very delicious, but sometimes we will worry about the food safety. The service quality should systematical be further improved. It needs training. There is a long way for the mainland to go. Some restaurants' hygiene is not good and so is the food.
Shopping	I like shopping in the mainland, especially there are lots of choices, and I can buy gifts. It's cheap to buy some gifts for friends in the mainland.	Too many fake products which have poor quality. Nothing is special but expensive. I don't like to spend much time on shopping.
Immigration	It's very convenient from HK to Chinese Mainland.	It's very crowded and inconvenient when passing the border gate.
Destination image	Metropolitans are good, such as Beijing, Shanghai. It's modern and attractive. Most cities are clean. There are different kinds of amazing attractions in the mainland, such as historical attractions, nature scenery, hot spring attractions, world nature and culture heritages etc.	The sanitary condition in some cities are poor, such as the toilet. The shops in some attractions cheat customers, and force them to consume. Some attractions provide two types of ticket prices for local and foreigners.

内容	表示满意的实例	表示不满意的实例
当地居民	很多人蛮勤快的。 在沟通方面比较顺畅,文化上大家都可以聊在一起,距离不会很远。 现在很多人都有文化了,很有礼貌,很友善。我们真的很喜欢那个气氛。	有些居民不守规则,例如:乱扔垃圾,说话很大声,照相的时候不按次序来。文明程度不太高,有些父母让孩子在街上小便。
导游	我觉得导游都还可以,我跟的廉价团都很热情,讲解很专业。 导游很多时候是不错的,非常勤快。	有些导游强迫游客消费。

2.9 政策建议

通过分析比较来自对接待方和旅游者的建议内容,从中得到对两者共同提出的建议和对两方分别提出的不同建议,供各方决策者参考(见图 2-6)。

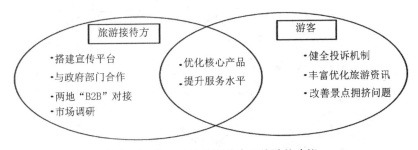

图 2-6 吸引香港游客赴内地旅游的建议

1. 接待方与旅游者共同提出的建议

(1) 优化核心产品

从接待方的角度出发,一些旅游产品的核心价值并没有得到充分挖掘。例如,有受访者反映,海南岛旅游的核心产品部分做得不好,目的地文化方面的价值没有得到充分的开发与宣传。与泰国、柬埔寨等地以及我国台湾地区的海岛旅游产品相比,除了大家共有的阳光、海水与沙滩,这些地方各自的地方文化才是旅游产品中最为核心的部分。上述几个地方的旅游产品开发模式是值得海南借鉴的。另外,旅游产品的细分也是优化旅游产品的一个重要

Continued

Content	Satisfaction examples	Dissatisfaction examples
Local residents	Most people work hard. It's easy to communicate, with short cultural distance. Most people are kind and polite, and friendly.	Some residents don't follow rules, for example, littering, speaking loudly and taking pictures out of order. Some residents are not so civilized, for example, some parents told children to pee on the street.
Tour guide	I think the tour guides are very enthusiastic even I join the cheap group. The tour guide is very good, and hard working.	Some tour guides force tourists to consume.

2.9 Policy Suggestions

There is a comparative analysis on the suggestions from the reception and tourists, from which we could get their common and different suggestions to support different decision-makers (see Figure 2 – 6).

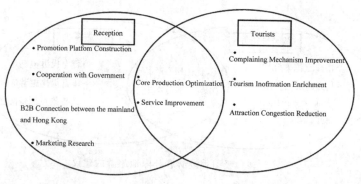

Figure 2 – 6　Suggestions to Attract Tourists of Hong Kong to Chinese Mainland

1. Common Suggestions from the Reception and Tourists

（1）Core Product Optimization

From the perspective of the reception, the core values of some tourism products have not been completely explored. For example, some respondents reflected that the core tourism products in Hainan are not good as the cultural value of the destination was not developed and promoted effectively. Compared with the island tourism products of destinations such as Thailand, Cambodiaetcetc., and Chinese Taiwan different local culture and custom are the most valuable parts of the products, apart from the similar sunshine, seas and beaches. Essentially, such destinations provide a great model for Hainan to improve tourism products. In addition, products subdivision plays a significant role to optimize tourism products. It is important for tourism destinations to design targeted products

方面。如果旅游目的地希望吸引香港不同群体的游客，他们首先要根据目标市场的年龄结构及特殊需求，设计出一些针对这一人群的旅游产品，而不是直接推荐一般的大众旅游产品给他们。

（2）提升服务水平

在景区方面，尤其是在旅游旺季，可以针对有特殊需求的游客增添一些便捷服务，比如快速通道或等候室，以减少他们的站立等候时间。在餐饮配套方面，接待方可以根据香港人的口味，进行一些调整，以满足这一人群的特殊需求。服务人员的专业素质同样是需要改进的方面。接待方可以对一线服务人员进行系统的专业培训及定期考核以使他们达到并保持较高的服务水准，从而减少由人员服务问题引发的投诉。

2. 接待方提出的其他建议

（1）搭建宣传平台

由于市场不同，内地的旅游接待方对香港市场所惯用的宣传渠道并不是很了解。例如，在内地很受欢迎的微博等社交平台在香港地区并不被广泛使用。而香港地区很受欢迎的"脸书（Facebook）"及"What's App"在内地却不常用（或无法使用）。香港理工大学 2015 年的研究结果显示，互联网、报纸杂志、电视节目以及旅游展是香港游客获得赴内地旅游信息的主要途径。因此，内地景区可以选择通过这些平台向香港游客宣传，并积极参加各种旅游展，从而最大可能地与目标市场进行互动，扩大目的地的知名度。

（2）与政府部门合作

政府部门在两地旅游发展中扮演着至关重要的角色。首先，上级政府可以利用自己的资源，对各旅游目的地进行统一的营销宣传，将各种旅游资源加以整合，从而进行统一的一站式服务，以期达到最佳的宣传推广效果。其次，内地与香港特区政府也应进行更紧密的合作，通过政府间合作提高宣传促销活动的影响力，以及内地旅游目的地在港澳地区的知名度。

（3）两地 B2B 对接

B2B 对接主要是指两地的旅游运营方在一定的平台上进行直接的沟通。

according to age structure and special requirements of their target market if they want to appeal to different segments of tourists from Hong Kong, rather than recommending mass tourism products to them.

(2) Service Improvement

In tourism attractions, especially in the peak season, it could increase some special service, such as express entry and waiting room for tourists with special needs to reduce their standing time. In terms of catering service, the reception could adjust their supply to meet unique needs based on the taste of Hong Kong residents. Meanwhile, the quality of service staff need to be improved. The reception could provide systematic training and periodical assessment for front-line employees to achieve and maintain high-standard service, and consequently reduce complaints that are caused by service problems.

2. Other Suggestions from the Reception

(1) Promotion Platform Construction

Because of the different markets, the reception of the mainland is not familiar with the promotion channels that are used in Hong Kong. For instance, social networks, such as Weibo, which is popular in the mainland, but not widely used in Hong Kong. In contrast Facebook and What's App that are welcomed in Hong Kong are not popular in the mainland (or cannot be used). The research of The Hong Kong Polytechnic University in 2015 indicated that the Internet, newspapers and magazines, television programs and tourism exhibitions are main channels for Hong Kong tourists to acquire tourism information in the mainland. Therefore, tourism attractions in the mainland could use such channels, and actively participate in various tourism exhibitions, so as to maximize the connection with the target market and increase its popularity.

(2) Cooperation with Government

Government plays a significant role in the tourism development of Hong Kong, and the mainland. Firstly, government can make use of their resources and promote tourism destinations consistently by integrating resources to offer unified one-stop service in order to achieve the best pubeicity and promotion effect. Secondly, government cooperation between the mainland and Hong Kong needs to be further enhanced through boosting the promotional influence and reputation improvement of the mainland tourism destinations in Hong Kong.

(3) B2B Connection between the mainland and Hong Kong

B2B connection mainly refers to the tour operators of the mainland and Hong

这种对接可以使两地的旅游运营方共享资源,互通有无。例如,旅游接待方的受访者表示,他们希望跟香港当地的旅游平台直接联系,因为当地的平台对香港市场比较熟悉。这样,香港游客可以通过香港的平台直接进行预订,然后平台可以将预订信息直接传递过来,由接待方进行落实。另外,接待方也希望多参与一些像旅游展之类的交流活动,这样可以在这些交流平台上认识更多的潜在合作伙伴。

（4）市场调查

旅游接待方表示对香港的市场没有一个整体的认识,不了解这些人的出游习惯和需求。这也是内地大部分旅游产品在开发及设计中所遇到的问题。针对这一问题,系统的市场调查和产品可行性分析是较好的解决方案。

3. 旅游者提出的其他建议

（1）健全投诉机制

首先,投诉机制要透明公开,相关部门要公开投诉的相关信息,使赴内地旅游的游客都了解相关程序,从而使游客更加便捷地行使此类权利。这也有助于旅游行业的自我监督与健康发展。另外,反馈的程序需要简单化、便捷化。例如,可以借用当今的信息技术,使游客进入一个目的地时,手机可以自动收到当地旅游部门的提示信息,包括一些游客常用的旅游信息,以及投诉或表扬的快速链接等。

（2）丰富优化旅游信息

对于旅游者而言,尤其是对于自由行的旅游者来说,旅游信息的准确性与及实时性非常重要。有些地区的交通状况已经发生了改变,但是旅游指南及当地的指示牌却仍然没有及时更新,这给游客出行带来了很多不必要的困扰。另外,旅游信息的翻译准确度需要提高。部分受访者反映,一些旅游标识直接使用汉语拼音充当英文翻译,而没有使用标准的英文翻译。

（3）改善景点拥挤问题

拥挤现象在内地的旅游景区中比较严重,节假日时更为突出,很多

Kong who have a direct communication through platforms. This can help them to share resources and keep connections. For example, the respondents from the reception said that they would like to connect with tourism platforms of Hong Kong directly, as these platforms are more familiar with the local market. Hence Hong Kong tourists could book tourism services through the local platforms, and then these platforms also could directly transfer reservation information to the reception of the mainland. Moreover, the reception hopes to participate in various exchange activities, such as tourism exhibitions, so that they could build up a good relationship with potential partners.

(4) Marketing Research

The reception of the mainland indicated that without an overall understanding of the tourism market, they could not better understand Hong Kong tourists' travelling habits and demands. This is a common problem with the design and development of tourism product in the mainland. Tackling this problem, a better method is to produce a systematic marketing research and a feasibility analysis.

3. Other Suggestions from Tourists

(1) Complaint Mechanism Improvement

On one hand, the complaining mechanism is required to serve the public, which means that the relevant departments need to provide full information to tourists. Based on the information, tourists gain a better understanding of the complain procedure and could make it into practice more conveniently and effectively if necessary, which is beneficial to the self-supervision and development of tourism industry. On the other hand, it is important to have a brief and convenient feedback procedure. For instance, when tourists come to a tourism destination, they could automatically receive short message service from local tourism departments through information technology, including some tourism information and useful links for complain and praising.

(2) Tourism Information Enrichment

The accuracy and timeliness of tourism information is particularly important for tourists, especially for free walkers. Traffic conditions in some regions have been changed, but the travelling guides and local signs are not updated in time, which results in a lot of unnecessary troubles to the tourists. In addition, the accuracy of tourism information translation needs to be improved. Some respondents suggested that some tourism logos are translated directly in Chinese Pinyin instead of standardized English translation.

(3) Attraction Congestion Reduction

Congestion is a serious problem in tourism attractions in the mainland,

地区会出现人满为患的情况。旅游景区可针对这一问题,利用科学分流的方法,尽量缓解局部地区过于拥挤的现象。同时,香港游客也意识到,他们可以选择在香港放假而同时内地非节假日的时间出游。对此,接待方可以与旅行社合作,向港澳中老年旅游者宣传这种"错高峰旅游"的概念。

especially on public holiday，it is overcrowded in many areas. To address this problem，tourism attractions could adopt distribution methods to ease the overcrowding in some areas. At the same time，the tourists of Hong Kong are aware that they could travel to the mainland on holidays of Hong Kong but not the holidays in the mainland. Therefore，the reception could cooperate with travel agencies to promote a perception of travelling at off-peak season to the middle-aged and elderly tourists in Hong Kong and Macao.

中国内地出境旅游
Outbound Tourism of Chinese Mainland

第3章 中国内地出境旅游概况

 学习目标

- 了解经济发展对中国内地出境旅游的影响
- 了解政策对中国内地出境旅游的影响
- 了解中国内地游客的热门目的地

3.1 经济发展对中国内地出境旅游的影响

在经济持续快速增长和居民收入显著增加的推动下,中国内地的出境旅游在过去的 20 年中经历了前所未有的发展。

如图 3-1 所示,进入新世纪以来,中国人均国内生产总值一直保持着较快的增长速度,从 2001 年的 1047 美元增长到 2015 年的 7590 美元,平均年增长速度为 16.5%。当人们变得富有、不必担心吃穿等基本生活需求时,他们就会去旅行。由于收入的提高和假期的增加,旅游已成为中国内地居民生活的一部分(联合国世界旅游组织 UNWTO,2006)。他们开始在国内旅行,并前往全球的其他国家或地区。欧睿信息咨询公司(2012)发现,中国内地的中产阶级更喜欢出国旅行,因为他们相信海外旅游经验可以帮助他们感受不同的文化,学习新知识,相较国内旅游可以更好地放松自己。联合国世界旅游组织 UNWTO(2012)也报道,国际旅游目的地忽视中国内地游客是不合理的,因为他们将来会成为出境旅游的主力军。事实上,中国内地出境过夜游客在 2014 年便突破了一亿大关,达到 1.17 亿人次,比 15 年前的数量高出10 倍。即使在 2009 年,当全球遭受金融危机时,中国内地的出境旅游也保持了正增长。自 2013 年起中国内地便已成为世界上最大的出境旅游市场。

Chapter 3   Overall Outbound Tourism of Chinese Mainland

 ## Learning Outcomes

■ Understanding the impact of economic development on the outbound tourism of Chinese Mainland

■ Understanding the impact of policies on the outbound tourism of Chinese Mainland

■ Understading the top destinations of visitors from Chinese Mainland

3.1   *The Impact of Economic Development on the Outbound Tourism of Chinese Mainland*

Driven by the sustained and rapid economic growth and significant improvement of income of the residents, the outbound tourism of Chinese Mainland has enjoyed an unprecedented growth in the last two decades.

As shown in Figure 3 – 1, GDP per capita of China has maintained a fast growth rate since the new century, increasing from $1,047 in 2001 to $7,590 in 2015 with an average annual growth rate of 16.5%. When people become rich and do not need to worry about food and clothing, they will start to travel. Due to the increase of income and longer holidays, travel has become part of the residents' lives in Chinese Mainland (UNWTO, 2006). They start to travel within the country and then to explore other countries/regions in the world. Euromonitor International (2012) noticed that the middle classes in Chinese Mainland prefer to travel aboard because they believe that oversea travel experience could help them to enjoy different cultures, learn new knowledge and get better relaxation than domestic tourism. UNWTO (2012) also reported that it is not reasonable for international destinations to overlook the tourists from Chinese Mainland as they will become the main force of the outbound tourism in the next fature. As a result, overnight departures from Chinese Mainland broke through 100 million in 2014 for the first time, peaking at 116.59 million, which was 10 times more than the figure of 15 years ago. Even in 2009 when the Chinse economy suffered from the Global Financial Crisis, the outbound tourism of Chinese Mainland still kept a positive growth. Chinese Mainland has been the world's largest outbound tourism market since 2013.

从图 3-1 也可以看出，由于中国的汇率改革，从 2005 年开始，中国内地出境游客和旅行支出的增长速度便开始提升。人民币自汇率改革以来对美元升值 25%，这意味着中国内地游客有了更多的购买力。随着收入的快速增长，旅行支出的年增长率达到 20.9%，比同期出境过夜游客（19.0%）还高。与出境游客规模的扩大相类似，中国自 2012 年以来已成为世界上最大的旅游支出国，与作为第二大消费国的美国之间的差距在 2014 年进一步增加到 540 亿美元（联合国世界旅游组织 UNWTO，2015）。

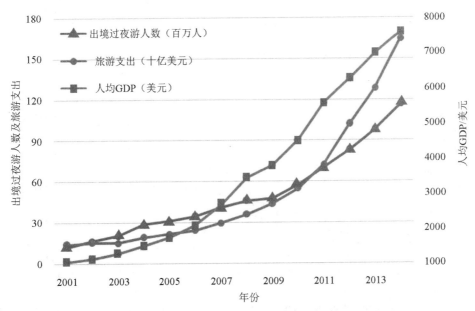

图 3-1　中国内地出境旅游和中国人均 GDP
（资料来源：联合国世界旅游组织，2016；中国经济产业数据库，2016）

3.2　中国内地出境旅游政策的影响

除了经济的快速增长和汇率的增值，出境旅游政策的放松也在中国内地出境旅游发展中起到了重要的作用。

1. 旅游目的地许可计划

在中国内地出境旅游的发展过程中，最重要的政策是旅游目的地许可计划。该计划首先在 1990 年与新加坡、马来西亚和泰国等东南亚国家签署实施。虽然赴港澳的旅行团在 1983 年便已开放，但出游目的仅限于探访港澳亲属，同时费用需由亲属支付。这项限制分别于 1997 年和 1999 年香港和澳

It can also be seen in Figure 3 – 1 that the growth rates of both departures from Chinese Mainland and the travel expenditure started to accelerate in 2005 due to the exchange rate reform of China. Chinese RMB has appreciated more than 25% against US Dollars, since then which gives Chinese tourists more purchasing power than previously. Together with the rapid increase of income, the growth of travel expenditure is 20.9% per annum which is even higher than overnight departurers (19.0%) in the same period. Similar to the expansion of outbound visitors, China has become the largest spender in the world since 2012 and the gap with the USA, which is the second largest spender, was further widened to $ 54 billion in 2014 (UNWTO, 2015).

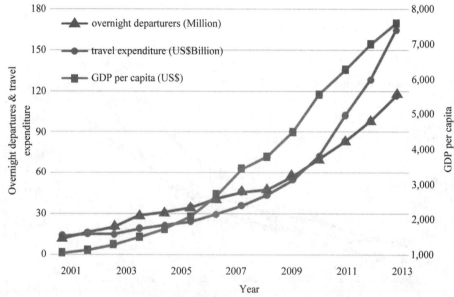

Figure 3 – 1   The development of outbound tourism of Chinese Mainland and GDP percapita of China
(Data source: United Nations World Tourism Organization, 2016; China Economic and Industry Data, 2016)

3.2   *The Relaxed Policies on the Outbound Tourism of Chinese Mainland*

Inspite of the rapid economic growth and exchange rate appreciation, the relaxing outbound policies also play an important role in the development of the outbound tourism of Chinese Mainland.

1. The Approved Destination Status

The most important policy for outbound tourism of Chinese Mainland is the ADS system which was launched in 1990 with southeast Asian countries such as Singapore, Malaysia and Thailand. Although group tours to Hong Kong and Macao were carried out in 1983, the purpose was limited to visiting relatives in Hong Kong and Macao and the expenses should be paid by the relatives there. This limitation was abolished by Hong Kong in 1997

门回归后被废除,中国内地居民可以以休闲度假、探亲访友和商务等理由前往香港和澳门特别行政区。

旅游目的地许可计划是中国和目的地政府签订的协议。根据该协议,只有符合资质的旅行社可以经营出境旅游团到签署协议的目的地,同时也只有签署协议的目的地境内符合资质的旅行社才能接待中国内地旅行团。这样做的目的是确保游客的安全,同时,还可以防止非法移民。此外,在中国内地和签署协议的目的地,只有通过认证的旅行社可推广和组织旅游团,为游客申请签证,并使用外币进行国际支付(Hsueh,2013)。该协议只适用于休闲旅游,不适用于商务旅行。在本书写作之前,已有 146 个国家和地区与中国签署了该协议,覆盖亚洲、欧洲、美洲、大洋洲和非洲等旅游目的地。

2. 自由化签证政策

虽然旅游目的地许可计划显著地刺激了中国内地的出境旅游发展,但游客数量受到严格控制。为了促使香港从"非典"(SARS)导致的经济衰退中复苏,中国政府于 2003 年推出了自由行计划(IVS),允许来自北京、上海和广东省的 8 个城市的居民以自由行的方式赴香港或澳门旅行。这是签证自由化与中国内地出境旅游发展的一个里程碑,因为这是中国内地游客第一次可以以自由行的方式出境旅游,而不必参加旅行团。该政策的效果可谓立竿见影。2003 年赴香港的内地旅客增加至 847 万,较上年增长24.1%。此后自由行政策进一步放开,2004 年增加了另外 22 个城市。在本书写作之际,已有来自于 49 个城市的居民,包括广东省的所有城市和其他 28 个城市,覆盖中国内地一线和二线城市,可以自由前往香港或澳门。香港旅游发展局估计,香港三分之二的内地游客来自于自由行计划,并相信自由行是香港旅游发展在过去十年保持快速增长的最重要的因素(Liu 和 McKercher,2014)。

在 2009 年自由行进一步放开时,中国政府宣布在深圳和珠海这两个与香港和澳门接壤的边境城市的居民可以申请多次往返签证,没有访问次数的限制。这项政策不仅是对过夜游客起作用,更是有效地刺激了一日游的游客。据 Liu 和 McKercher(2014),自 2009 年自由行政策进一步放宽以来,中国内地当天往返的访港旅客的年均增长速度超过了 30%。

and Macao in 1999 after the handovers to China respectively so that the residents of Chinese Mainland could travel to the two SARs for any purposes including leisure, visiting relatives and friends, business etc.

The ADS scheme is an arrangement signed between China and the destination governments. According to ADS, only qualified travel agencies could operate outbound group tours to the ADS destinations and only qualified tour operators in the destinations could host Chinese Mainland group tours. The aim is to ensure the safety of the tourists and also to prevent illegal immigration. Furthermore, only such certified ADS travel agencies of Chinese Mainland and destinations are available to promote and organize tour groups, apply visas for tourists and conduct international payment using foreign currencies (Hsueh, 2013). ADS only works for leisure tourism, and is not applicable for business travel. At the time of writing, 146 countries/regions have signed the ADS with China covering the destinations in Asia, Europe, Americas, Pacific and Africa.

2. Liberalization of Visa Policies

Although the ADS scheme stimulates the outbound tourism of Chinese Mainland significantly, the number of visitors are strictly controlled. To help Hong Kong recover from the recession caused by the severe acute respiratory syndrome (SARS), the Individual Travel Scheme (IVS) was introduced in 2003 by the Chinese government, allowing residents from Beijing, Shanghai and eight cities in Guangdong province to visit Hong Kong and Macao as independent tourists. This is a milestone in the visa liberalization and the development of the outbound tourism of Chinese Mainland, because this is the first time that visitors of Chinese Mainland could travel outbound individually without any restrictions from the tour groups. The policy effect emerged immediately. The numbers of visitor arrivals from the mainland to Hong Kong surprisingly increased to 8.47 million in 2003, showing a 24.1% annual growth rate. The IVS policy was further introduced to another 22 cities in 2004 and at the time of writing, residents from 49 cities including all the cities in Guangdong province and another 28 cities covering the first and second tiers of the mainland are free to visit Hong Kong and Macao. Hong Kong Tourism Board (HKTB) estimated that two-thirds of the tourists from the mainland are under the IVS and believes the IVS is the most important trigger for Hong Kong tourism to maintain a rapid growth in the last decade (Liu & McKercher, 2014).

The IVS was further liberalized in 2009 when Chinese government announced that permanent residents in Shenzhen and Zhuhai, the two border cities with the two SARs, could apply for multi-entrance visa to Hong Kong and Macao respectively without any restriction on the number of visits. This policy stimulates not only the overnight visitors, but more effectively on the same-day visitors. According to Liu and McKercher (2014), the average annual growth rate of the same day visitors from the mainland to Hong Kong is more than 30% since 2009 when the IVS was further relaxed.

作为中国内地出境游的两大旅游目的地,香港和澳门在 2014 年占据了 60% 以上的出境游市场份额,不断放松的签证政策对这两个特别行政区的影响是显著的。这些政策不仅促进了香港入境旅游的发展,同时也带动了整个中国内地出境旅游市场的发展。

中国的签证自由化仍在继续。赴台自由行的政策于 2011 年执行。来自北京、上海和厦门的居民有资格申请赴台自由行签证,配额为每天 500 人。赴台自由行城市数量由 2012 年的 10 个增长到本书写作时的 42 个。其结果是,大陆赴台游客从 2012 年到 2014 年年平均增长率为 22.8%。据预计,赴台自由行政策在不久的将来将扩大到更多的城市,这有助于台湾吸引更多的大陆游客。

长途旅游目的地签证政策也在不断放松。赴美国和英国的多次入境签证有效期已延长至 10 年。其他目的地如法国、意大利、澳大利亚和泰国也在与中国商讨简化和放宽签证政策。

在放宽签证政策的推动下,我们相信,即使中国经济目前面临较大的增长压力,中国内地的出境旅游也会得以高速发展。

3.3　中国内地游客的热门目的地

表 3-1 展示了中国内地游客赴五大洲的市场份额。中国内地出境市场的结构在过去十年基本稳定。亚洲是中国内地游客的主要目的地,占据超过 80% 的市场份额。随着中国内地出境旅游的发展,越来越多的中国游客在积累了国内和短途出境的旅游经验后开始前往长途目的地。其结果是,欧洲和美洲的市场份额有所扩大,在 2014 年分别达到 12.18% 和 3.46%。

表 3-1　中国内地出境旅游市场份额

市场	2005 年	2010 年	2014 年
非洲	0.54%	0.96%	0.72%
美洲	1.60%	2.56%	3.46%
亚洲	83.99%	84.39%	81.97%
欧洲	12.39%	10.56%	12.18%
大洋洲	1.47%	1.54%	1.67%

（资料来源：联合国世界旅游组织 UNWTO,2016）

As Hong Kong and Macao are the top two destinations for the mainland, occupying more than 60% outbound market share in 2014, the impact of the specific policies to the two SARs is significant. It not only triggers the development of the inbound tourism in Hong Kong, but also stimulates the whole outbound market of the mainland as well.

The visa liberalization of the mainland is still going on. The IVS was introduced to outbound tourism to Taiwan in 2011. Residents from Beijing, Shanghai and Xiamen are eligible to apply for independent visa to Taiwan with a quota of 500 people per day. The number of cities in IVS with Taiwan rolled to 10 cities in 2012 and reached 42 at the time of writing. As a result, arrivals from the mainland to Taiwan increased 22.8% per annum from 2012 to 2014. It is expected that cities under the IVS with Taiwan would be further expanded in the near future which helps Taiwan to attract more visitors from the mainland.

The liberalization of visa polices to long-haul destinations has also been carried out. The multi-entrance visa with the valid period of 10 years is available for both the USA and the UK. Other destinations are also discussing with China to simplify and liberalize the visa policies such as France, Italy, Australia and Thailand.

Driven by the relaxed visa policies, it is believed that the outbound tourism of Chinese Mainland would further develop with a high rapid growth even though the pressure on economic growth in China nowadays is higher than previous years.

3.3 Top Destinations of Visitors of Chinese Mainland

Table 3 – 1 presents the market shares of Chinese Mainland visitors to the five continents. The structure of the outbound market of Chinese Mainland is stable in the last decade. Asia is the dominant region for Chinese Mainland's visitors, occupying more than 80% market share. As to the development of the outbound tourism in Chinese Mainland, more and more Chinese travelers started to visit long-haul destinations after they accumulate enough travelling experience from short-haul or domestic experience. As a result, the market shares of Europe and Americas enjoyed a little expansion to 12.18% and 3.46% in 2014 respectively.

Table 3 – 1   Market share of Chinese Mainland outbound market

Market	2005	2010	2014
Africa	0.54%	0.96%	0.72%
Americas	1.60%	2.56%	3.46%
Asia	83.99%	84.39%	81.97%
Europe	12.39%	10.56%	12.18%
Pacific	1.47%	1.54%	1.67%

(Date Source: United Nations World Tourism Organization, 2016)

如果我们从目的地国家/地区的角度看,就可以发现,中国内地出境游客的五大目的地分别是韩国、日本和中国的香港、澳门、台湾地区(见图 3-2)。这五个目的地在 2014 年吸引了 8102 万中国内地游客,占中国内地出境旅游市场的 69.5%。

香港在中国内地游客的出境市场中占据主导地位,这得益于其与内地相邻的地理位置和相似的文化。在自由行政策的刺激下,赴港的内地游客呈现出持续快速的增长。从图 3-2 可以观察到,赴港旅客不管是数量还是增长速度都比其他四个目的地高得多。

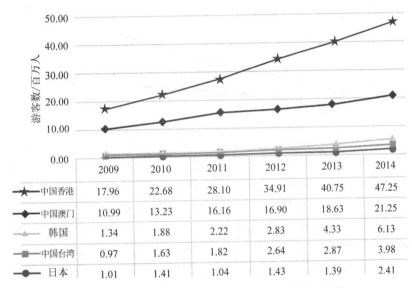

	2009	2010	2011	2012	2013	2014
中国香港	17.96	22.68	28.10	34.91	40.75	47.25
中国澳门	10.99	13.23	16.16	16.90	18.63	21.25
韩国	1.34	1.88	2.22	2.83	4.33	6.13
中国台湾	0.97	1.63	1.82	2.64	2.87	3.98
日本	1.01	1.41	1.04	1.43	1.39	2.41

图 3-2　中国内地游客赴五大目的地游客数量(百万)
(资料来源:联合国世界旅游组织,2016)

作为中国的另一个特别行政区,澳门是中国内地出境游市场第二热门的目的地。澳门也从自由行政策中受益,2014 年内地赴澳游客增加至 2125 万人,虽然游客数量还不到香港的一半,但比其他三个目的地多得多。

韩国是除港澳地区以外,最受中国内地游客欢迎的目的地。这受益于其对中国成功的文化输出,如明星、电视剧、食品和化妆品。许多中国内地游客喜欢去韩国体验完全不同的文化。此外,韩国著名的度假胜地济州岛对中国内地游客免签证,这也可能有助于韩国吸引更多的中国内地游客。

随着台湾地区和大陆自由行政策的不断放开,台湾地区在大陆出境游市场中扮演着越来越重要的角色。大陆赴台游客数量由 2009 年

If we look at the market share from country/region level, it can be found that the top five destinations of Chinese Mainland visitors are R.O.Korea, Japan and Hong Kong, Macao, Taiwan of China respectively (see Figure 3 – 2). The five destinations attracted 81.02 million visitors of Chinese Mainland, accounting for 69.5% share of all the departures from Chinese Mainland in 2014.

Hong Kong is the dominant outbound market for the mainland's tourists. Thanks to the stimulus of the IVS policy and the close distance and similar culture to the mainland, the number of visitors from the mainland to Hong Kong has shown a rapid and sustained grouth. It can be observed in Figure 3 – 2 that either the number of visitors to Hong Kong or the growth rate of Hong Kong is much higher than the other four destinations.

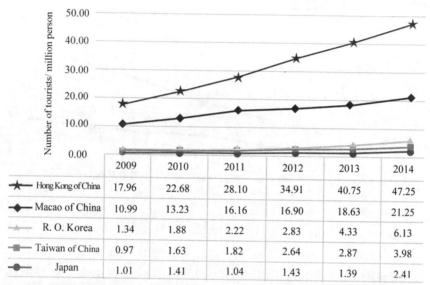

Figure 3 – 2　The number of visitors from Chinese Mainland to top five destinations（Million）
(Data source: United Nations World Tourism Organization, 2016)

As the other SAR of China, Macao is the second most popular destination in the outbound market of the mainland. Macao also benefits from the IVS policy and visitors from the mainland increased to 21.25 million in 2014. Although the number is less than half of Hong Kong, it is much more than the other three destinations.

R.O.Korea is the most popular destination for the visitors of the mainland except after the two SARs. Benefited from the successful culture exports to China such as the pop stars, TV dramas, food and cosmetics, many Chinese Mainland's visitors prefer to go to R.O.Korea to experience different culture in a completely foreign country. In addition, Jeju Island, which is a famous holiday destination in R.O.Korea, is visa-free for Chinese Mainland's visitors. This may also help Korea to attract more Chinese Mainland's visitors.

As the expansion of IVS between Taiwan of China and Chinese Mainland, Taiwan has played a more and more important role in the outbound market of the mainland. Visitors from the mainland to Taiwan increased from 0.97 million in 2009 to

的97万人增加到2014年的398万人,年均增速为32.6%。与港澳相比,游客数量依然不大,但增长速度却令人印象深刻。可以预计,台湾地区在大陆的出境旅游市场中的市场份额将在未来进一步扩大。

日本是中国内地出境游客的第五大目的地。与韩国类似,日本同样凭借不同的文化、食品和化妆品等特色吸引中国游客。特别是如果考虑到日元的大幅贬值,赴日本的中国游客数量将会有较快的增长。然而,赴日的旅客人数往往对两国间的政治纠纷,如领土争端等问题比较敏感。这也是2013年赴日中国游客数量显著下跌的最主要原因。

总体来说,中国内地的出境旅游在过去几十年取得了令人瞩目的发展。这不仅得益于中国内地强劲的经济增长和居民收入水平的不断提高,也得益于对中国内地游客日益简化的签证政策,如旅游目的地许可计划和对港澳台地区的自由行政策。

毫无疑问,香港地区是中国内地出境游市场中最受欢迎的目的地,在五个热门目的地中,拥有最大的游客数量和最快的增长速度。可以预测,香港将在内地出境旅游发展中发挥最重要的作用。因此下一章将选取香港作为例子来全面介绍中国内地的出境旅游。

3.98 million in 2014 with an average annual growth rate of 32.6%. Compared with Hong Kong and Macao, the volume is still small whereas the growth rate is impressive. It could be expected that the market share of Taiwan in the outbound market of the mainland will further expand in the future.

Japan is the fifth largest destination of Chinese Mainland. The advantages of Japan to attract Chinese Mainland's visitors is similar to R.O. Korea such as the different culture, food and cosmetics. Particularly, if the depreciation of Japanese Yen is taken into consideration, the growth of Japan would be even faster. However, visitor arrivals from Chinese Mainland to Japan is very sensitive to the political issues such as the ongoing territorial disputes. This is the main reason to explain the significant drop of visitors from Chinese Mainland in 2013.

In summary, the outbound tourism of Chinese Mainland has enjoyed unbelievable development in the past decades. The expansion is not only stimulated by the strong economic growth and the improvement of income level of residents, but also driven by the visa liberalization in Chinese Mainland such as the ADS and IVS with Hong Kong, Macao and Taiwan.

There is no doubt that Hong Kong SAR is the most popular destination in the outbound market of Chinese Mainland with largest arrivals and fastest growth rate in the top five largest destination of Chinese Mainland. It can also be predicted that Hong Kong will play the most essential role in the development of outbound tourism of the mainland for quite a long time in the future. Thus the next chapter takes Hong Kong as an example to introduce the outbound tourism of Chinese Mainland comprehensively.

第4章　赴港出境游

学习目标

- ■ 掌握社会可持续发展的测度指标
- ■ 掌握经济可持续发展的测度指标
- ■ 学习研究可持续发展的研究方法

4.1　中国内地赴港出境游现状

本章的内容摘自香港理工大学 2016 年的一份研究报告《从中国内地居民赴香港旅游的角度探索经济与社会的可持续发展之路》。内地游客对香港旅游业的成功至关重要。如图 4-1 所示,为了消除 2003 年"非典"危机带来的不良国际影响,中国政府试图通过推出自由行计划以刺激旅游业发展,帮助香港经济复苏。根据该计划,获得批准的城市的内地游客可以以自由行的方式到香港旅游,如上海、北京和广州。该方案随后扩展至 49 个内地城市,包括整个广东省(所有 21 个城市)、北京、上海、天津、重庆、南京和苏州等。2009 年,为了应对全球金融危机给香港带来的影响,自由行政策进一步放宽,约有 400 万深圳居民可以申请"一年多签"。中国内地游客访问香港人(次)数从 2003 年的 847 万增加到 2014 年的 4720 万,占香港入境游客的 77.7%(香港旅游发展局 HKTB,2014)。毫无疑问,如此大的游客规模对香港这个仅拥有 700 万常住人口和 1104 平方公里面积的城市的影响是巨大的。如此大规模的旅游通常称为"大众旅游",因为游客数量的增加,对居民和基础设施会产生许多影响。然而,在现有的研究中并没有评估游客数量及其影响的具体方法。

尽管内地游客赴港旅游为香港带来了可观的经济效益,但入境客流

Chapter 4   Outbound Tourism to Hong Kong

 Learning Outcomes

- Understanding the measurements of social sustainability
- Understanding the measurements of economic sustainability
- Learning the research method to analyse sustainable development

4.1   Current Status of Mainland's Tourists Outbound to Hong Kong

The content of this chapter is referred to *Towards Sustainability*: *Exploring the Social and Economic Dimensions of Travel to Hong Kong by Mainland Chinese*, a report issued by the Hong Kong Polytechnic University in 2016. Tourists from the mainland are crucial to the success of Hong Kong's tourism industry. As indicated in Figure 4 – 1, after the negative international publicity from the SARS crisis in 2003, the Chinese government attempted to help the Hong Kong economy recover by stimulating the tourism sector with the introduction of the Individual Visit Scheme (IVS). Under the IVS scheme, the tourists of the mainland from approved cities, such as Shanghai, Beijing, and Guangzhou, may visit Hong Kong on an individual basis. This scheme has subsequently expanded to 49 cities of the mainland, including the entire Guangdong province (all 21 cities), Beijing, Shanghai, Tianjin, Chongqing, Nanjing, and Suzhou etc. The further expansion of IVS in 2009, which was a response to the impact of the global financial crisis in Hong Kong, about four million Shenzhen residents were endorsed for one-year multiple-entry visits to Hong Kong. The number of the mainland's tourists in Hong Kong increased from 8.47 million in 2003 to 47.2 million in 2014, accounting for 77.7% of tourist arrivals in 2014 (HKTB, 2014). These figures would certainly affect the resident population of seven million in a city like Hong Kong with only 1,104 square kilometers. This volume of tourism is often called as "mass tourism" because the increase of the number of tourists affect residents and infrastructure. However, there is no agreed formula which can help to evaluate the the impact on communities of particular volumes of tourists relative to the community population.

Although the tourists from the mainland have brought considerable economic benefits to Hong Kong, the visitor inflow also causes some problems such as the increase

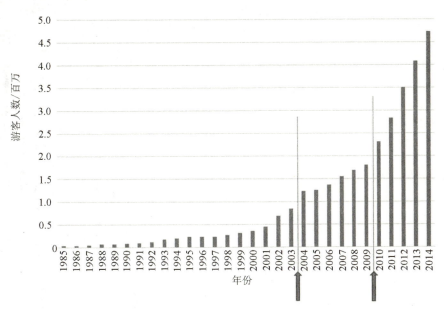

图4-1 1985—2014年赴香港的内地游客数量
(资料来源：香港旅游发展局，2014)

也引起了一系列问题，例如消费品和房地产价格的上涨（Chow，2012）以及公共资源的过度使用（Ye、Zhang和Yuen，2012）。旅游业的快速增长也带动了中国内地游客前往香港的非旅游区，进而影响社区发展。这些香港居民所面临的负面影响，促使当地政府考虑如何平衡入境游客所带来的正面和负面的社会和经济影响。从当地居民和游客之间存在的与潜在的紧张局势来看，研究旅游业对香港未来旅游发展所产生的社会影响是很有必要的。内地入境游客给香港带来的经济效益和社会效益已引起研究者的关注。内地市场的长远可持续发展，将有赖于当地社区福利的改善、主客关系的和谐以及与赴港旅游者相关的其他方面的问题的改善。为了能够评估香港旅游业在社会和经济方面的可持续性，当前研究的目标是：

● 系统地分析中国内地游客到港旅游的发展过程；

● 根据世界旅游组织的基线指标，评估中国内地游客到港旅游的可持续发展水平；

● 为政府制定未来与内地游客赴港旅游相关的政策提供建议，从而提高

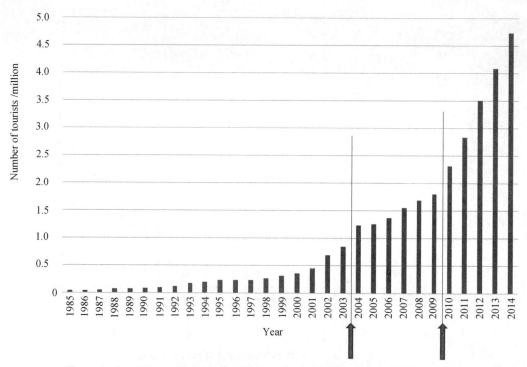

Figure 4 – 1   Chinese Mainland's tourist arrivals in Hong Kong (1985—2014)

(Data source: Hong Kong Tourism Board, 2014)

of the price for consumer goods and properties (Chow, 2012) and the over-use of public resources (Ye, Zhang & Yuen, 2012). The rapid growth of tourism has also driven the tourists of the mainland to visit the non-tourism areas of Hong Kong, affecting the development of local communities. The negative effects faced by local Hong Kong residents have pushed the authorities to consider how to balance the positive and negative social and economic impact which is brought to Hong Kong by the travelers from the mainland. If we look at the current and potential intense situation between residents and tourists, we believe that it is urgent to review the social impact of tourism on the development of Hong Kong in the future. The economic and social effects that the tourists from the mainland brought to Hong Kong have recently aroused the attention of researchers. The sustainable development of the mainland market in the long-run depends on the improvement of the welfare in local communities, the harmonious relationship between hosts and tourists and other tourism related fields. To facilitate the assessment of social and economic sustainable development of tourism in Hong Kong, the research objectives are as follows:

● to systematically analyze the development process of the travelers from the mainland to Hong Kong;

● to assess the sustainability level of the travelers from the mainland to Hong Kong based on the baseline indicators developed by UNWTO;

● and to draw necessary implications for the formulation of future policies on the

香港旅游业长期的可持续发展水平。

4.2　出境游的相关研究

从大量有关旅游可持续发展的相关研究中我们可以得出以下结论。首先,虽然学者们已开发建立了一些定量测度旅游业可持续发展程度的指标,但很少有研究讨论旅游业在社会发展方面的可持续性。此外,根据联合国环境规划署和世界旅游组织的建议,把社会因素简化成单一指标来度量社会发展方面整体的可持续性不能全面反映可持续发展的全部信息。其次,旅游业的社会可持续性和社会影响的概念在很大程度上仍然是相互独立的。因此,本研究对理论和实践的一个潜在贡献便是开创性地将社会影响引入旅游在社会方面可持续发展的评估中。再次,正如文献所指出的,社会可持续性在不同的目的地的定义往往不同。但目前鲜有研究使用严谨的统计技术检验旅游可持续性测度指标在不同目的地的结构稳定性。在这种情况下,测度指标的匮乏阻碍了学术界和从业者对旅游业在社会可持续发展的概念方面的研究。针对上述的研究空白,本研究旨在以香港作为目的地,建立一套有效可靠的指标体系,来评估旅游业发展的社会可持续性。

现有文献对旅游的经济可持续性的研究尚不够深入,对经济可持续性本身的概念和影响因素都没有达成共识。尽管人们都认为经济可持续性是一个需要从多角度去度量的概念,但却很少有研究去探讨旅游发展过程中经济可持续发展的维度。文献中度量差异也很大。现有的研究往往强调经济表现的客观定量指标(如国内生产总值、就业率),其他非市场化的福利指标却被忽视(如目的地吸引力,高质量的游客经验)。值得注意的是,目前只有少数的研究采用了主观指标来反映当地利益相关者对经济可持续性的判断。为了填补上述研究空白,本研究旨在为经济可持续性制定一个更广义的定义,并制定一套有效可靠的测量指标来评估旅游业发展的经济可持续性。

4.3　研究方法

为了评估香港旅游业在社会和经济方面的可持续,本研究将采用文献综述、深入访谈和电话调查多种方法来增强结论的可靠性。本研究按表 4-1 中的 10 个步骤来开发和建立有关社会和经济可持续发展的测度指标。

development of the mainland market to Hong Kong in such a way that the sustainable development of tourism in Hong Kong can be enhanced in the long run.

4.2 Relevant Research

Several conclusions may be drawn from the substantial body of work on the measurement of sustainable tourism. Firstly, although some measurement instruments have been developed to quantify the extent to which tourism is sustainable, few studies have focused on the social aspects of sustainable tourism. Moreover, scales that view the social element as simply a single dimension of overall sustainable measurement are insufficient to deliver comprehensive information according to the broad guidelines provided by UNEP and UNWTO. Secondly, the concepts of social sustainability and social effects in tourism have remained largely independent of the other. On this basis, it is timely to undertake an integrated study that introduces social effects into the assessment of social sustainability as a potential contribution to both the theoretical and practical literature. Thirdly, as noted in the literature, social sustainability may vary in different destination settings. Unfortunately, few researchers have tested the structural stability of measurements of tourism sustainability in different contexts using rigorous statistical techniques. In such cases, the lack of measurement has hindered the development of social sustainability concepts for both academics and practitioners. To address the aforementioned research gaps, the present study uses Hong Kong as the host location to develop a valid and reliable measurement tool for assessing the social sustainability of tourism development.

Regarding the economic sustainability, the literature only scratches the surface of tourism economic sustainability. There is little agreed definition of either the phenomenon itself or its main drivers. Although perceived as a multi-faceted concept, few studies have explored the dimensionality of tourism economic sustainability. Inconsistency of indicators for measuring tourism economic sustainability is revealed in the literature. Existing research tends to rely on objective financial indicators of economic performance (e.g., GDP, employment rate). Other non-market criteria that contribute to economic well-being (e.g., destination attractiveness, high quality experience for visitors) is overlooked. It is worthy of note that only a few studies have employed subjective indicators which emphasize the perceptions of local stakeholders. To address the aforementioned research gaps, this study aims to provide a more inclusive definition and develop a valid and reliable measurement tool for assessing the economic sustainability of tourism development.

4.3 Methodology Adopted

In order to assess the social and economic sustainability of tourism in Hong Kong, the present study involved a literature review, in-depth interviews, and a telephone-based poll for enhancing the reliability of the conclusions. A 10-step approach was

表 4－1　测度指标的建立步骤

步骤	研究方法
1.明确研究范围	文献检索
2.构建备选指标	文献检索 深度访谈
3.筛选指标和设计问卷	专家讨论 预调查(测度问卷内容的有效性)
4.收集数据	CAST(香港理工大学社会政策研究中心计算机辅助调查团队)
5.维度探索	探索性因子分析
6.可靠性评价	Alpha 系数
7.因子结构稳定性的评价 (1)	数据拆分：将数据按居民—旅游景点密度分组,在高密度和低密度组分别执行步骤 5 和 6
8.可靠性评价	复合可靠性
9.有效性评价	收敛效度 判别效度 理论效度
10.因子结构稳定性的评价(2)	数据拆分：在居民—旅游景点的高密度组和低密度组分别执行步骤 8 和 9

4.4　赴港出境游的研究结果

1. 调研的执行

问卷调查的对象是 18 岁及以上的香港永久居民。由香港理工大学社会政策研究中心(CSP)计算机辅助调查团队(CAST)于 2014 年 7 月 15 日到 2014 年 8 月 14 日实施。团队使用结构化的问卷和口语化的中文对受访对象进行电话访问。采用计算机辅助电话访问(CATI)系统的目的是收集所需信息以进行数据分析。在调查过程中,以简单随机抽样的方法获取电话号码,然后选取最近过生日的家庭成员为受访对象。对于无法联系到的受访者,访问员需要随机至少联系受访者三次。本次调查共收集 1839 份有效问卷。电话调查的详细情况见表 4－2。

adopted to develop the social and economic sustainability and its measurement instrument as indicated in Table 4 – 1.

Table 4 – 1　Procedures for developing the measurement instruments

Procedures	Techniques
1. Specify the domain of the construct	Literature search
2. Generate a sample of items	Literature search In-depth interviews
3. Purify items and design a questionnaire	Panel of experts，pilot study(content validity)
4. Collect data	CAST （computer-assisted survey team by PolyU Center for Social Policy Studies)
5. Explore dimensionality	Exploratory factor analysis
6. Assess reliability	Coefficient Alpha
7. Assess factor structure stability （1）	Data split：Conduct steps 5 and 6 in both high and low resident-tourism density groups
8. Assess reliability	Composite reliability
9. Assess validity	Convergent validity
	Discriminant validity Nomological validity
10. Assess factor structure stability （2）	Data split：Conduct steps 8 and 9 in both high and low resident-tourism density groups

4.4　The Research Findings of the Outbound Tourism to Hong Kong

1. The implementation of the survey

The survey target is permanent Hong Kong residents aged 18 years or above. It was conducted from July 15，2014 to August 14，2014 by the computer-assisted survey team （CAST） from the Centre for Social Policy Studies （CSPS） of The Hong Kong Polytechnic University. The CAST was responsible for conducting the telephone interviews using a structured questionnaire for respondents in colloquial Chinese. The computer assisted telephone interviews （CATI） system was used in order to collect the required information for analysis purposes. The telephone numbers were identified via simple random sampling，and the respondents were selected using the last-birthday method. Before considering a respondent as unreachable for interviewing，the interviewers were required to make

表 4-2 电话访问结果

样本类型	所拨电话数量
完成访谈	1839
部分访谈	131
拒绝且符合条件的单位	2366
不符合条件的单位	1056
无联系但已知符合条件的单位	7401
其他非访问单位	40207
所拨电话号码总数	53000

2. 人口统计学特征

我们用配额抽样法随机抽取三个地区的受访者。在 1839 份有效答卷中,女性受访者的人数(55.5%)超过男性受访者(44.5%),两组受访者在年龄上都分布广泛。大约分别有 44.5% 的女性受访者和 31.9% 的男性受访者持有中学/预科及本科或更高级别的学位。大部分受访者(56.6%)从事管理或专业工作,其中近三分之一从事与旅游业直接或间接相关的工作,这意味着,受访者中约有三分之二的人从事与旅游业无关的工作。因此本研究的受访者能提供代表香港居民的独立观点,而不会受到对旅游业了解程度的影响。由于话题的敏感性,只有一半左右的受访者(51.1%)愿意透露自己的收入。约有 28% 的受访者的月收入为 1 万~3 万港币。考虑到调查的普遍性,将受访者的人口状况与香港 2011 年的人口普查进行对比后,发现两个样本的性别、婚姻状况、年龄、受教育程度、工作状况、行业职业以及个人月收入是相似的。由于在普查中关于旅游就业的信息有限,旅游行业从业比例这一指标无法与普查报告比较。

3. 影响因素

我们总结出了主客冲突、社会宽容度和社会认同度三个影响旅游发展过

contact on at least three occasions. As a result，a total of 1,839 valid responses were collected. Further details on the telephone survey are shown in Table 4 – 2.

Table 4 – 2　Results of the telephone interviews

Types	Number of calls
Complete interviews	1,839
Partial interviews	131
Refused eligible units	2,366
No eligible units	1,056
Not contacted，but known eligible units	7,401
Other non-interviewed units	40,207
Total number of dialed telephone numbers	53,000

2. Demographical characteristics

Following quota sampling，the respondents were randomly selected from three regions. A total of 1,839 valid responses were collected. Female respondents（55.5%）outnumbered the male counterparts（44.5%），and both groups were widely distributed in terms of age. Approximately 44.5% and 31.9% of the respondents were holding secondary/matriculation and bachelor or higher-level degrees，respectively. Most respondents were working（56.6%），of whom nearly one-third occupied in managerial or professional roles and 13.3% were working in jobs that were either directly or indirectly related to the tourism industry which means that about 87% of the respondents were from non-tourist related sectors. This provided independent views of all Hong Kong residents without being affected by how much they know about the tourism industry. Given the sensitivity of the topic，only half of the respondents（51.1%）were willing to disclose their income on the phone. Roughly 28% of the respondents earned a monthly income ranging from 10,000HKD to 30,000HKD. Considering the generalizability of the survey，the demographic profile of respondents in the current study was comparable to the Hong Kong 2011 Population Census，as indicated in Table 4. The comparison revealed that two samples are similar for gender，marital status，age，educational attainment，working status，industry occupation as well as monthly personal income. Because of limited information about jobs in relation to tourism，this particular category cannot be aligned with the census report.

3. Affecting factors

Three factors were generated for affecting the social sustainability in the process of

程中社会可持续性的因素。主客冲突作为旅游业的社会可持续标准的重要组成部分,由代表当地居民对旅游业的投诉、调控和对旅游业的看法等八个指标来测度。这些指标主要是从文献中获取的,尤其是负面影响(Allen 等,1993;Lankford 和 Howard,1994;Latkova 和 Vogt,2012;Perdue 等,1990)、限制(Perdue 等,1990;Latkova 和 Vogt,2012)和社会成本(Choi 和 Sirakaya,2005)。社会影响存在于旅游产品生命周期的每个阶段,并因承载能力的枯竭而在整合和停滞阶段加剧(Aledo 和 Mazon,2004;Yang 等,2014)。游客的大幅增加和旅游设施的快速发展可能会引起当地居民的不满和冲突,也可能产生其他不利影响导致居民福利减少(Diedrich 和 Garc'a-Buades,2009)。

以香港为例,主客冲突主要指客源地居民对游客的抱怨,特别是对来自中国内地的游客的不恰当的行为,如大声喧哗、随地吐痰和在禁止饮食的公共场所吃东西,以及香港居民与内地游客的利益冲突。内地游客经常被指责在公共场所做出不当行为,如在列车上进食和大声说话。文化和社会规范的差异可能是导致这种冲突的主要原因。虽然香港是中国的一部分,但它有150 年被殖民的历史,所以内地和香港存在着明显的文化差异(Ye 等,2013)。文化背景的差异会扭曲行为所表达的含义(Triandis;1977),导致沟通问题的发生(Pearce,1977;1982)和幸福感的降低(Lynch,1960),从而影响社会交往(Robinson 和 Nemetz,1988)。大众游客数量的急剧增加,也使居民被迫与游客分享自己的资源(即交通和医疗设备),并导致商品短缺、消费品价格上涨,如奶粉、日用品和先进的技术设备(Chow,2012)。当地环境的拥挤和变化也增加了香港居民的不安。

社会容忍度涉及居民幸福感和与游客相处的能力。这一因素在本研究中被首次发现,它主要指居民对目的地旅游承载能力的反馈。考虑到大量的游客可能产生的影响,该因素主要从交通设施、医疗设施和社会公平等方面对容忍度进行评估。这种方法为从居民的角度来评估旅游容量水平提供了一种有效的解决方案。例如,由于香港政府的推动,医疗旅游从 2003 年到 2012 年得以迅速发展。2009 年共有 58994 位孕妇在香港产子,其中 29766 位(50%)来自中国内地(Ye、zhang 和 Yuen,2011)。当地的孕妇抱怨医院房间缺乏

tourism development, namely, Host-Guest Conflict, Social Tolerance, and Social Acceptance. Host-Guest Conflict acts as a major component of social sustainable scale in tourism. The eight items in this construct represent local complaints, control and perceptions of tourism. These were mainly adopted from the literature, notably negative impacts (Allen, et al., 1993; Lankford & Howard, 1994; Latkova & Vogt, 2012; Perdue et al., 1990), restriction (Perdue, et al., 1990; Latkova & Vogt, 2012) and social cost (Choi & Sirakaya, 2005). As discussed in the literature review, social impact exists in each stage of the cycle and are exacerbated during the consolidation and stagnation stages due to the exhaustion of carrying capacity (Aledo & Mazon, 2004; Yang et al., 2014). The great volume of tourists and speedy development of tourism facilities may arouse discontent and conflicts among local residents and may adversely lead to the decline of the welfare of the local residents (Diedrich & Garcl'a-Buades, 2009).

Taking Hong Kong as an example, host-guest conflicts emphasize the complaints by local residents about tourists, especially those from the mainland (i.e., inappropriate behavior such as shouting, spitting, and eating at forbidden public areas) and the perceived conflict of interest between local residents and the tourists from the mainland. The mainland's tourists are frequently accused of displaying improper behaviors in public areas, such as eating in trains and speaking loudly. Differences in culture and social norms may be the main reasons for such conflicts. Though Hong Kong is apart of China, it had 150 years of colonial history, and cultural differences have been identified between the two regions (Ye, et al., 2013). The dissimilarity in cultural background distorts the meanings of behaviors (Triandis, 1977), leads to communication problems (Pearce, 1977; 1982) and loss of emotional wellbeing (Lynch, 1960), and inhibits social interaction (Robinson & Nemetz, 1988). The dramatic increase in the number of mass tourists has also required residents to share their resources (i.e., transportation and medical facilities) with tourists, and has resulted in a shortage of goods and price inflation for consumer goods, such as milk powder, daily necessities, and advanced technological devices (Chow, 2012). The overcrowding and change in the local appearance of their environment also increased the anxiety of Hong Kong residents.

Social Tolerance relates to residents' wellbeing and the competence to get together with tourists. This factor has been newly explored in the present study which considers host feedback towards destination tourism capacity. Considering the possible influence of large number of tourists, items under this dimension represent the host evaluations of the transportation facilities, medical facilities and social equity. Adopting such an approach provides an efficient solution to appraise the tourism capacity level from a resident's viewpoint. For instance, as a service promoted by the Hong Kong government, medical tourism developed rapidly from 2003 to 2012. A total of 58,994 mothers gave birth in Hong Kong in 2009, of whom 29,766 (50%) were from the mainland (Ye, Zhang & Yuen, 2011). The local mothers complained about the lack of vacant rooms in hospitals

且住院费用高昂,这些都被归因为香港医疗服务的需求增加(*Wen Wei* *Po*,2010)。这种现象不利于当地居民对当地设施的使用,从而引发了他们对游客的敌对态度。

社会认同度意味着当地居民接受和支持游客和旅游发展的程度。根据之前对旅游可持续发展测度指标的研究,这一因素主要从游客满意度(Choi 和 Sirakaya,2005)、欢迎情况(Woosnam,2012)和积极影响(Allen 等,1993;Lankford 和 Howard,1994;Latkova 和 Vogt,2012;Perdue 等,1990)方面来评估当地居民对游客的看法和游客为当地带来的积极影响。一个有趣的发现是,并不是当地居民因保护(Latkova 和 Vogt,2012)和与游客共享(Boley 和 McGehee,2014)本地文化而欣慰,反而是游客让他们更深入地理解了文化的多样性。这种差异揭示了旅游的一个独特魅力,它能够提高东道主的文化竞争力(Ye 等,2013)。关心游客出游的满意度和感激游客为自身带来的利益的程度决定了当地居民能在多大程度上接受游客作为社会的一部分。要建立社会可持续的旅游业,居民对旅游业的积极态度是必需的,这需要采取具体的措施落实,如在社区和学校举办宣传活动。

按照同样的步骤,我们还识别出了三项影响经济可持续的因素,即发展调控、积极的经济作用和市场了解程度。发展调控是指对香港旅游可持续发展潜在负面影响的关注。特别是,香港居民认为游客太多可能会导致环境的破坏和旅游资源的过度消耗以及商品价格的上升。因此,他们更担心负面影响,也更愿意政府调控旅游业的发展,如限制内地和其他国家的来港旅游人数。然而,旅游业发展的影响,不能仅由负面因素决定,它应该同时从正面和负面进行评估。

旅游业在香港经济发展中显现出重要的积极作用。作为支柱产业之一,旅游业对香港的发展具有重要作用。尤其是在现今社会,港口行业和金融市场的形势不乐观。自 2003 年以来,随着自由行政策的落实,来自中国内地的游客数量保持了超过 10 年的持续增长。这不仅扩大了香港的入境市场,也在劳动力市场上提供了更多的就业机会,显著地增加了政府收入。旅游业的贡献,尤其是内地游客在过去 10 年对香港经济发展所起到的作用是不可忽视的。

and the high cost of hospitalization, which were both attributed to the increased demand for medical services in Hong Kong (*Wen Wei Po*, 2010). This phenomenon unfavorably affected the right of residents to use local facilities, hereby triggering their hostile attitude towards tourists.

Social Acceptance represents the extent to which local residents accept and appreciate tourists and tourism development. Building on previous reporting about visitor satisfaction (Choi & Sirakaya, 2005), welcoming nature (Woosnam, 2012) and positive impacts (Allen et al., 1993; Lankford & Howard, 1994; Latkova & Vogt, 2012; Perdue, et al., 1990) in the measurement of sustainability, this factor mainly assesses perceptions toward tourists and their positive impacts. It is of interest that, rather than preserving (Latkova & Vogt, 2012) and sharing (Boley & McGehee, 2014) the local culture, this factor identifies host appreciation that tourists will help them to understand the diversity of culture. Such difference reveals a unique appreciation of tourism, which has the potential to improve host cultural competences (Ye, et al., 2013). Caring about tourist travel satisfaction and appreciating the benefits brought by tourists are indicators of accepting the tourists as part of the host society. To create a socially sustainable tourism, residents' positive attitude towards tourism is essential, which requires specific intervention such as awareness campaigns in the community and schools.

Following the same procedure, three economic indicators were generated in this research, namely Development Control, Economic Positivity and Market Understanding. Development control refers to the concern of the potential negative impact of tourism on the sustainable development of Hong Kong. Particularly, Hong Kong residents believe that too many tourists may lead to the disruption of environment and over consumption of tourism resources and the increase of the commodity price. Thus they are more worried about the negative impact and they are more willing to suggest to the government to control the development of tourism such as the number of visitors from both the mainland and other countries. However, the impact of the development of tourism cannot be determined only by negative factors, it should be comprehensively evaluated from both the negative and positive sides comprehensively.

Economic positivity depicts the benefits to the economic development of Hong Kong brought by tourism. As one of the pillar industries, the tourism industry plays an important role for the development of Hong Kong, particularly in nowadays when port industry and financial markets do not go very well. Since 2003 when IVS was launched, the number of visitors from Chinese Mainland has enjoyed a rapid and sustained growth for more than one decade. This enlarged the internal market of Hong Kong, providing more employment opportunities and expanded government revenues significantly. The contribution of tourism, particularly from visitors from the mainland, to the economic development of Hong Kong cannot be overlooked based on the economic fact of the last decade.

市场了解程度是指居民感受到的因中国内地游客数量增加对自身带来的影响。例如,居民把收入增长归功于自由行政策落实后旅游业的发展。研究指出,自由行政策执行后,中国内地游客的数量从 2003 年的 847 万人次增加到 2014 年 4720 万人次,占旅游人数的 77.7%(香港旅游发展局,2014)。在有着亚洲的"购物天堂"美誉的香港,随着游客人数的巨大增长,旅游业收入当然也迅速增加。研究人员了解旅游业对个人经济的影响,可以促进政府有效采取相应的策略来应对旅游业的风险和变故。

为了评估社会和经济可持续性测度指标的结构稳定性,整体样本根据居民—景点密度和以下公式,被进一步划分为两个子样本:

$$居民-景点密度 = \sqrt{\left(\frac{地区人口}{地区面积}\right)\left(\frac{区域内景点数}{地区面积}\right)}$$

我们用两个子样本的数据来重新检验由整体样本得到的因子模型。其结果是,社会和经济的可持续性测度指标在高居民—景点密度和低居民—景点密度两个子样本中是一样的。

如表 4-3 和表 4-4 所示,这些因子的平均分数是根据社会和经济因素系数计算得出的。有趣的是,在低密度地区的居民,与那些高密度地区的居民相比,对游客有着相对较高程度的冲突感和较低程度的容忍度和认同感。同时,在高密度区域的居民,与低密度地区的居民相比,对旅游业积极的经济作用有较高的认同度,而对旅游业发展进行控制的愿望较小。本研究所得结果似乎有悖于人们的普遍认知,即传统的旅游地区的居民更反对旅游发展,对游客和旅游业的发展持有更多消极观念,因为他们的日常生活倍受旅游干扰。相反,研究表明,低密度旅游地区的居民对当前旅游业的可持续发展水平持有更多负面看法。与高密度的旅游地区的居民相比,低密度旅游地区的居民长期按自己的节奏生活而不受外人的干扰。随着旅游业在香港快速发展,相当数量的游客已经前往传统的非旅游区旅游。居民已意识到这些游客所带来的负面影响,如不当行为、拥挤的公共设施以及被推高了的日用品价格。但是,低密度地区旅游业的发展所带来的经济利益并没有得到认可。在这种情况下,低密

Market understanding refers to residents' perceptions toward the personal influences brought by the considerable amount of tourists from the mainland. For instance, residents credit their income increase to the development of tourism after IVS. As indicated in the research context, after the IVS, the number of tourists from the mainland in Hong Kong increased from 8.47 million in 2003 to 47.2 million in 2014, accounting for 77.7% of tourist arrivals in 2014 (HKTB, 2014). Such a great increase in tourist number leads to the increase in tourism income, especially for Hong Kong, which is called the "shopping paradise" in Asia. Residents' understanding of the personal economic impact brought by the tourism industry can facilitate the government to take efficient strategies to cope with any risk or change of the tourism industry.

To assess the factor structural stability in both the social and economic sustainable measurements, the overall sample was further divided into two subgroups based on the resident-attraction density according to the following equation:

$$\text{Resident-attraction density} = \sqrt{\left(\frac{\text{District population}}{\text{District area}}\right)\left(\frac{\text{No. of attractions in district}}{\text{District area}}\right)}$$

The factor model that was derived from the overall sample was re-examined in both subgroups. As the result, the dimensionality of the social and economic sustainability measurement instruments was generally consistent between the high and low resident-attraction density groups.

As demonstrated in Table 4 - 3 and Table 4 - 4, factor mean scores were calculated from both the social and economic factors. It was interesting to notice that, residents in low-density areas have a relatively higher feeling of conflicts and a lower degree of tolerance and acceptance with the tourists, compared with those from high-density areas. Meanwhile, residents in high-density areas have a relatively higher recognition of the positive aspects of tourism and a lower desire of development control of tourism, compared with those from low-density areas. The result seems to decline a common assumption that residents from traditional tourism areas are more rabid against the tourism development and are holding more negative perceptions toward the tourists and tourism development in the host community as their daily life is more disturbed by tourists. On the contrary, as argued in the study, residents from the low tourism density areas are holding more negative views toward the current tourism sustainability level. Compared with those from high tourism density areas, residents from the low tourism density areas have been long living on their own pace without being disturbed by the outsiders. As the tourism industry developed dramatically in Hong Kong, the traditional non-tourism areas have been visited by a considerable number of visitors. The negative impact brought by those tourists, such as improper behaviors, overcrowded public facilities, and pushing up the prices for daily commodities, are well realized by those residents. However, due to the tourism development level in the low density areas, the economic benefits from the tourism are not commonly recognized. In that case, residents

度旅游地区居民的主客冲突和旅游发展调控的想法的分数更高,社会容忍度、社会认同度、积极的经济作用和对市场的了解程度的分数更低。对于高密度旅游地区的居民来说,他们已经习惯了游客参与生活的现象了。由于其丰富的与游客相处的经验,他们已经经历过了严重的主客冲突的阶段。他们对游客抱以更宽容的态度并了解旅游发展也能带来的好处。

表4-3 社会可持续性构面平均值

	问 题	总体平均值	高密度地区平均值	低密度地区平均值
因素一 主客冲突		3.66	3.62	3.69
问题7	内地游客造成大量的社会问题	3.93	3.91	3.95
问题11	香港因为旅游业变得拥挤不堪	4.10	4.08	4.10
问题12	听到关于内地游客的抱怨	4.06	4.00	4.11
问题13	看到部分内地游客的不文明行为	3.72	3.67	3.76
问题16	内地游客给当地管理带来挑战	3.51	3.44	3.56
问题17	香港居民与游客的利益冲突	3.10	3.05	3.14
问题18	香港居民与内地游客的利益冲突	3.47	3.43	3.49
问题19	内地游客占用社区资源	3.39	3.37	3.40
因素二 社会容忍度		3.01	3.10	2.94
问题20	尽管游客多,我对政府所提供的交通设施仍然满意	3.03	3.11	2.97
问题21	尽管游客多,我对政府所提供的医疗设施仍然满意	3.09	3.20	3.01
问题24	香港旅游业以公平的社会化方式发展	2.91	3.01	2.83
因素三 社会认同度		2.69	2.77	2.63
问题2	内地游客可以帮助香港居民了解文化的多样性	2.79	2.90	2.71
问题3	大部分内地游客可以保持公共场所整洁	2.43	2.51	2.37
问题4	我认为大部分内地游客对香港旅游持满意态度	2.85	2.91	2.81

from low tourism density areas are generally holding higher scores of host-guest conflict and desire of controlling the tourism development, and lower scores of social tolerance, social acceptance, economic positivity and market understanding. For residents from high tourism density areas, they are getting used to the life with tourists participated as such phenomenon has been on for a while. Due to their rich experience of dealing with the tourists, they already pass the severe conflict stage between hosts and guests. They are holding more tolerance toward the tourists and are more aware of the benefits brought by the tourism development.

Table 4 – 3 Mean scores for social sustainability constructs

Questions		Overall mean	High-density mean	Low-density mean
Factor One Host-Guest Conflict		3.66	3.62	3.69
Q7	Visitors from the mainland cause a great number of social problems.	3.93	3.91	3.95
Q11	Hong Kong becomes overcrowded because of tourism.	4.10	4.08	4.10
Q12	I heard a lot of complaints about visitors from the mainland.	4.06	4.00	4.11
Q13	I saw some uncivilized behavior by visitors from the mainland.	3.72	3.67	3.76
Q16	Visitors from the mainland bring challenges to local control.	3.51	3.44	3.56
Q17	There are conflicts of interest between Hong Kong residents and visitors.	3.10	3.05	3.14
Q18	There are conflicts of interest between Hong Kong residents and outsiders from the mainland.	3.47	3.43	3.49
Q19	Community resources are occupied by visitors from the mainland.	3.39	3.37	3.40
Factor Two Social Tolerance		3.01	3.10	2.94
Q20	I am satisfied with transport facilities provided by the government even though there are many visitors.	3.03	3.11	2.97
Q21	I am satisfied with medical facilities provided by the government even though there are many visitors.	3.09	3.20	3.01
Q24	The tourism in Hong Kong is developed in a fair and socially just way.	2.91	3.01	2.83
Factor Three Social Acceptance		2.69	2.77	2.63
Q2	Visitors from the mainland can help Hong Kong residents understand diversity of cultures.	2.79	2.90	2.71
Q3	Most mainland visitors can keep public places clean and tidy.	2.43	2.51	2.37
Q4	I think most visitors from the mainland are satisfied with travelling in Hong Kong.	2.85	2.91	2.81

表 4 - 4　经济可持续性构面平均值

问　题		总体平均值	高密度地区平均值	低密度地区平均值
因素一　发展调控		3.60	3.53	3.65
问题 42	香港需要限制游客数量	3.32	3.22	3.39
问题 43	香港需要限制内地游客数量	3.79	3.67	3.87
问题 44	政府应该加强限制，保护环境和旅游资源	4.03	3.93	4.11
问题 46	政府应该限制价格	3.21	3.19	3.23
问题 47	内地游客对当地商品价格产生负面影响	3.64	3.62	3.66
因素二　积极的经济作用		3.41	3.43	3.38
问题 25	总体上从经济角度来说，入境旅游对香港很重要	3.62	3.66	3.58
问题 31	内地游客扩大了香港旅游市场	3.32	3.36	3.28
问题 33	内地游客带来更多就业机会	3.42	3.45	3.40
问题 34	如果香港旅游业收缩，许多香港居民将失去工作	3.28	3.29	3.26
问题 36	与旅游业相关的税收增加，将会增加政府收入	3.32	3.30	3.33
问题 50	自由行给香港带来了经济效益	3.49	3.53	3.46
因素三　市场了解程度		1.88	1.94	1.84
问题 35	在自由行政策执行后，我收入的增加与旅游业的发展相关	1.84	1.92	1.78
问题 37	我在内地游客示范效应的带动下购买了额外的商品	1.59	1.64	1.56
问题 40	即使在旅游旺季，我在旅游景点也感觉舒适	2.22	2.27	2.18

Table 4 – 4   Mean scores for economic sustainability constructs

Questions		Overall mean	High-density mean	Low-density mean
Factor One Development Control		3.60	3.53	3.65
Q42	Hong Kong has to limit the number of visitors.	3.32	3.22	3.39
Q43	Hong Kong has to limit the number of visitors from the mainland.	3.79	3.67	3.87
Q44	Government should impose restriction to preserve the environment and to conserve tourism resources.	4.03	3.93	4.11
Q46	The Government should impose restriction to suppress prices.	3.21	3.19	3.23
Q47	Visitors from the mainland negatively impact local commodity price.	3.64	3.62	3.66
Factor Two Economic Positivity		3.41	3.43	3.38
Q25	Overall，inbound tourism is important to Hong Kong economically.	3.62	3.66	3.58
Q31	Visitors from the mainland enlarge Hong Kong's tourism market.	3.32	3.36	3.28
Q33	Visitors from the mainland bring more job opportunities.	3.42	3.45	3.40
Q34	A great number of Hong Kong residents will lose their jobs when tourism declines in Hong Kong.	3.28	3.29	3.26
Q36	The increase of taxes related to the tourism industry has raised the government revenue.	3.32	3.30	3.33
Q50	The Individual Visit Scheme brought economic benefits to Hong Kong.	3.49	3.53	3.46
Factor Three Market Understanding		1.88	1.94	1.84
Q35	The increase of my income was related to the development of the tourism industry after the Individual Visit Scheme.	1.84	1.92	1.78
Q37	I bought some extra commodities，which is affected by the demonstration effect of mainland's visitors.	1.59	1.64	1.56
Q40	I feel comfortable in tourism attractions even in the peak tourist season.	2.22	2.27	2.18

4.5　政策含义和建议

社会和经济可持续性发展的指标体系为我们提供了一个测度飞速增长的游客数量对香港当地社区影响的工具。游客数量的增加不仅对基础设施的使用产生压力，也影响居民的生活质量，包括更拥挤的交通、更多的垃圾和噪音，以及所感知到的不断消失的社区价值观和传统。如果不能合理控制游客数量，则很可能导致居民对这些游客产生敌意并造成对游客不友好的环境。许多国家都因为没有处理好这一点而产生了一系列的问题。对于空间本就狭小的香港，这些问题任一方面的恶化都会增加公众对内地游客的不满并加剧现有的紧张局势。本研究最重要的贡献就是为量化反映这些问题提供了测度方法，并为旅游业的管理和发展政策提供数据支持。为了使这套指标体系行之有效，应通过定期收集数据建立一个监控体系，让社区参与到监控体系的构建中，也为政策制定者及时了解相关信息提供渠道。随着内地游客数量的增加，本研究的成果能帮助政府抓住时机去主动回应而不是被动接受这些因内地游客过快增长所产生的经济和社会压力。

本研究发展建立的六个经济社会可持续发展影响因素有助于旅游规划者和决策者评估香港旅游行业现阶段的发展，并制定适当的战略来支持旅游业的平衡发展。世界各地的旅游规划者和决策者普遍强调旅游业发展所带来的积极经济效应，而忽视了当地居民在旅游发展过程中的声音，直到他们与游客的冲突和对游客的抱怨产生了严重的后果。旅游目的地的长期可持续性取决于当地居民对旅游发展、社区福利的改善以及和谐的主客关系的接受程度。社会和经济的可持续性直接影响到居民，是旅游业成功和可持续性发展的关键。因此，旅游规划者和决策者应该定期监测社会可持续性，以从宏观上把握旅游市场的发展和其对社会的影响，而不是完全依赖于国内生产总值和就业率等客观指标。在制定未来的旅游政策和战略时也应考虑社会和经济的可持续性问题，以确保旅游业的平衡健康发展。

4.5 Policy Implications and Suggestions

The development of the social and economic sustainability scale has provided an instrument to measure the impact on local communities arising from rapidly increasing numbers of tourist arrivals. Such increases not only put pressure on infrastructure but also on resident's quality of life including an intolerance of more traffic, littering, noise, and a perception of diminishing community values and traditions. Without some control over tourist numbers then it is probable that residents will become hostile to these visitors and engender an unwelcoming environment. In many countries these effects are not well-recognized. In a small territory like Hong Kong, any increase in these problems can increase public disaffection with visitors from Chinese Mainland and exacerbate existing tensions. An important output of this research is a means of measuring these problems and to use this data to facilitate policies for the development and control of tourism. To make this effective, a monitoring system to collect the data periodically should be established, to include community participation, and provide a conduit to tourism policy-makers. With tourists from Chinese Mainland likely to continue to increase, the output of this research provides an opportunity to be proactive rather than reactive to these pressures.

Six social and economic sustainable indicators empirically developed and further tested from this study may help tourism planners and policy makers in evaluating the current development of the tourism industry and in developing appropriate strategies that support balanced tourism development. Tourism planners and policy makers worldwide generally emphasize the positive economic effects of tourism development. However, residents' voices have been largely overlooked until their conflicts with and complaints against tourists have generated serious consequences. Long-term destination sustainability depends on acceptance by residents of territorial plans for tourism development, improvements in community wellbeing, and harmony between hosts and guests. Social and economic sustainability, with their direct influence on residents, is crucial to the success and sustainability of tourism. Therefore, tourism planners and policy makers should regularly monitor social and economic sustainability to obtain a holistic opinion of the tourism market and its effect on society, instead of relying exclusively on objective data, such as GDP indices and employment ratios. Social and economic sustainability issues should also be considered and addressed in forthcoming tourism policies and strategies to ensure balanced and healthy tourism development.

　　如何监督,以及由谁监测旅游在经济和社会方面的可持续性是一个仁者见仁智者见智的问题。有大量的文献支持社区(旅游活动发生的地方)应在这个问题上起主导作用。然而,人们对社区在哪里并由谁构成的认识并不统一。"利益相关者"的概念可能并不明确,因为这些团体包括私营部门和公共部门,而公共部门的类别可能是难以确定的。本研究试图解决的问题是如何识别和测度旅游业发展的社会和经济可持续性。我们建立的指标体系应能够从社会和经济方面来共同测度香港旅游业的可持续发展问题。同时,另一个重要的问题是,这一监测进程对最终用户是否有用,最终用户当然包括社区,但也包括能够建议进行必要改革的决策者。总体来说,这一监测体系如何得以真正运行非常重要,因为它可以用来检验本研究的研究成果。

The question of how and who should monitor social and economic sustainability in tourism is open for debate. There is an extensive literature which advocates the community（where tourism activity takes place）play a leading role in this process. However，there is much debate on where and whom constitutes a community. Reference to "stakeholders" can be ambiguous as these groups cover both the private and public sectors，and later category could be difficult to be identified. A further problem，hopefully mitigated by this research，is how to identify and measure social and economic sustainability of tourism development. The proposed instrument should be able to measure the sustainable development issues in Hong Kong from both social and economic aspects of views. Another important issue is the usefulness of this monitoring process to end-users who would certainly include the community but also policy makers who can recommend needed changes. Collectively，these implementation issues are important because they justify the output of the research.

中国内地酒店的发展
——过去与现在

Hotel Development in Chinese Mainland
—Past and Present

第5章　中国内地酒店的发展

学习目标

- ■ 了解中国内地酒店的发展史
- ■ 了解中国内地酒店的星级评定系统
- ■ 了解中国内地酒店的地理分布

5.1　中国内地酒店数据 (1978 — 2013 年)

自 1978 年中国改革开放以来,中国内地酒店业的发展与国家经济的发展并驾齐驱。中国国家旅游局的数据显示(见图 5-1),在不到 40 年的时间里,中国内地酒店数量自 1978 年的 137 家酒店、共 30740 张床位,发展到

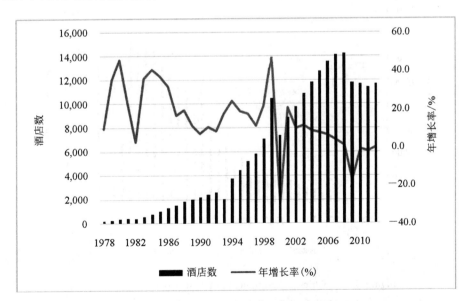

图 5-1　中国内地酒店统计(1978—2013 年)

(1. 资料来源:国家旅游局,2014;2. 2001 年开始营业的非星级酒店不在统计范围内)

Chapter 5 Hotel Development in Chinese Mainland

 Learning Outcomes

- Understanding the hotel development history of Chinese Mainland
- Understanding the hotel star-rating system of Chinese Mainland
- Understanding the geographical distribution of hotels in Chinese Mainland

5.1 The Statistical Data of Chinese Mainland's Hotel (1978—2013)

Since 1978, when China opened up to the world, the development of the hotel industry has shown a parallel path of the development of the economy in the country. As the CNTA statistics show in Figure 5 - 1, within less than 40 years' time, the number of hotels has increased from 137 hotels, with 30,740 beds in total in Chinese Mainland in 1978, to 11,687 hotels, with 2,705,013 beds in 2013, excluding non-star-rated hotels. The cumulative growth has been 8,430.7% in number of hotels.

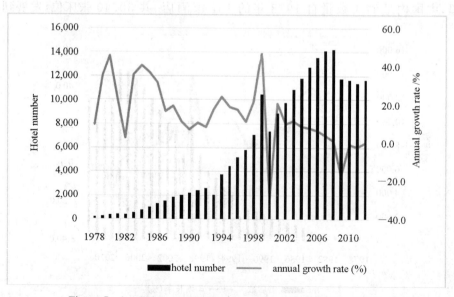

Figure 5 - 1　Chinese Mainland's hotel statistics (1978—2013)

(1. Source: China National Tourism Administration, 2014; 2. Starting in 2001 non-star rated hotels are not included in the statistics)

2013 年的 11687 家酒店、2705013 张床位,不包括不在星级评定范畴内的酒店。酒店数量累计增长率达到 8430.7%。

1. 酒店数量的增长

由图 5-2 可知,中国内地酒店数量的增长在 1984 年到 1987 年间达到高峰,增长率保持在 30%～40%;在 2000 年世纪之交时达到第二次高峰,年增长率到达 49%。进入 21 世纪以来,随着中国加入世界贸易组织,酒店数量继续攀升。2008 年的北京奥林匹克运动会和 2010 年上海世博会进一步推动酒店数量的增长。到 2009 年年末,星级酒店数量达到 14237 家 。

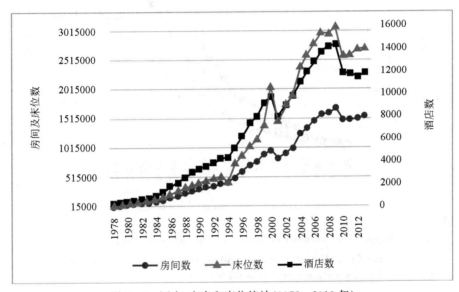

图 5-2　酒店、客房和床位统计(1978—2013 年)
(1. 资料来源:国家旅游局,2014;2. 2001 年开始营业的非星级酒店不在统计范围内)

2013 年以后的星级酒店数量对于中国内地酒店总量来说已经不那么具有代表性了。由于各种原因,很多酒店不再选择挂星,但是酒店增长的趋势依旧。

2. 业绩

尽管这么多年中国内地酒店的平均入住率保持在 56% 左右,但是这些酒店的业绩并不总能保持连续增长。尤其在 21 世纪初,由于酒店数量供大于求、1997 年东南亚金融危机、酒店分销管理不当等原因(袁宗堂,2001),中国内地酒店业经历了行业性的亏损。2008—2009 年的经济下滑再一次冲击了中国内地酒店业的业绩。以 2009 年为例,三星级的平均房价低至 151～200 元,四星

1. The growth of hotels in number

As shown in Figure 5 - 2, the growth rate of Chinese Mainland peaked during the time period of 1984—1987, when the annual growth kept between 30% ~ 40%; the growth rate reached a record high at the turn of the century, 49% in 2000. In the new century, as China's joint of WTO, the number of hotels continue to climb. And the mega events—the 2008 Beijing Olympics and the 2010 Shanghai World Expo have further pushed the growth of hotels. By the end of 2009, the number of star-rated hotels had increased to 14,237 in total.

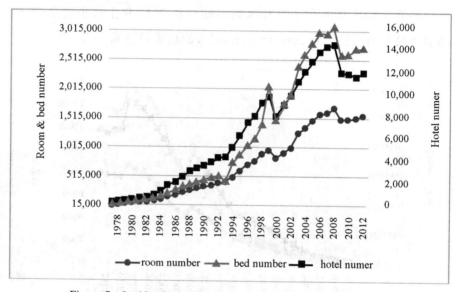

Figure 5 - 2   Number of hotels, rooms and beds (1978—2013)

(1. Source: China National Tourism Administration, 2014; 2. Starting in 2001 non-star rated hotels are not included in the statistics)

Since 2013 the number of star-rated hotels recorded has been less representative of the total number of hotels in Chinese Mainland, since many hotels choose not to take any stars for various reasons. However, the increasing trend of the hotels continues.

2. Financial performance

Although, the occupancy has been averaged at 56 % over the years, the financial performance of the hotels does not always reflect positive growth. Especially toward the end of last century, hotel industry in Chinese Mainland faced with industry wide financial loss, due to various reasons including the oversupply of hotel rooms, the 1997 financial crisis in Southeast Asia, and the poor management of the hotel distributors (Yuan, 2001). The financial downturn in 2008—2009 has further influenced the financial performance of the hotels in Chinese Mainland. Taking 2009 for example, the average daily rate (ADR) of three-star hotels was as

级酒店的平均房价也不过 250～400 元,而五星级酒店的平均房价仅为 450～550 元(谷慧敏和秦宇,2010)。

5.2 中国内地酒店业发展大事记

表 5-1 简要回顾了中国内地酒店业的发展历程。尽管中国内地的酒店业一直都存在,但是其真正的发展应该是从 1978 年改革开放后才开始的。这些年来,中国内地的酒店业发生了翻天覆地的变化:从以国有企业为主导的经营模式到以私有制为主体;从独立经营到连锁经营;从以经营管理为主导到侧重资本运作;以及从国内扩张到国际并购(国家旅游局监督管理司、中国旅游研究院,2011)。另外,有预测说中国内地会成为世界第一大旅游目的地,到 2020 年中国内地的酒店房间数将增长到 370 万(Chen 和 Kim,2010)。

表 5-1 中国内地酒店业发展大事记

1978 年	—改革开放
1982 年	—北京建国饭店落成、并引进香港半岛酒店管理集团管理建国饭店
1983 年	—合资企业白天鹅宾馆开业,此为第一家内地与香港的合资企业 —洲际酒店集团进入中国 —南京金陵饭店开业——一座由中国人借贷外资、自己建造、自己经营管理的大型酒店
1984 年	—以上海锦江饭店为骨干的上海锦江联营公司成立,成为我国第一家国际性的饭店管理公司;东湖、华亭及新亚于同一年成立 —广州中国大酒店开业 —北京喜来登长城饭店开业(第一家五星级的合资饭店)
1985 年	—上海新亚(集团)联营公司成立 — 广州花园酒店开业
1986 年	—中国旅游饭店业协会(CHTA)在北京成立
1987 年	—中国饭店联谊集团成立,是我国的第一个饭店联合体 —华龙旅游饭店集团成立 —友谊旅游饭店成立
1988 年	—酒店星级评定生效 —北京饭店集团成立 —广州白天鹅饭店管理公司成立
1989 年	—国家旅游局公布全国第一批 22 家星级饭店(一家四星级、七家三星级、13 家二星级、1 家一星级)
1990 年	—中国国家旅游局评出首批三家五星级酒店 —北京中国大饭店开业
1993 年	—国家旅游局颁布《饭店管理公司管理暂行办法》

low as 151~200 RMB, and the ADR of four-star hotels was at an average of 250~400 RMB, and the ADR of five star hotels was only 450~550 RBM (Gu and Qin, 2010).

5.2 Key Milestones of Hotel Development History in Chinese Mainland

Table 5 – 1 illustrates the development history of the hotel industry in Chinese Mainland. Although hotels existed long before the opening and reform policy in 1978, the development of this industry is generally believed to have started after 1978 when China was re-opened up to the world. Over the years, Chinese domestic hotel groups have experienced dramatic changes: from state-owned business domination to the emergence of the private hotel companies; from independent hotel domination to chained hotel management; from focusing on operation and management to the operation of fund; from domestic expansion to international acquisition (CNTA Monitoring Department & CTA, 2011). Moreover, since it is predicted that Chinese Mainland will become the number one destination in the world, the number of hotel rooms is projected to reach 3.7 million by 2020 (Chen & Kim, 2010).

Table 5 – 1   Timeline of milestones of hotel development in Chinese Mainland

1978	—Reform and opening policy
1982	—The establishment of Jianguo Hotel, and the introduction of the Hong Kong Peninsular Group as the management company for Jianguo Hotel
1983	—The opening of the White Swan Hotel in Guangzhou—the first joint venture between the mainland and Hong Kong —Inter Continental Hotel Group entered China market —The opening of Jinling Hotel in Nanjing, a big hotel that was built and operated by Chinese
1984	—Establishment of Shanghai Jinjiang International, which was the first international hotel management company in Chinese Mainland, followed by Donghu, Huating, and Xinya, in the same year. —The opening of China Hotel in Guangzhou —The opening of the Great Wall Sheraton in Beijing
1985	—The establishment of Xinya in Shanghai —The opening of the Garden Hotel in Guangzhou
1986	—The establishment of China Hotel and Tourism Association (CHTA) in Beijing
1987	—The first hotel consortia got established—Lianyi Hotel Consortia —The establishment of Hualong Tourist Hotel Group —The establishment of Friendship Tourist Hotel
1988	—Star Rating System began in Chinese Mainland —The establishment of Beijing Hotel Group —The establishment of Guangzhou White Swan Hotel Management Company
1989	—The first batch of 22 star-rated hotel were approved by CNTA (1 four-star, 7 three-star, 13 two-star, and 1 one-star hotels)
1990	—The first three five-star hotels were approved by CNTA —The opening of the Beijing China Hotel
1993	—CNTA issued the "Administration of the hotel management companies"

续　表

1997 年	—万豪进入中国内地 —第一家经济型酒店——锦江之星在上海开业 —我国申请加入国际饭店金钥匙组织,成为第 31 个成员
1998 年	—世界顶级品牌"丽嘉"接手管理上海波特曼大酒店
2006 年	—如家于美国纳斯达克上市
2010 年	—锦江集团与 Thayer 一起收购美国的州逸,成为迄今为止中国内地对外最大的收购案例

马勇和陈雪钧(2008)将中国内地酒店集团的发展分为以下三个阶段。

1. 开放引进阶段(20 世纪 80 年代)

1978 年前,中国内地几乎没有符合国际标准的酒店(Pine,2002)。酒店数量的不足和质量的不合格无法满足改革开放后涌入中国内地的旅游者。

1978 年改革开放后,中国内地将酒店发展放在优先发展的位置上,降低对于外商投资的政治壁垒、税收,并给予优惠的工商管理政策(马勇和陈雪钧,2008)。在如此众多的优惠政策下,不少国际知名的酒店公司开始通过建立合资企业的方式进入中国内地。香港半岛酒店管理公司于 1982 年开始管理北京建国饭店,这标志着国际酒店管理公司开始进入中国内地(国家旅游局监督管理司、中国旅游研究院,2011)。在香港半岛酒店集团管理模式的基础上,建国饭店集团于 1984 年成立了中国内地第一家中国酒店管理公司。在半岛的管理下,建国饭店取得了巨大的成功。中央政府很快发文号召中国内地所有酒店向建国饭店学习——《关于推广北京建国饭店经营管理方法有关事项的请示》。这之后,50 家酒店被批准进行酒店管理大改革(袁宗堂,2001)。

引进国际酒店公司管理中国内地的酒店为中国酒店业在发展的初始阶段提供了强有力的管理支持。与此同时,中国内地酒店业派管理团队赴海外酒店公司学习先进的管理知识和技能。比如,南京的金陵集团曾经派 13 人的管理团队前往香港文华东方酒店进行为期 6 个月的学习(袁宗堂,2001)。

1984 年,洲际酒店集团旗下的假日酒店开始管理北京丽都假日酒店。不久便在很多其他城市建立了合作关系,包括拉萨、桂林、广州、西安、厦门、

Continued

1997	—Marriot entered Chinese Mainland —The opening of the first budget hotel —Jinjiang Inn in Shanghai —China joined the Golden Key Association, becoming 31st member country
1998	—(The Ritz-Carlton) World top brand—The Ritz-Carlton took over the Shanghai Portman Hotel
2006	—Home Inns got listed in NASDAQ
2010	Jinjiang Hotels and Thayer jointly completed the acquisition of Interstate, marking the success of the largest overseas acquisition

Ma & Chen (2008) have summarized the development of Chinese Mainland hotel corporations into three stages.

1. Opening up and the introduction stage (1980s)

Before 1978, there were only few lodging facilities in Chinese Mainland that could meet international standard (Pine, 2002). The poor quality and insufficiency of the hotels could not accommodate the sudden influx of tourists to Chinese Mainland after the open-door policy.

After the opening and reform policy in 1978, prioritizing hotel development, Chinese Mainland gave favorable conditions to foreign capital in terms of political fortress, tax, and industrial and commercial administration issues (Ma & Chen, 2008). Under these favorable conditions, quite a few world famous hotel companies entered the market of Chinese Mainland through the forms of joint venture and collaboration. The Hong Kong Peninsular Hotel Group started to manage Beijing Jianguo Hotel in 1982, which was the first international hotel operator (CNTA Monitoring Department & CTA, 2011). Jianguo Hotel Group thus became the first Chinese domestic hotel group in 1984, establishing its unique management model based on the management model of the Hong Kong Peninsular Hotel Group. The management model of Jianguo Hotel, managed by the Peninsular group, was a great success. The central government soon issued a policy calling for all the hotels in the country to learn from Jianguo hotel. The name of the policy is called *The Instruction Regarding the Popularization of the Management Method of Beijing Jianguo Hotel*, under which 50 more hotels were approved to have management reforms (Yuan, 2001).

Inviting international hotel groups to manage hotels in Chinese Mainland has provided strong managerial support at the early stage. At the same time, management teams were sent to overseas hotel companies to study advanced management know-how. For example, the Jin Ling Group from Nanjing sent a team of thirteen to study in Mandarin Oriental in Hong Kong within a period of six months (Yuan, 2001).

In 1984, Holiday Inn (under InterContinental Hotel Group) started to manage Lidu Holiday Inn in Beijing, and soon established joint relationship with hotels in many cities

大连、成都以及重庆(马勇和陈雪钧,2008)。在这之后,不少国际知名酒店公司如凯悦、雅高、喜达屋、希尔顿等纷纷通过合资企业的模式或者委托管理模式涌入中国内地市场。这些国际酒店公司为中国内地酒店业带来了先进的管理模式、标准的操作流程、先进的设备和技术以及世界级的酒店人才。这些都在很大程度上推动了中国内地酒店业的发展。

在这样的发展势头下,一部分中国民族酒店集团开始起步,比如像目前在中国内地酒店业扮演重要角色的上海锦江酒店集团,另外还有东湖集团、华亭集团以及新亚集团(国家旅游局监督管理司、中国旅游研究院,2011)。1987 年中国内地成立了三家饭店经济联合体,分别是中国联谊饭店集团、中国华龙旅游饭店集团、和友谊饭店集团(马勇和陈雪钧,2008)。

2. 学习、模仿、快速发展阶段 (20 世纪 90 年代)

为了促进中国民族酒店集团的发展,中央政府出台了一系列政策。其中包括《国务院办公厅转发国家旅游局关于建立酒店管理公司及有关政策问题请示的通知》。这项政策明确说明,国企酒店公司也可以享受相似的诸如减税、进口优惠、经营自主权和信贷优惠等政策(马勇和陈雪钧,2008)。同时,在 20 世纪的最后 10 年,中国内地经济腾飞,大幅度带动了国内游的发展,国际游客到达数量亦大幅度增加。市场对酒店的需求空前增长,远远大于供给。这 10 年成了酒店发展的黄金时期。在向国际酒店公司学习的同时,一大批国内酒店公司在这个时期涌现。到 1999 年年底,中国内地共有 49 个酒店管理公司,共管理 350 个酒店(马勇和陈雪钧,2008)。

3. 品牌竞争阶段 (21 世纪)

随着中国经济改革日趋稳定以及中国加入国际世贸组织,这个时期,在中国内地酒店市场中,国际酒店公司与国内酒店公司并存,中国内地酒店业进入竞争时代。诸如 2008 年北京奥林匹克运动会及 2010 年上海世界博览会这样的大型活动进一步推动了中国内地酒店业的发展,导致酒店过多开发(Yu 和 Gu,2005)。这个阶段,中国内地酒店及房地产市场完全对外开放,这也加剧了酒店业的竞争,尤其是国内外酒店集团之间的竞争。然而,许多国内酒店公司依然很难抗衡国际酒店公司,究其原因主要还是

including Lasa，Guilin，Guangzhou，Xi'An，Xiamen，Dalian，Chengdu，and Chongqing （Ma & Chen，2008）. Soon after，a great number of well-known hotel companies such as Hyatt，Accor，Starwood，Hilton，etc. find their ways to Chinese Mainland through the form of joint venture or entrusted management mode. These international hotel companies brought with them the advanced management model，standard operation procedures，advanced facility and technology，as well as world level hotel talents. All these have helped the development of hotel industry in Chinese Mainland tremendously.

Under this momentum，a few Chinese domestic hotel groups emerged，such as the Shanghai Jinjiang Hotel Group，which is now playing a leading role in Chinese domestic hotel development，Donghu Hotel Group，Huating，and Xinya （CNTA Monitoring Department & CTA，2011）. In 1987，three Chinese hotel consortia were established：China Lianyi Hotel Group，Hualong Tourist Hotel Group，and Friendship Tourist Hotel Group （Ma & Chen，2008）.

2. Learning，imitating and fast developing stage （1990s）

In order to promote the development of domestic hotel groups，the central government issued a few policies including，for example，*The Notice of Launching Hotel Management Company and the Instruction of the Related Policies*. This policy has specified that domestic hotel groups could enjoy similar tax reduction，import favoritism，autonomous administration，mortgage favoritism，etc. （Ma & Chen，2008）. Meanwhile，the last decade of last century has seen flying economic development in Chinese Mainland，which consequently brought up domestic travel，as well as international arrivals，to a great extent. The demand for hotels was at historical high，which far surpassed the supply at this time period. This has made the decade the golden period for hotel development. Having been learning from the international hotel groups，a great number of domestic hotel companies appeared. By the end of 1999，there were 49 hotel management companies in Chinese Mainland，managing 350 hotels （Ma & Chen，2008）.

3. Brand competition stage （21st Century）

Along with the stabilization of the economic system in China，and China joint in the WTO，huge number of both international and domestic hotel companies co-exists in the Chinese Mainland market，and the development of this industry has entered a highly competitive stage. The world mega events such as the 2008 Olympics in Beijing and the 2010 World Expo in Shanghai have further pushed the hotel industry in Chinese Mainland to a greater extent，resulting in overbuilding of hotels （Yu & Gu，2005）. In this stage，China has been completely opened up to the international investors for hotels and other real estate projects，which has also intensified the competition of hotel industry，especially between the international hotel groups and the domestic ones. However，many domestic hotel companies are not able to compete against their international counterparts，largely due to low management

管理能力不足而导致服务质量低下(Yu 和 Gu，2005)。因此，政府启动了许多包括所有制转变的改革。

中国内地酒店市场，尤其是高端市场，已经接近饱和，这使得竞争日益激烈。入住率、平均房价及可出租客房平均房价开始下滑。于是酒店间的竞争上升到品牌竞争阶段。

在这个阶段，经济型酒店发展迅速。第一家经济型酒店为 1997 年上海的锦江之星。中国内地酒店市场的主要经济型酒店——如家、华住、7 天(如今已是铂涛酒店集团旗下的品牌)及锦江之星几乎让中国内地酒店业的版图翻新一遍。

5.3　中国内地酒店星级评定

1988 年，中国国家旅游局启动了星级评定的工程，旨在加强酒店管理以及保持服务标准，以保障酒店从业者、顾客及旅游公司的利益（Yu，1992）。1990 年，中国国家旅游局宣布了第一批包括上海希尔顿和广州白天鹅宾馆在内的星级酒店（Yu，1992）。这个酒店评星系统融合了国际酒店标准和中国特色。根据 Yu（1992）的研究，这套评星系统包括六大块内容：(1) 建筑和服务档次；(2) 设施；(3) 维护；(4) 清洁卫生；(5) 服务质量；(6) 客户满意度。自从启用这套评星系统，中国内地酒店数据基本以星级酒店统计数据为准。中国国家旅游局每年提供星级酒店的分类数据。

酒店星级评定系统是政府致力于提高酒店产品和服务水平并追求卓越的举措。这套评星系统分别于 1993 年和 1997 年进行修改和更正，并于 2000 年通过旅游局发文《关于进一步加快饭店星级评定工作的通知》进一步改善（袁宗堂，2001）。

比较表 5-2 的数据，三到五星级酒店的数量呈上升趋势。三星级酒店的数量从 2007 年的 5307 家上升到 2013 年的 5631 家，四星级酒店从 2007 年的 1595 家上升到 2013 年的 2361 家，而五星级酒店则从 2007 年的 369 家上升到 2013 年的 739 家。

proficiency, corporate governance, and consequent poor service quality (Yu & Gu, 2005). In response, the government initiated various reforms including the shifting of the ownership, which will be elaborated later.

The hotel market in Chinese Mainland, especially the high end segment, has come to a saturation, which makes the competition even more intense. Occupancy, ADR, and Revenue per available room (RvePAR) began to decline. This has brought the hotel companies competing against each other in terms of branding.

In this stage, budget hotels began to develop and prosper, the beginning of which was marked by the first Jinjiang Inn opened in Shanghai in 1997. The development of the leading budget hotel chains such as Home Inns, China Lodge, 7 Days Inn (now a brand under the Plateno Hotel Group), and Jinjiang Inn, has largely restructured the hotel industry in Chinese Mainland.

5.3 *Star-rating of Hotels in Chinese Mainland*

In 1988, CNTA launched the star-rating program in Chinese Mainland, with the aim of both enhancing hotel management and maintaining service standard (Yu, 1992), so that the interest of the hoteliers and the travel companies, as well as the travelers, could be ensured. In 1990, CNTA announced the first batch of star-rated hotels, including Shanghai Hilton and the White Swan Hotel in Guangzhou (Yu, 1992). The development of the star-rating system incorporates both the international standard and national characteristics of Chinese Mainland. According to Yu (1992), the criteria of the star-rating system includes six categories: (1) architecture and level of service; (2) facilities; (3) maintenance; (4) sanitation and hygiene; (5) service quality; and (6) guest satisfaction. Since the launch of the star-rating system, hotel statistics have been mostly based on the system. For example, CNTA provides annual statistics on hotels in terms of star-rated categories.

Establishing the star-rating system in the country shows the effort of the government to maintain consistency of hotel product and service, as well as the determination to strive for excellence in the hotel industry. The system underwent a few further revisions and reforms through the years, for example, 1993 and 1997. In 2000, CNTA further improved the system by issuing *The Notice to Further Accelerate the Hotel Star-Rating* (Yuan, 2001).

Along the years, the number of three to five star hotels increased from 2007 to 2013 (See Table 5 - 2). Three-star hotels have increased from 5,307 in the year 2007 to 5,631 in the year 2013, four-star hotels from 1,595 in the year 2007 to 2,361 in 2013, and five-star hotels from 369 to 739.

表 5 - 2　2007 年与 2013 年按星级划分的中国内地酒店比较统计

星级	酒店数		房间数(间)		总收入(10 亿元)		总固定资产(10 亿元)		纳税额(10 亿)		入住率(%)	
年份	2007	2013	2007	2013	2007	2013	2007	2013	2007	2013	2007	2013
5 星	369	739	137327	261072	40.11	76.14	116.80	188.19	2.24	4.37	64.64	56.06
4 星	1595	2361	336910	462821	50.29	76.67	133.56	174.96	4.20	4.32	63.84	57.21
3 星	5307	5631	647583	620778	51.98	63.08	130.96	118.49	3.62	3.64	61.25	55.64
2 星	5718	2831	420399	188663	21.18	12.10	45.83	19.64	1.70	0.72	56.73	54.05
1 星	594	125	31565	5807	11.59	0.30	27.01	0.48	0.07	0.16	56.84	51.53
总计	13583	11687	1573784	1539141	175.15	228.29	454.16	501.76	11.83	13.21	* 60.96	* 55.97

（资料来源：国家旅游局，2014；* 整体平均入住房间数／总房间数）

另一方面，一、二星级酒店的数量急剧下滑。二星级酒店从 2007 年的 5718 家下滑到 2013 年的 2831 家，而一星级酒店从 2007 年的 594 家下滑到 2013 年的 125 家。经济型酒店绝大多数不评星级，因此不被包含在中国国家旅游局酒店数据当中。关于经济型酒店的内容，下一章将详细描述。图 5 - 3所示是 2013 年中国内地星级酒店各等级的百分比。

如图 5 - 3 所示，2013 年，中国内地的三星级酒店数量最多，占所有星级酒店的 48%，其次是二星级和四星级酒店，各占 24% 和 20%。五星级酒店占 7%，而一星级酒店仅为 1% 左右。

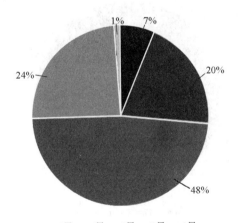

■5星　■4星　■3星　■2星　▨1星

图 5 - 3　2013 年中国内地星级酒店分布
（资料来源：国家旅游局，2014）

近年来星级酒店数量增长速度减缓，相反，非星级酒店数量急剧上升。原因诸多。首先，在 21 世纪之初，经济型酒店开始迅速发展，但是经济型酒

Table 5 – 2   Comparative statistics of Chinese Mainland hotels by star rating in year 2007 & 2013

Star Rating	No. of Hotels		No. of Rooms		Total Revenue (RMB Billion)		Total Fixed Assets (RMB Billion)		Tax (RMB Billion)		Occupancy (%)	
Year	2007	2013	2007	2013	2007	2013	2007	2013	2007	2013	2007	2013
5 Star	369	739	137,327	261,072	40.11	76.14	116.80	188.19	2.24	4.37	64.64	56.06
4 Star	1,595	2,361	336,910	462,821	50.29	76.67	133.56	174.96	4.20	4.32	63.84	57.21
3 Star	5,307	5,631	647,583	620,778	51.98	63.08	130.96	118.49	3.62	3.64	61.25	55.64
2 Star	5,718	2,831	420,399	188,663	21.18	12.10	45.83	19.64	1.70	0.72	56.73	54.05
1 Star	594	125	31,565	5,807	11.59	0.30	27.01	0.48	0.07	0.16	56.84	51.53
Total	13,583	11,687	1,573,784	1,539,141	175.15	228.29	454.16	501.76	11.83	13.21	* 60.96	* 55.97

(Source: China National Tourism Administration, 2014; * Overall average occupancy / size)

On the other hand in the year 2013, the number of two star hotels decreased from 5, 718 to 2,831 in 2013 whereas one star hotels from 594 to 125. Budget hotels are mostly non-star rated hotels, which are not included in the CNTA hotel statistics. The development of the budget sector will be elaborated in the later part of this book. Figure 5 – 3 shows the percentages of star-rating hotels in Chinese Mainland in 2013.

As Figure 5 – 3 shows, three-star hotels represent the biggest share in Chinese Mainland (48%), followed by two-star (24%) and four-star hotels (20%). Five star hotels account for 7% in total, whereas one-star hotels only 1% in total share.

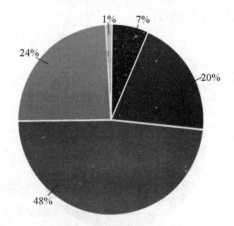

Figure 5 – 3   Numbers of hotels by star rating in 2013
(Source: China National Tourism Administration, 2014)

However, in the past decade, the growth rate of the star-rated hotels declined. On the contrary, the market has seen an increasing trend of the non-star-rated hotels. There are a few reasons that the number of non-star-rated hotels has been increasing. Firstly, at the beginning of the twenty-first century, the budget hotel sector started to develop in

店不评星。其次,许多国外品牌酒店也选择不参与评星,这个类别的酒店数量很庞大。再者,近几年的政策对公务消费有诸多限制,导致很多酒店不希望挂星,更有已经评星的酒店希望摘星。

5.4　中国内地酒店的区域分布

图 5-4 描述了中国内地星级酒店的地理分布。大多数酒店分布在经济发达的省份。广东省 917 家、浙江省 828 家、山东省 792 家、江苏省 735 家,这些省份多数在沿海地区。相反,中国内陆省份如宁夏、青海以及西藏由于旅游业不发达,酒店数量较为稀少。

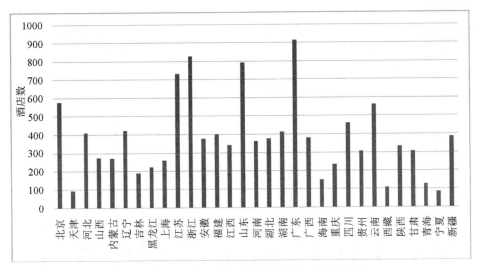

图 5-4　2013 年中国内地星级酒店地区分布情况
(资料来源:国家旅游局,2014)

Chinese Mainland. The expansion of this hotel segment has been tremendous. Most budget hotels are not star-rated. Secondly, many foreign branded hotels are not star-rated. Thirdly, recent government policies on the limitation of governmental expense (restricting government travel and accommodating—maximum four star hotels) restrained many hotels from being star-rated. Some existing star-rated hotels, especially five star hotels, even apply to have the star removed.

5.4 Geographical Distribution of the Hotels in Chinese Mainland

Figure 5 – 4 shows the geographic location of the star-rated hotels in Chinese Mainland. Majority of the hotels are located in economically developed provinces. Guangdong province (917), Zhejiang province (828), Shandong province (792), and Jiangsu province (735) have the biggest numbers of hotels among all provinces and autonomous regions in Chinese Mainland. These provinces are mostly along the coastal areas in Chinese Mainland. On the other hand, inner provinces such as Ningxia, Qinghai, and Tibet have smallest numbers of hotels due to less developed tourism industry in these regions.

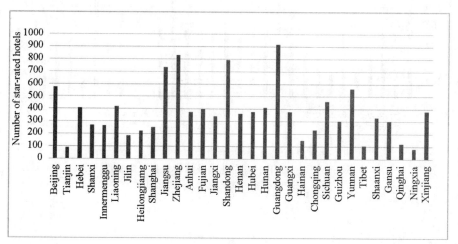

Figure 5 – 4　Geographical distribution of star-rated hotels in Chinese Mainland, 2013
(Data source: China National Tourism Administration, 2014)

第6章 中国内地酒店集团

 学习目标

- 了解中国内地酒店行业的国际化趋势
- 了解中国内地酒店行业的发展趋势

2014年6月,第十一届中国饭店集团化发展论坛暨第八届饭店品牌建设国际论坛发布了"2013年度中国饭店集团60强"(中国旅游报,2014)。如表6-1所示,从酒店规模来说,国际酒店集团不再占据中国内地酒店业的主导地位。排名在前五位的均是中国本土酒店集团,它们纷纷超过国际酒店巨头名列前茅,尽管它们大多以经济型酒店为主要产品。

表6-1 2013年度中国内地饭店集团60强

排名	名 称	门店数	客房数	备注
1	如家酒店集团	2341	275875	
2	华住酒店集团	1852	194779	
3	铂涛酒店集团	1998	188646	
4	格林豪泰酒店管理集团	1698	171498	
5	上海锦江国际酒店(集团)股份有限公司	1178	160777	
6	洲际酒店集团	360	115745	英国
7	温德姆酒店集团	695	82140	美国
8	喜达屋酒店与度假酒店国际集团	231	75492	美国
9	希尔顿酒店管理(上海)有限公司	184	63739	美国
10	雅高酒店集团	260	61333	法国
11	万豪国际集团	158	56605	美国
12	开元酒店集团	154	48750	

Chapter 6　Chinese Domestic Hotel Groups

 Learning Outcomes

- Understanding the internationalization of the hotel industry in Chinese Mainland
- Understanding the development trend of the hotel industry in Chinese Mainland

According to China Tourism News (2014), in June of 2014, the 11th China Hotel Development Group Forum and the 8th International Forum on Hotel Brand Building released "2013 China Top 60 Hotel Groups". As Table 6 – 1 shows, international hotel groups are no longer in the dominating position in hotel industry in Chinese Mainland, in terms of scale. The first five hotel groups have surpassed the international hotel giant, although these five groups all have a focus on budget hotel products.

Table 6 – 1　Top 60 hotel groups in Chinese Mainland 2013

Rank	Name	Number of hotels	Number of rooms	Notes
1	Home Inns & Hotels Management Inc.	2,341	275,875	
2	China Lodge	1,852	194,779	
3	Plateno Hotel Group	1,998	188,646	
4	Green Tree Inns Hotel Management Group	1,698	171,498	
5	Shanghai Jin Jiang International Hotels（Group）Co., Ltd.	1,178	160,777	
6	InterContinental Hotel Group	3,60	115,745	UK
7	Wyndham Hotel Group	695	82,140	USA
8	Starwood Hotels and Resort International Group	231	75,492	USA
9	Hilton Hotel Management (Shanghai) Co., Ltd.	184	63,739	USA
10	Accor Hotel Group	260	61,333	USA
11	Marriott International Inc.	158	56,605	USA
12	New Century Hotels & Resorts	154	48,750	

续　表

排名	名　　　称	门店数	客房数	备注
13	青岛尚客优城际酒店管理有限公司	732	43920	
14	维也纳酒店集团	265	42305	
15	金陵酒店管理有限公司	136	35747	
16	山东蓝海酒店集团	89	30099	
17	北京首旅酒店（集团）股份有限公司	119	28575	
18	城市便捷酒店集团	306	28535	
19	碧桂园凤凰国际酒店管理公司	84	27219	
20	港中旅酒店有限公司	78	27168	中国香港
21	凯悦酒店集团	88	26295	美国
22	香格里拉酒店集团	54	24161	中国香港
23	杭州住友酒店管理有限公司	326	22976	
24	万达酒店及度假村	71	21232	
25	山东银座旅游集团有限公司	187	20736	
26	海航酒店集团	77	18363	
27	湖南华天国际酒店管理有限公司	70	18163	
28	广州岭南国际企业集团有限公司	65	17472	
29	湖南和一酒店连锁有限公司	87	17016	
30	君澜酒店集团	54	15650	
31	中州国际酒店管理集团有限公司	74	15536	
32	康年国际酒店集团	53	15526	
33	北京国宾友谊国际酒店管理有限责任公司	48	13495	
34	凯莱酒店集团	55	13320	中国香港
35	雷迪森旅业集团有限公司	56	13197	
36	粤海（国际）酒店管理集团有限公司	43	12885	
37	绿地国际酒店管理集团	44	12106	

Continued

Rank	Name	Number of hotels	Number of rooms	Notes
13	Qingdao Excellent Choice for Intercity Hotel Management Co., Ltd.	732	43,920	
14	Vienna Hotel Group	265	42,305	
15	Jingling Hotels & Resorts Corporation	136	35,747	
16	Blue Horizon Hotel Group	89	30,099	
17	BTG Hotels (Group) Co., Ltd.	119	28,575	
18	City Comfort Hotel	306	28,535	
19	Phoenix International Hotel Management Company	84	27,219	
20	HK CTS Hotels Co., Ltd.	78	27,168	HK(China)
21	Hyatt Hotels and Resorts	88	26,295	USA
22	Shangri-La Hotels and Resorts	54	24,161	HK(China)
23	Hangzhou Sumitomo Hotel Management Co., Ltd.	326	22,976	
24	Wanda Hotels and Resorts	71	21,232	
25	Shandong Ginza Tourism Group Co., Ltd.	187	20,736	
26	HNA Hotels and Resorts	77	18,363	
27	Hunan Huatian International Hotel Management Co., Ltd.	70	18,163	
28	Guangzhou Lingnan International Enterprise Group Co., Ltd.	65	17,472	
29	Hunan Heyi Hotel Chain Co., Ltd.	87	17,016	
30	Narada Hotel Group	54	15,650	
31	Zhongzhou International Hotel Management Group Co., Ltd.	74	15,536	
32	Conifer International Hotel Group	53	15,526	
33	Beijing State Guest Friendship International Hotel Management Co., Ltd.	48	13,495	
34	Gloria Hotels & Resorts	55	13,320	HK(China)
35	Landison Tourism Group Co., Ltd.	56	13,197	
36	Guangdong (international) Hotel Management Holdings Limited	43	12,885	
37	Greenland International Hotel Management Group	44	12,106	

排名	名称	门店数	客房数	备注
38	贝斯特韦斯特国际酒店管理有限公司	63	11891	美国
39	四川锦江旅游饭店管理有限责任公司	39	10752	
40	雅阁酒店集团(澳大利亚)	47	10700	澳大利亚
41	浙江南苑控股集团有限公司	76	10365	
42	明宇酒店集团	27	10339	
43	世纪金源酒店集团	20	10167	
44	桔子水晶酒店集团	81	9629	
45	白天鹅酒店集团有限公司	37	9595	
46	上海衡山集团饭店管理公司	37	9473	
47	驿家365连锁酒店	115	9255	
48	陕西旅游饭店管理(集团)股份有限公司	48	8334	
49	阳光酒店管理集团有限公司	37	7673	
50	东莞市八方连锁酒店集团有限公司	70	7000	
51	华侨城国际酒店管理有限公司	40	6985	
52	尊茂酒店集团	42	6900	
53	深航酒店管理有限公司	25	6338	
54	福建中旅饭店管理有限责任公司	29	6257	
55	远洲酒店集团	18	5821	
56	恒大酒店集团	15	5750	
57	北京天伦国际酒店管理有限公司	23	5356	
58	中青旅山水酒店投资管理有限公司	41	5234	
59	城市名人酒店管理(中国)股份有限公司	20	4593	
60	玉渊潭酒店集团	17	3986	

注：表中备注的为国际酒店管理公司，并备注其总部所在地。

Continued

Rank	Name	Number of hotels	Number of rooms	Notes
38	Best Western International Hotel Management Co., Ltd.	63	11,891	USA
39	Sichuan Jinjiang Tourism Hotel Management Co., Ltd.	39	10,752	
40	Argyle Hotel Group (Australia)	47	10,700	AUS
41	Zhejiang Nanyuan Holding Group Co., Ltd.	76	10,365	
42	Mingyu Hotel Group	27	10,339	
43	Empark Hotels & Resorts	20	10,167	
44	Crystal Orange Hotel Group	81	9,629	
45	White Swan Hotel Group Limited	37	9,595	
46	Shanghai Hengshan Group Hotel Management Company	37	9,473	
47	Yijia 365 Hotel Chain	115	9,255	
48	Shanxi Tourism Hotel Management (Group) Co., Ltd.	48	8,334	
49	Sunshine Hotel Management Group Co., Ltd.	37	7,673	
50	Dongguan Octagon Hotel Chain Group Co., Ltd.	70	7,000	
51	OCT International Hotel Management Co., Ltd.	40	6,985	
52	Luxemon Hotel Group	42	6,900	
53	SZA Hotel Management Co., Ltd.	25	6,338	
54	Fujian China Travel Hotel Management Co., Ltd.	29	6,257	
55	S&N Hotels & Resorts	18	5,821	
56	Hengda Hotel Group	15	5,750	
57	Beijing Tianlun International Hotel Management Co., Ltd.	23	5,356	
58	CYTS Shanshui Hotel Investment Management Co., Ltd.	41	5,234	
59	Celebrity City Hotel Management (China) Co., Ltd.	20	4,593	
60	Yuyuantan Hotel Group	17	3,986	

Note: The table notes the international hotel management companies and notes the location of its headquarters.

　　另一方面,就品牌而言,尤其是豪华酒店这一块,国际酒店公司依然处于主导地位。表6-2为2017年中国内地国际酒店高端品牌10强排行榜。

表 6-2　2017 年中国内地国际酒店高端品牌 10 强排行榜

排名	品牌名称	所属集团	客房数(间)	门店数(家)
1	皇冠假日	洲际酒店集团	27938	77
2	喜来登酒店	喜达屋全球酒店及度假村集团	27022	73
3	香格里拉	香格里拉酒店集团	18514	43
4	希尔顿酒店	希尔顿酒店集团公司	16682	41
5	洲际酒店	洲际酒店集团	15130	36
6	豪生大酒店	温德姆酒店管理集团	14794	46
7	万豪酒店	万豪国际酒店集团	10503	27
8	凯宾斯基	凯宾斯基酒店集团	8796	21
9	铂尔曼	雅高酒店集团	8113	26
10	威斯汀	喜达屋全球酒店及度假村集团	7523	21

(资料来源:中国饭店协会、盈蝶,2018)

　　表6-3列出了2017年中国内地高端酒店国内品牌10强排行榜。

表 6-3　2017 年中国内地高端酒店国内品牌 10 强排行榜

排名	品牌名称	所属集团	客房数(间)	门店数(家)
1	锦江酒店	锦江国际酒店集团	33000	109
2	首旅建国	首旅如家酒店集团	19318	65
3	金陵饭店	金陵饭店集团	16946	61
4	碧桂园凤凰	碧桂园集团	13726	45
5	开元名都	开元酒店集团	11697	32
6	万达嘉华	万达集团	11213	38
7	华天大酒店	华天实业控股	10726	39
8	世纪金源	世纪金源酒店	9702	29
9	维景酒店	港中旅酒店有限公司	7991	21
10	开元大酒店	开元酒店集团	6492	24

(资料来源:中国饭店协会、盈蝶,2018)

On the other hand, in terms of branding, especially in luxury hotel sector, international hotel groups are still in the dominating position. According to the most recent statistics, the top ten international hotel brands in Chinese Mainland are as follows (Table 6 – 2).

Table 6 – 2 Top 10 international hotel brands in Chinese Mainland in 2017

Ranking	Hotel brand	Parent group	Number of rooms	Number of hotels
1	Crown Plaza	IHG (InterContinental Hotel Group Co.)	27,938	77
2	Sheraton	Starwood Hotel & Resorts	27,022	73
3	Shangari-La	Shangari-La Hotels and Resorts	18,514	43
4	Hilton	Hilton	16,682	41
5	InterContinental	IHG (InterContinental Hotel Group Co.)	15,130	36
6	Howard Johnson	Wyndham Hotel Group	14,794	46
7	Marriot	Marriott International	10,503	27
8	Kempinski	Kempinski Hotels	8,796	21
9	Pullman	AccorHotels	8,113	26
10	Westin	Starwood Hotel & Resorts	7,523	21

(Data source: CHA & Innite, 2018)

Table 6 – 3 is a list of top ten Chinese domestic hotel brands in 2017.

Table 6 – 3 Top 10 Chinese domestic hotel brands in 2017

Ranking	Hotel brand	Parent group	Number of rooms	Number of hotels
1	Jinjiang Hotel	Jinjiang International (Group) Company Limited	33,000	109
2	Jianguo Hotel	BTGHomeinns Hotels Group	19,318	65
3	Jinling Hotel	Jinling Hotels & Resorts	16,946	61
4	Phoenix Hotel	Country Garden	13,726	45
5	New Century	New Century Hotels & Resorts	11,697	32
6	Wanda Jiahua Hotel	Wanda Group	11,213	38
7	Huatian Hotel	CHHT	10,726	39
8	Empark	Century Golden Resources	9,702	29
9	Metropark	HKCTS Hotels	7,991	21
10	New Century Grand	New Century Hotels & Resorts	6,492	24

(Data source: CHA & Innite, 2018)

总体来说,与国际酒店相比,中国内地的本土酒店在高端酒店市场还是落后的。尽管中国内地的本土酒店企业在过去的 10 年内取得了长足的进步,其前途还是任重道远。国际酒店公司在全球的知名度、关系网络、先进的管理和技术等优势(Pine,2002)都令国内酒店难以望其项背。为了更好地了解中国酒店业,Yu 和 Gu(2005)对中国内地酒店业进行了 SWOT 分析。他们的分析结果如下:中国内地酒店业有着良好的发展前景,因为中国内地作为旅行目的地的知名度越来越高,中国内地酒店业产品多样化,可以满足不同层面的需求,服务和产品的质量都有所提高,国际酒店数量有所增加。然而,国内酒店公司仍然存在诸如所有制结构、债务和经济效益低下等问题。相比之下,国际酒店公司管理的酒店,尤其是高端酒店,在平均房价和可出租客房平均房价方面的业绩可以高出 35%(Yu 和 Gu,2005)。

随着酒店行业的日渐成熟,在国际品牌的优势冲击和国内新型酒店发展的双重影响下,一些老牌的星级酒店开始迎来了"倒闭潮"。比如在 2014 年年初,宁波的老牌四星级酒店——宁波文昌大酒店以及运营了 32 年的甬港饭店永久退出了酒店市场(《中国酒店采购报》,2015)。这些老牌酒店的倒闭正是中国内地酒店业发展到一定阶段后不可避免的结果。与国际酒店以及中国新兴的连锁酒店相比,这些老牌酒店显得竞争力低下,品牌竞争力、销售平台、人力资源和采购系统等都无法与后两者相提并论。另外,国有体制的束缚也是这些老牌星级酒店难以为继的主要原因之一(《中国酒店采购报》,2015)。

6.1　中国内地酒店公司的国际化前景

在获得大量酒店管理经验之后,部分中国内地的民族酒店企业日渐强大。我们甚至可以看到中国酒店跨出国门走向世界的前景。上海锦江集团在这个方面又率先行动。作为中国内地民族酒店企业的老大,锦江酒店集团有着良好的声誉,其产品受到国内外旅客的一致好评(Gross 和 Huang,2011)。截至 2013 年年底,锦江酒店集团共有 1566 家酒店、235000 个房间,分布在中国内地的 31 个省份的 280 个城市。在海外市场,锦江拥有美国州际酒店公司的 50% 股份,其旗下管理 10 个国家的 400 家酒店(锦江集团官网,2015)。对于锦江来说,其公司的业务能力、政府的支持、营销及品牌战略、关系网络

Generally speaking, Chinese indigenous hotel groups are still lagging behind in competitiveness, compared with their international counterparts, especially in the high-end hotel segment. Although the former has achieved dramatically in the past few decades, there is still a long way to go. Foreign hotel companies enjoy advantages such as global recognition, networking, well-established managerial and technological advancement (Pine, 2002). Yu and Gu (2005) conducted a SWOT analysis trying to understand the hotel industry in Chinese Mainland better. Summarizing their analysis, the hotel industry in Chinese Mainland has positive prospects since the country enjoys strengths such as the growing popularity as a destination, the diversity of hotel products in the country to cater for varied needs, improved service and product quality, and increase in the number of international hotel companies; however, the domestic hotel companies still have the weaknesses such as ownership structures, debt issues, and low financial performance. Comparatively, hotels, especially high-end ones, perform better if they are managed by international hotels, in terms of ADR and RevPAR, and the performance gap could be as big as 35% (Yu & Gu, 2005).

Along with the maturity of hotel industry in Chinese Mainland and the advantage of international hotel companies, as well as the development of the new hotel types, some old star-rated hotels begin to decline. For example, at the beginning of 2014, the old four-star hotel Wenchang Hotel, and Yonggang Hotel exited the market after their operation in the market for 32 years (*China Hotel Purchasing Paper*, 2015). This is an inevitable consequence of the development of hotel industry in Chinese Mainland. These old branded hotels are not able to compete against their international counterparts in many aspects including branding, marketing, human resource, and purchasing. In addition, their state ownership adds up to their reasons of exit from the market (*China Hotel Purchasing Paper*, 2015).

6.1 The Internationalization Prospects of the Hotel Companies in Chinese Mainland

Having obtained substantial hotel management expertise, some of the Chinese domestic hotel groups are getting stronger. We can now see the potential of Chinese hotel companies to expand to the world. Jinjiang Hotel Group takes the initiative in this respect. Being one of the earliest hotel groups in Chinese Mainland, Jinjiang Hotel Group has well-established reputation in domestic market, and its product is also well accepted by both domestic and international customers (Gross & Huang, 2011). By the end of 2013, there were 1,566 hotels under Jinjiang, with 235,000 hotel rooms, covering 280 cities in 31 provinces in Chinese Mainland. In overseas markets, Jinjiang has the 50% of share of the Interstate Hotels and Resorts in the United States, managing 400 hotels in 10 countries (Jinjiang official website, 2015). For Jinjiang, factors such as strengthened company abilities, government support, marketing and brand strategy, as well as network and

及管理水准等都是该公司走向国际化的重要前提（Gross 和 Huang，2011）。2014 年 11 月，该集团以 12 亿欧元收购法国卢浮酒店集团（盈蝶咨询，2015）。

除了锦江以外，酒店专家非常看好中国内地酒店集团走向全球的前景。在 2013 年迈点品牌风云榜上国内酒店排名第一的开元酒店在国际拓展方面亦不落后。2013 年是开元积极向外拓展的一年，该集团以 1050 万欧元收购德国金郁金香饭店；同时，在法兰克福建造的酒店也已经封顶（《中国旅游报》，2014）。

2013 年，其他海外投资的项目还包括海航收购西班牙 NH 集团的 24% 股权、绿地集团在德国法兰克福的铂骊酒店、君澜酒店集团在澳大利亚珀斯水边收购套房酒店、万达在英国的游艇和酒店计划等（《中国旅游报》，2014）。2014 年 7 月，富华国际集团完成对墨尔本地标建筑柏悦酒店的收购（《中国酒店采购报》，2015）。2014 年 10 月铂涛与法国巴黎酒店共同创立安铂酒店（《中国酒店采购报》，2015）。

除了上述海外收购及投资，中国内地酒店业的国际化还体现在中国内地酒店企业与国际顶级酒店集团的战略联盟上。例如，2014 年希尔顿酒店集团宣布铂涛酒店集团为希尔顿酒店集团欢朋品牌的中国内地总代理；2014 年 12 月，华住与雅高达成战略合作协议——雅高的部分品牌，如美爵、诺富特、美居以及宜必思将成为华住在中国内地的一部分，也就是说华住将成为这些品牌在中国内地的总代理（《中国酒店采购报》，2015）。

随着中国出境游市场的井喷，国内酒店集团往外发展的势头也将越来越旺盛。据估计，2013 年中国内地对外直接投资达 1078 亿美元，是 2002 年的40 倍（《中国酒店采购报》，2015）。

6.2　中国内地中档酒店的崛起

高端酒店市场一直以来是国内外酒店公司在中国内地市场的投资和开发重点。然而，近年来随着国家政策的调整，高端酒店在市场中遭到了冷遇。政府部门不再青睐五星级豪华酒店。相反，消费者对中档酒店的需求越来越高，此类酒店也随着高档酒店的业绩下滑迅速出现在消费者面前。中档酒店的快速崛起跟国家出台的限制"三公"消费、中等收入阶层的快速增长和现有酒店经营时间过长等因素有着很大的关系。不少国际酒店集团及时调整在

management standards have contributed to its capability of internationalization (Gross & Huang, 2011). In November 2014, the company acquired de Louvre from France with 1.2 billion Euro(Inntie,2015).

Apart from Jinjiang, hotel experts in Chinese Mainland foresee a big potential for the Chinese hotel companies to expand to the world in the near future. Kaiyuan, which was listed on the top of the branding list by Meadin in 2013, is not lagging behind in internationalization. 2013 was a year when the company actively expanded to the international market. The company acquired the Golden Tulip in Germany, with 10.5 million Euro, and its hotel in Frankfurt is topping its roof (*China Tourism News*, 2014).

In 2013, there were a few other overseas hotel investment projects including HNA's acquisition of 24% stock share of NH Corporation from Spain, Greenland's "The Qube Frankfurt" in Germany, Narada's acquisition of Suite Hotel in the waterfront in Perth, Australia, and Wanda's yacht and hotel project in Britain (*China Tourism News*, 2014). In July 2014, Fu Wah Group completed its acquisition of the landmark hotel in Melbourne-Park Hyatt (*China Hotel Purchasing Paper*, 2015). And in October 2014, the Plateno and the Paris Inn Group from France jointly founded the ALBAR Hotel (*China Hotel Purchasing Paper*, 2015).

Apart from the above overseas acquisition and investment, the internationalization prospect of the Chinese hotel industry can also be reflected from the strategic alliance of Chinese hotel companies and the world top hotel groups. For example, in 2014, Hilton announced that Plateno Hotel Group was going to be the overall agent in Chinese Mainland for the hotel brand of Hampton Inn under Hilton; and in December 2014, China Lodge and Accor reached strategic alliance agreement that partial brands under Accor were going to be part of China Lodge, including the Grand Mercure, Novetel, Mercure, and Ibis, which means that China Lodge is going to be the overall agent for these brands in China (*China Hotel Purchasing Paper*, 2015).

Along with the drastically increasing trend of outbound tourism in Chinese Mainland, the internationalization momentum of Chinese hotel companies will grow. It is estimated that the direct investment in overseas market in 2013 has reached 107.8 billion USD, which is 40 times that of 2002 (*China Hotel Purchasing Paper*, 2015).

6.2　The Rise of the Mid-scale Hotels in Chinese Mainland

High-end hotel market has always been the focus of investment and development in Chinese Mainland over the years. However, along with the new government policy, the high-end hotels become less popular. The government departments have been avoiding five star hotels or luxury hotels. On the contrary, there is an increasing demand for mid-scale hotels. This type of hotels have almost immediately emerged in the market in response to the demand, which is also attributed to the government's spending limit policy, the burgeoning middle class in Chinese Mainland, and the aging of the existing hotels. In view of this, quite a few international hotel companies have adjusted their

华发展战略,推出适合大众消费的中档及中高档酒店品牌。例如,希尔顿酒店集团推出花园酒店和欢朋酒店、万豪推出万怡等;香格里拉推出中档酒店品牌——金旅;凯悦旗下两大中高端酒店品牌进入中国(《中国酒店采购报》,2015)。国内的中档酒店品牌也不示弱,例如,维也纳、山水时尚、富驿以及华住、如家和锦江旗下的中档品牌业绩均较好。据迈点网预测,中档酒店在未来的 3～5 年内的增长速度将超过任何其他板块的酒店增长(迈点旅游研究院,2014)。科尔尼(2013)研究预测,未来的 10 年内,中国内地主要酒店集团的中档酒店的市场份额将由 2011 年的 3% 增长到 2022 年的 28%。盈蝶酒店咨询在 2015 中国酒店连锁发展与投资报告中也做出类似的分析和预测——国内外各大酒店公司都将于 2015 年加大对中端酒店市场的投入和开发。专家们认为,外资酒店将把中档酒店作为未来的发展战略目标,中国内地的酒店业将会迎来新一轮的洗牌。

6.3　资本重构:以首次公开募股(IPO)方式融资

近年来,"上市""融资"成了中国内地酒店业的热门话题。"上市"这个词也似乎成了酒店公司变大、变强的一条必经之路。锦江集团于 2006 年率先在香港上市(Gross 和 Huang,2011),如家也于 2006 年 10 月在美国纳斯达克成功上市。"7 天"和华住亦相继上市。开元酒店集团在 2013 年也做出了上市的举动。

上市能够让酒店企业融得更多资金,但是同时对于酒店公司也提出了新的要求,如酒店业绩、质量保障、严格的财务审计等,这也使得公司的管理变得更加严谨。上市也把酒店公司的运营放到公众的眼皮底下(Gross 和 Huang,2011)。

6.4　向二、三、四线城市进军

一线城市向来是酒店投资者们的首选。然而,近年来由于市场竞争的日益激烈、物业价格的不断提升和各类成本增加等原因,投资者们已经将目标转移到二、三线城市,甚至是四线城市。比如,在宁波这样的二线城市,各大国际酒店巨头均已在该城市有了各自的酒店,如万豪、柏悦、洲际、喜达屋、温德姆、雅高、香格里拉等。国内酒店公司也不落后,开元、南苑等酒店公司在这样的城市也是很活跃的。专家认为,二、三线城市成本低,因此还有大量的机遇和潜力。

developing strategy in Chinese Mainland, promoting mid to upper-mid scale hotels to cater for the demand. The examples include the Garden Inn and Hampton Inn under Hilton, Courtyard under Marriot, etc. Shangri-La also has its mid-scale hotel called Hotel Jen. Hyatt has similar plans (*China Hotel Purchasing Paper*, 2015). Chinese domestic hotel companies have also been trying hard to catch the opportunity of developing mid-scale hotels. For instance, Vienna Hotel, Shanshui Hotels, FX Hotels Group, China Lodge, Home Inns, and Jinjiang Hotel Group are all performing well in the mid-scale hotel category. According to the prediction of Meadin, the mid-scale hotel sector will undergo fastest increase in the next $3 \sim 5$ years' time (Meadin Tourism Institute, 2014). According to Kearney (2013)'s prediction, in the next 10 years, the leading hotel companies in Chinese Mainland will increase their market share in mid-scale hotel sector from 3% in 2011 to 28% in 2022. Inntie has similar analysis in its report on China Hotel Chain Development and Investment in 2015. Experts agree that foreign hotel companies will also target mainly at the mid-scale hotel sector in the years to come, and the hotel industry in Chinese Mainland will be restructured.

6.3 Capital Restructure: Fund Raising through Initial Public Offers (IPO)

In recent years, "being listed on stock market" and "fund raising" have been buzzwords in the hotel industry in Chinese Mainland. Apparently, being listed on stock market has become a MUST in order to make the hotel company strong in the market. Jinjiang Hotel Group was listed on the Hong Kong Stock Exchange in 2006 (Gross & Huang, 2011). Home Inns was successfully listed on NASDAQ in October 2006. 7 Days Inn and China Lodge have also been listed on stock market subsequently. Kaiyuan Hotel Group made similar attempt in 2013.

Being listed in the stock market allows the hotel companies access to new sources of capital. On the other hand, being listed in the stock market poses new requirements on issues such as performance, quality assurance, rigorous auditing, etc., which strengthens the management and administration of the companies. This has brought the companies to the scrutiny of the public at large (Gross & Huang, 2011).

6.4 Entering the 2nd, 3rd, and 4th Tier Cities

First-tier cities have been the focus of hotel investors. However, as the market competition gets intensified, the price of the properties goes up, as well as the increase of various costs, the investors have shifted their target onto the second, third, and even the fourth tier cities. For example, in a second tier city such as Ningbo, you can already see hotel brands from big hotel companies including Marriot, Park Hyatt, Starwood, Wyndham, Accor, Shangri-La, etc. Domestic hotel companies are also active in this type of cities, examples include Kaiyuan, Nanyuan and many others. Experts argue that the cost in these cities are lower, and there are abundant other opportunities and potentials.

(宁波万豪酒店,图片来自万豪酒店集团官网)

6.5　更多的兼并和收购

在过去的 10 年内,中国内地酒店业见证了多起兼并和收购,主要集中在经济型酒店这一板块,比如如家酒店集团对七斗星和莫泰的收购(如家官网,2015);华住(原名汉庭)于 2012 年收购了星程连锁酒店(科尔尼,2013)。也有其他类型的收购和兼并,比如首旅对宁波南苑的股份收购。首旅酒店于 2014 年 6 月以 2.4 亿元购得南苑股份的 70% 股份(《中国酒店采购报》,2015)。

6.6　走多品牌发展之路

市场多变,而酒店公司对市场变化的敏感度也越来越高。多家知名酒店公司纷纷开始走多品牌发展的道路。该举措也是众酒店公司未来发展的战略之一。2013 年"7 天"退市、铂涛酒店集团成立并推出系列酒店品牌;锦江集团除去现有的高端酒店品牌及经济型酒店品牌,推出锦江都城等中档品牌;如家及华住亦纷纷开发多个系列品牌。

(Ningbo Marriot Hotel, from the Marriot official website)

6.5 More Mergers and Acquisitions

In the past decade, the hotel industry in Chinese Mainland has witnessed quite a few mergers and acquisitions, mostly in budget hotel sector. For example, Home Inns acquired Top Star and Motel (Home Inn Official Website, 2015). China Lodge acquired Starway Hotels (Kearney, 2013). There are other types of acquisition and mergers. Beijing Tourism Group acquired 70% of shares of Nanyuan, with 240 million RMB in June 2014 (*China Hotel Purchasing Paper*, 2015).

6.6 Multi-branding Development

The market has been changeable, but the hotel companies have become more sensitive to the market change. Many renowned hotel companies have opted for multi-branding development strategy. For example, Plateno, which has 7 Days Inn under the company, recently announced a whole series of brands. Jinjiang Hotel group, Home Inns, and China Lodge have similar strategies.

第四篇（Part Ⅳ） <<<

国际酒店
International Hotels

第 7 章　国际酒店公司简介

 学习目标

- 了解处于世界领先地位的酒店公司

由于全球出境游和国内游的快速发展,全球酒店行业也得以迅速发展。根据最新的史密斯旅行研究(STR)数据,截至 2015 年 2 月,全球共有 1064 家不同层次的酒店连锁集团(STR,2015)。酒店连锁公司,尤其是主要酒店连锁公司的增长率,间接见证了酒店行业的快速增长。以雅高酒店集团为例,该公司平均每两天开一家新的酒店(雅高,2015)。

根据《酒店》杂志(*Hotels*)发布的《2017 年酒店 325 特别报道》(*Hotels 325 Special Report 2017*),我们在表 7-1 中罗列了以客房数排名的前 10 大国际酒店公司。其中,万豪国际酒店集团在合并了喜达屋全球酒店及度假村集团之后荣升为世界第一。这也是有史以来国际酒店公司首次突破 100 万客房数。除了万豪国际酒店集团,希尔顿和洲际分别排名第二和第三。另有其他酒店公司如中国的上海锦江国际酒店集团、北京首旅如家酒店集团、华住酒店集团等在经历几轮并购后增幅迅速。

表 7-1　国际十大酒店公司

排名	酒店公司	客房数(间)	酒店数(家)
1	万豪国际酒店集团	1164668	5952
2	希尔顿酒店集团公司	796440	4875
3	洲际酒店集团	767135	5174

Chapter 7   Introduction to International Hotel Companies

 Learning Outcomes

■ Understanding the leading hotel companies in the world

World hotel industry, as a whole, has been developing at a fast pace, thanks to the fast growing international and domestic tourism worldwide. According to the most updated Smith Travel Research (STR) statistics alone, there are 1,064 hotel chains of different tiers, by February 2015 (STR, 2015). The increase of the hotels can also be witnessed by the growth of the hotel companies, especially the leading hotel chains. Accor, for example, claims that the company opens 1 hotel in every 2 days (Accor, 2015).

Based on the most updated statistics from *Hotels 325 Special Report 2017*, the top ten international hotel companies based on number of rooms are shown in Table 7 - 1 below. Marriot, after combining Starwood, now has become No. 1, and this is the first time that any hotel company's number of rooms has surpassed one million. A few other companies are following right after Marriot, such as Hilton and the InterContinental Hotel Group. A few Chinese hotel companies are also catching up fast. Companies such as Shanghai Jin Jiang International Hotel Co., BTG Homeinns Hotels Group, and China Lodging Group, have come up fast in recent years due to fast expansion and their merging and acquisition activities.

Table 7 - 1   Top ten international hotel companies

Ranking	Hotel companies	Number of rooms	Number of hotels
1	Marriott International	1,164,668	5,952
2	Hilton	796,440	4,875
3	IHG (InterContinental Hotel Group Co.)	767,135	5,174
4	Wyndham Hotel Group	697,607	8,035

续　表

排名	酒店公司	客房数（间）	酒店数（家）
4	温德姆酒店管理集团	697607	8035
5	上海锦江国际酒店集团	602350	5977
6	雅高酒店集团	583161	4144
7	国际精品酒店集团	516122	6514
8	北京首旅如家酒店集团	373560	3402
9	华住酒店集团	331347	3269
10	最佳西方酒店及度假村	293059	3677

（资料来源：《2017 年酒店 325 特别报道》（*Hotels 325 Special Report 2017*））

Continued

Ranking	Hotel companies	Number of rooms	Number of hotels
5	Shanghai Jin Jiang International Hotel Co.	602,350	5,977
6	AccorHotels	583,161	4,144
7	Choice Hotels International Inc.	516,122	6,514
8	BTGHomeinns Hotels Group	373,560	3,402
9	China Lodging Group	331,347	3,269
10	Best Western Hotels & Resorts	293,059	3,677

（Data source：*Hotels 325 Special Report 2017*）

第8章　世界主要酒店公司的全球性扩张

 **学习目标**

- 了解世界知名酒店的主要品牌
- 了解知名酒店全球扩张的主要方式

全球主要的国际酒店公司还在不断地扩张。它们意识到在当今的轻资产年代,要想通过各种收费盈利,公司的规模变得很重要(HNN,2015)。扩张的途径之一自然是国际化,于是酒店公司纷纷以占据市场为目的通过国际化来实现扩张。全球扩张的好处包括市场增大、规模经济、更多的学习机会、更多的资源和更多的合作机会,而对酒店经理来说也有更多升职的机会(Enz,2010)。

表8-1具体呈现了以酒店所分布的国家数量排名的十大酒店公司。万豪国际酒店集团、希尔顿酒店集团公司、最佳西方酒店及度假村以及洲际酒店集团已经达到并超过100个国家。其他酒店集团正在努力赶上。

表8-1　十大跨最多国家数的酒店公司

排名	酒店公司	国家数
1	万豪国际酒店集团	122
2	希尔顿酒店集团公司	104
3	最佳西方酒店及度假村	101
4	洲际酒店集团	100
5	海航酒店集团	96
6	雅高酒店集团	95
7	璞富腾酒店及度假村	89

Chapter 8　Global Expansion of the World Leading Hotel Companies

 Learning Outcomes

- Understanding the key brands of the world leading hotel companies
- Understanding the ways of the main global expansion of the leading brands

The big players of the international hotel industry are still striving to expand. It is realized that size does matter when this industry has entered into an asset-light era, when the companies obtain profit increasingly through fees (HNN, 2015). One way to expand is internationalization. Hotel companies have strived to make their presence in as many counties / markets as possible. The benefits of global expansion include increased market size, economies of scale, more opportunity for learning, more resources, more partnership opportunities, and more opportunities for managers to advance their career (Enz, 2010).

Table 8 – 1 below illustrates top ten hotel companies in terms of number of countries they have entered. Marriott, Hilton, Best Western Hotels & Resorts, and IHG have made their presence in 100 and plus countries, while the rest companies in the list are also catching up.

Table 8 – 1　Top 10 hotel companies in number of countries

Ranking	Hotel companies	Number of countries
1	Marriott International	122
2	Hilton	104
3	Best Western Hotels & Resorts	101
4	IHG(InterContinental Hotel Group Co.)	100
5	HNA Hospitality Group	96
6	AccorHotels	95
7	Preferred Hotels and Resorts	89

续　表

排名	酒店公司	国家数
8	世界小型豪华酒店	80
9	温德姆酒店管理集团	77
10	立鼎世酒店集团	75

（资料来源：《2017 年酒店 325 特别报道》(*Hotels 325 Special Report 2017*)）

　　酒店公司扩张的主要方式有：特许加盟、合资企业、委托管理、直接拥有及并购(Enz，2010)。其中以合同为基础的模式有：许可、特许加盟及委托管理；直接投资的模式有：合资企业、全资控股子公司以及并购。

　　在所有的模式当中，特许加盟和委托管理是发展最快也最受欢迎的商务模式。以万豪为例，该公司把自己定位成"全球范围的酒店管理公司、酒店加盟公司、执照许可和分时度假酒店"。万豪直接拥有的酒店数量很少(万豪年度报告，2015)。喜达屋也有类似的说法。自 2006 年起，喜达屋把商务模式转向轻资产的模式，渐渐将直接拥有的酒店卖掉(喜达屋年度报告，2015)。

8.1　委托管理

　　根据 Eyster 和 deRoos (2009)的定义，管理合同是一个管理公司和完全服务型或者有限服务型酒店业主之间的书面协议，通过该协议，酒店业主聘用酒店管理公司全权管理及经营酒店。在这个商业模式下，酒店管理公司通常不做任何投资。所有的费用和投资均由业主承担，而业主通常不干涉酒店的经营活动。在理想状态下，合同双方都是受益的。酒店管理公司有专业管理知识和技能、市场资源以及其他具附加值的特质，为业主盈利，而业主也能为管理公司提供利润的来源(Dev 等，2010)。

8.2　特许加盟

　　从定义上看，特许加盟是两个独立的公司通过合同形式由授予特许者给予加盟者在特定时间、地点和品牌下经营特定业务的商业模式 (Enz，2010)。在特许加盟模式下，加盟者按照销售比例付给授予特许者加盟费，名曰综合费、冠名费及广告费。特许加盟在美国最受欢迎，大约 70% 的酒店通过特许加盟形式隶属于酒店公司(Enz，2010)。对于其他酒店市场，特许加盟也是颇受欢迎的商务模式。有些酒店公司专门做特许加盟，比如精品国际饭店公司 100% 以特许加盟为基础。

Continued

Ranking	Hotel companies	Number of countries
8	Small Luxury Hotels of the World	80
9	Wyndham Hotel Group	77
10	The Leading Hotels of the World	75

（Data source：*Hotels 325 Special Report 2017*）

To enter foreign markets, hotel companies usually rely on franchising, joint ventures, management contracts, ownership, and acquisitions (Enz, 2010). For contractual arrangement, there are licensing, franchising, and management contract, whereas for direct investment, there are joint venture, wholly owned subsidiary, and acquisition.

Among all, franchising and management contracts allow fastest expansion and are thus the most preferred business modes for the international giants to expand to foreign markets. Marriott, for example, defines the company as a "worldwide operator, franchisor, and licensor of hotels and timeshare properties" and owns only very few hotels (Marriott, 2015). Starwood has similar claims that, starting from 2006, the company has opted for asset light business mode, selling the properties that the company owns (Starwood, 2015).

8.1 Management Contracts

According to Eyster and deRoos (2009), management contract is defined as "a written agreement between the operator of a full-service hotel or select-service hotel by which the owner employs the operator to assume full responsibility for operating and managing the property". Under this arrangement, the operator usually does not make any investment. All the expenses and investment are made by the owner, while the owner does not involve in the operating process. Ideally, both parties are beneficial under this arrangement. The owner benefits from the operator's professional expertise, marketing resource, and other value added attributes; while the operator benefits from profitable source (Dev, et al., 2010).

8.2 Franchising

By definition, franchising is "two independent companies form a contractual agreement giving one (the franchisee) the right to operate a business in a given location for a specified period under the brand of the other firm (franchisor)" (Enz, 2010). Under franchising business format, the franchisee pays the franchisor a certain percentage of unit sales, in a form of combined fees and royalties, plus advertising contribution. Franchising is most popular in the USA, with around 70% of the hotels affiliated to hotel companies (Enz, 2010). It is also popular with other hotel markets. Some hotel companies such as Choice Hotel International solely rely on franchising for expansion.

表 8-2 和表 8-3 分别罗列了全球十大委托管理酒店公司及十大特许加盟酒店公司。

表 8-2　十大委托管理酒店公司

排名	酒店公司	酒店数
1	华住酒店集团	2473
2	万豪国际酒店集团	1911
3	上海锦江国际酒店集团	1110
4	雅高酒店集团	1085
5	北京首旅如家酒店集团	988
6	洲际酒店集团	845
7	希尔顿酒店集团公司	700
8	美国长住酒店	628
9	州际酒店及度假村	425
10	韦斯特蒙特酒店集团	410

（资料来源：《2017 年酒店 325 特别报道》(*Hotels 325 Special Report 2017*)）

表 8-3　十大特许加盟酒店公司

排名	酒店公司	酒店数
1	温德姆酒店管理集团	7924
2	国际精品酒店集团	6514
3	上海锦江国际酒店集团	4775
4	洲际酒店集团	4321
5	希尔顿酒店集团公司	4175
6	万豪国际酒店集团	4041
7	北京首旅如家酒店集团	2413
8	雅高酒店集团	1,877
9	马格努森酒店集团	1,274
10	红狮酒店公司	1,117

（资料来源：《2017 年酒店 325 特别报道》(*Hotels 325 Special Report 2017*)）

通过表 8-2 和表 8-3 可以看出，多数国际酒店公司巨头倾向于选择轻资产的特许加盟和委托管理商业模式，而不是直接投资。尽管目前特许加盟的数量多过委托管理，但后者的增长趋势在近年来日益明显（Eyster 和 de Roos，2009）。尤其是酒店公司选择向像中国这样的发展中国家扩展的时候，委托管理成了首选。比如说，喜达屋在中国内地的 146 家酒店中有 140 家是通过委托管理发展的（喜达屋年度报告，2015）。

The following two tables (Table 8 – 2 and Table 8 – 3) show the top ten hotel groups with management contracts and franchising respectively.

Table 8 – 2   Top 10 hotel companies with management contracts

Ranking	Hotel companies	Number of hotels
1	China Lodging Group	2,473
2	Marriott International	19,11
3	Shanghai Jin Jiang International Hotels Co.	1,110
4	Accor Hotels	1,085
5	BTG Homeinns Hotels Group	988
6	IHG (InterContinental Hotel Group Co.)	845
7	Hilton	700
8	Extended Stay America	628
9	Interstate Hotels & Resorts	425
10	Westmont Hospitality Group	410

(Data source: *Hotels 325 Special Report 2017*)

Table 8 – 3   Top 10 hotel companies with franchising

Ranking	Hotel companies	Number of hotels
1	Wyndham Hotel Group	7,924
2	Choice Hotels International Inc.	6,514
3	Shanghai Jin Jiang International Hotels Co.	4,775
4	IHG (InterContinental Hotel Group Co.)	4,321
5	Hilton	4,175
6	Marriott International	4,041
7	BTG Homeinns Hotels Group	2,413
8	AccorHotels	1,877
9	Magnuson Hotels	1,274
10	RLHC	1,117

(Data source: *Hotels 325 Special Report 2017*)

The above two tables show that most of the international hotel giants choose light asset business models of franchising and management contracts, instead of direct investment. Although the number of franchising still dominates, there is an increasing trend of management contracts in recent years (Eyster & de Roos, 2009). Management contract is a preferred mode for big companies to enter emerging markets like China. For example, of 146 hotels that Starwood operates in Chinese Mainland, 140 of them are under management contracts (Starwood, 2015).

8.3　品牌

世界上越来越多的酒店属于连锁酒店公司,品牌成了酒店产品的主要区分点。图8-1展示了在不同区域品牌酒店和非品牌酒店的比例。北美被品牌酒店主导,67%的酒店隶属于品牌连锁酒店公司,剩余33%依然是单体酒店。亚太紧跟北美,欧洲、中东和非洲以及南美品牌酒店过半。根据STR在建酒店研究报告,在建中的多数酒店属于品牌酒店,这也将成为未来酒店发展的主要趋势。

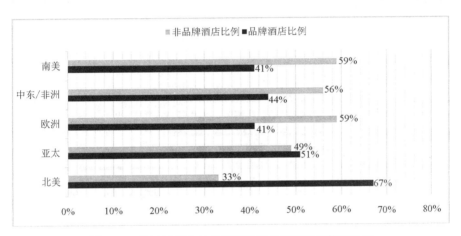

图8-1　按区域划分的品牌酒店和非平牌酒店数量对比
（资料来源：HNN,2015）

图8-2显示,69%的中档酒店、85%的中高档酒店、79%的高档酒店以

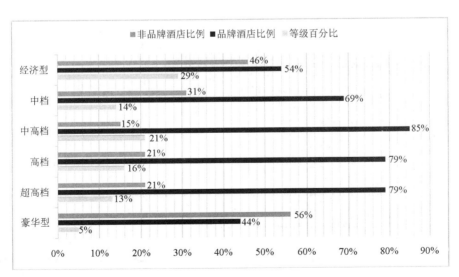

图8-2　按等级划分的品牌酒店与非品牌酒店数量对比
（资料来源：HNN,2015）

8.3 *Branding*

Worldwide, more and more hotels belong to chains, with branding as a main distinction of the hotel products. Figure 8 – 1 delineates the percentage of branded hotels vs. non-branded ones in different regions. North America is dominated by branded hotels, with 67% of the hotels belonging to branded hotel chains or companies, while the rest 33% are still mostly independent hotels. Asia/ Pacific is catching up, with slightly more than half of the hotels being branded. Europe, Middle East, Africa, and South America have slightly more non-branded hotels than branded ones. However, most of the new hotels being planned or in pipeline are branded ones, as it is shown by the STR pipeline report, and this is expected to be the future trend.

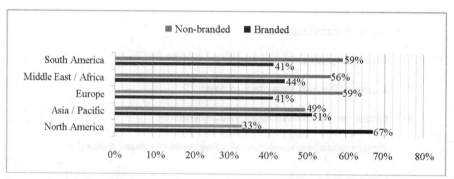

Figure 8 – 1　A breakdown of branded hotels and non-branded hotels by region

(Source: HNN, 2015)

Figure 8 – 2 shows that majority of hotels in midscale class（69%）, upper-midscale class（85%）, upscale class（79%）, and upper-upscale class（79%）are branded ones. For

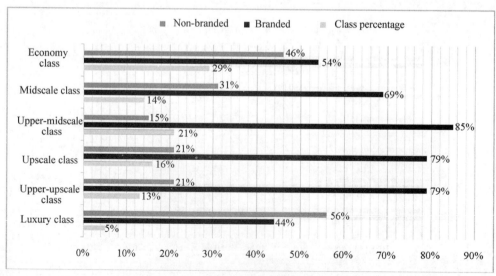

Figure 8 – 2　Percentage of global rooms by class: branded vs. non-branded

(Source: HNN, 2015)

及 79%的超高档酒店属于品牌酒店。在经济型酒店板块,54%属于品牌酒店,剩下的 46%属于非品牌酒店。豪华酒店中非品牌酒店(56%)的比例略高于品牌酒店(44%)。

酒店客户要求一致的酒店体验,这使得品牌化成为国际酒店公司的主要战略之一。图 8-3 显示了全球以房间数排列的前 20 位酒店品牌。

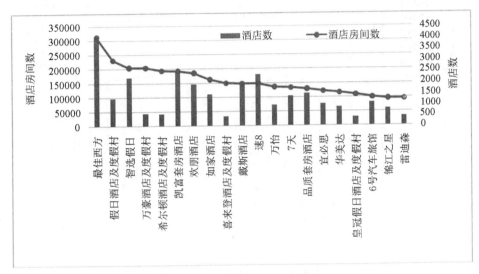

图 8-3　20 大酒店品牌

(资料来源:*Hotels*,*325 Special Report 2013*)

值得注意的是,排在前 20 位的酒店品牌中,经济型酒店占多数,如智选假日、凯富酒店、欢朋酒店、如家、戴斯、速 8、7 天、宜必思、6 号汽车旅馆、锦江之星等,这也体现了酒店行业发展的趋势。当今世界许多顾客选择简约的生活方式和不同的消费态度,这使得经济型酒店发展迅速。Guillet、Zhang 和 Gao(2011)的研究发现,90%的中国内地旅行者选择选择经济型酒店,这也解释了全球和中国内地经济型酒店快速发展的原因。中国的市场前景依旧被看好,被誉为是酒店,特别是经济型酒店最大的潜在市场。另一方面,与高档奢华的酒店相比,经济型酒店的发展更快、更灵活。这也是经济型酒店品牌能如此快速提升的原因之一。

8.4　多品牌发展战略

多数国际酒店巨头如今都追求多品牌战略,以满足不同的市场。一些公司发展或者并购许多品牌,将其纳入旗下。万豪如今拥有 19 个不同档次的品牌,以吸引不同市场。喜达屋目前有 9 个品牌,主要还是集中在豪华型和高档选择服务型板块。温德姆拥有 13 个品牌,几乎每个板块都已涉猎,从超

economy class, there are now more branded hotels（54%）than non-branded ones（46%）. The luxury class has slightly more non-branded hotels（56%）than branded ones（44%）.

Customers are constantly looking for consistent hotel experience, which has made branding the key development strategy for the major international hotel companies. Figure 8 – 3 shows the top 20 hotel brands ranked by number of rooms under each brand.

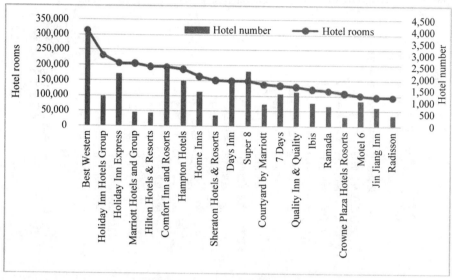

Figure 8 – 3   Top 20 hotel brands
（Data source：*Hotel*，*325 Special Report 2013*）

It is worth noting that many of the best performing hotel brands in terms of number of rooms are budget hotel brands—Holiday Inn Express, Comfort Inn, Hampton Hotels, Home Inns, Days Inn, Super 8, 7 Days, Ibis, Motel 6, Jinjiang Inn, etc., which has shown the development trend of hotel industry. There is a trend that many customers now choose simpler lifestyle, with changed consuming attitude, which makes budget hotel prosper. Guillet, Zhang and Gao（2011）have also identified that around 90% of the customers in Chinese Mainland choose to stay in budget hotels when they travel, which is another reason accounting for the fast development of budget hotels worldwide and in Chinese Mainland, which is the biggest potential market, especially in the budget hotel sector. On the other hand, the expansion of budget hotels are usually faster and easier than its luxury counterparts, which is probably another reason that budget hotel brands have crept on the top of the brand list.

8.4 Multi-branding

Majority of the international big players have been pursuing multi-branding developing strategy, catering for different market segments. Some of the companies have developed or acquired many brands under their portfolio. Marriot has currently 19 brands of various tiers targeting for different markets. Starwood has currently 9 brands, mainly

高档到中档再到经济型酒店,每个品牌又同时拥有系列子品牌,比如华美达和豪生品牌同时拥有系列子品牌,可谓是应有尽有。多品牌发展战略是一个不断演变的过程。2014 年 6 月,希尔顿开启新的品牌 Curio 希尔顿系列,是专门为寻找地方特色和体验的旅行者设计的品牌。同年 10 月,希尔顿再创新品牌—— Canopy,为住客提供简单、人性化、考虑周到和舒适的选择(希尔顿年度报告,2015)。这些新的品牌反映了希尔顿对不断演变的住客的生活方式的理解。其他酒店集团也有类似的品牌演变。雅高酒店集团刚刚购买了 Mama Shelter 37% 的股份,这个品牌是一个创新的城市度假潮流设计的酒店品牌。这个举动让雅高更加丰富了它的品牌组合(雅高年度报告,2015)。

in luxury and upscale selected-service segments. Wyndham has 13 brands, covering whole range of brand series from upper-upscale, midscale, to economy, and some of the brands such as Ramada and Howard Johnson have sub-brands to cater for different market segments. Multi-branding has been an ever evolving strategy for most of the big hotel companies. In June 2014, Hilton launched its new brand: Curio-A Collection by Hilton, created for travelers who seek local discovery and experiences, In October 2014, Hilton launched another new brand—Canopy by Hilton, "offering simple, guest-directed service, thoughtful local choices and comfortable spaces" (Hilton, 2015). These new brands reflect that Hilton understands the evolving lifestyle of the customers. Similar brand evolution is taking place with other hotel companies. Accor has recently acquired 37% stake in Mama Shelter which is a innovative lifestyle concept more like urban retreats with trendy design (Accor, 2015). This acquisition has further enriched Accor's brand portfolio.

第9章　国际酒店公司和中国内地市场

学习目标

- 了解国际酒店公司在中国内地的进入模式和商业模式
- 了解在中国内地的主要国际酒店品牌

多数酒店集团都把中国内地视为主要市场。中国内地享有快速增长的经济和稳定的政治环境,以及快速增长的中产阶级人群。中国疆土辽阔,拥有13亿人口,这对于酒店巨头来说确实是不可多得的优质市场。自从建国酒店——第一家由国际酒店公司(香港半岛酒店集团)管理的中国内地酒店开业以来,中国内地酒店业的发展一直受到国际酒店公司的影响。世界上几乎所有的酒店业大公司都已进入中国内地市场。事实上,目前中国内地酒店市场的豪华及高档市场仍然由洲际、希尔顿、万豪、雅高等国际酒店公司主导。这些酒店集团均对中国内地市场有着相当激进的扩张计划(Guillet、Zhang 和 Gao,2011)。根据中国饭店协会(CHTA)的数据,2011年,有40个国际酒店管理公司的70个酒店品牌管理着中国内地市场的1000家左右酒店。全球十大酒店公司均已落户中国内地,仅洲际酒店集团就有286家酒店在中国内地(CHTA,2011)。这些酒店公司已经不再把重心完全放在一线城市上,而是纷纷向二、三线城市转移,甚至还有四线城市。这些酒店公司在诸如酒店管理、人力资源管理、酒店科技、收益管理及酒店文化方面大大影响了中国内地酒店业的发展(CHTA,2011)。

9.1　进入模式/商业模式

在进入中国内地市场的时候,国际酒店公司比较多采用委托管理模式

Chapter 9 International Hotels Groups and the Market in Chinese Mainland

 Learning Outcomes

■ Understanding the entry mode and business format of the international hotels in Chinese Mainland

■ Understading the major international hotel brands in Chinese Mainland

Chinese Mainland has been recognized as a key market for most hotel companies. Enjoying quick economic growth and political stability, as well as the burgeoning middle class in such a vast country with 1.3 billion population, Chinese Mainland is indeed a lucrative market for the world hotel giants. Since the establishment of Jianguo Hotel, which is the first hotel managed by international hotel group—The Hong Kong Peninsular Hotel Group, the Chinese hotel industry has been growing under the influence of the international hotel companies. Almost all of the big players in the world have entered Chinese Mainland. As a matter of fact, the luxury and upper scale market is still dominated by the international hotel groups such as the InterContinental Hotel Group, Starwood Hotel Group, Hilton Hotels Corporation, Marriot International, and Accor Hotel Group. These hotel groups are all identified to have aggressive expansion plans within the market in Chinese Mainland (Guillet, Zhang, and Gao, 2011). According to statistics provided by China Hotel and Tourism Association (CHTA), in 2011, there were over 40 foreign hotel companies with more than 70 brands in Chinese Mainland, managing around 1000 hotels. The top ten hotel companies have all found their ways to Chinese Mainland, among which IHG(InterContinental Hotels Group) had managed 286 hotels in Chinese Mainland (CHTA, 2011). These hotel companies are no longer only focusing on first tier cities, but targeting at second and third tier cities, and even fourth tier cities increasingly. These foreign hotel companies have greatly influenced hotel development in Chinese Mainland through introducing all aspects of hotel management from human resource, hotel technology, to the management of revenue and service culture (CHTA, 2011).

9.1 Entry Mode / Business Model

When entering the market of Chinese Mainland, the preferred business format for

（Guillet、Zhang 和 Gao，2011）或者其他轻资产的商务模式，如特许加盟。例如，到 2013 年 9 月为止，洲际酒店集团的 198 家酒店中有 193 家采用委托管理模式，4 家特许加盟，1 家是租赁加直营的模式（洲际酒店集团官网，2014）。

9.2 在中国内地的主要国际酒店公司

根据《中国旅游报》的数据，2014 年排在前六名的国际酒店管理公司有洲际酒店集团、温德姆酒店管理集团、喜达屋全球酒店及度假村集团、希尔顿酒店集团、雅高酒店集团以及万豪国际酒店集团（见图 9-1）。

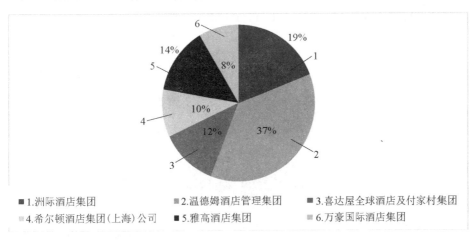

■1.洲际酒店集团　　　■2.温德姆酒店管理集团　　　■3.喜达屋全球酒店及付家村集团
■4.希尔顿酒店集团(上海)公司　　■5.雅高酒店集团　　　■6.万豪国际酒店集团

图 9-1　2013 年中国内地六大国际酒店公司
（资料来源：《中国旅游报》，2014）

2015 年 1 月中国饭店业协会和盈蝶咨询联合发布了中国内地 30 大外资酒店品牌。这些品牌多数属于上述六大酒店公司。表 9-1 列出了该 30 个品牌的明细。

表 9-1　2015 年中国内地 30 大外资酒店品牌

排名	品牌名称	所属集团	客房数	门店数
1	速 8 酒店	温德姆酒店管理集团	53838	706
2	皇冠假日	洲际酒店集团	25552	70
3	喜来登酒店	喜达屋全球酒店及度假村集团	23573	63
4	假日酒店	洲际酒店集团	21815	71
5	香格里拉酒店	香格里拉酒店集团	16139	35
6	华美达酒店	温德姆酒店管理集团	15218	58

the international hotel groups is management contract (Guillet, Zhang, and Gao, 2011) or other light asset business formats such as franchising. IHG, for example, has now 198 hotels in Greater China by September 2013, among which 193 are managed, 4 franchised, and only 1 hotel under owned & leased business format (IHG official website, 2014).

9.2 The Major International Hotel Players in Chinese Mainland

According to statistics released on *China Tourism News*, in 2014 the major international hotel players in Chinese Mainland include InterContinental Hotel Group, Wyndham Hotel Group, Starwood Hotels and Resort International Group, Hilton Hotel Management, Accor, and Marriott International (see Figure 9 - 1).

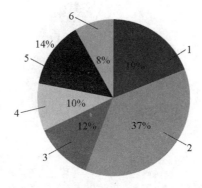

■ 1. InterContinental Hotel Group ■ 2. Wyndham Hotel Group ■ 3. Starwood Hotels and Resort
International Group
■ 4. Hilton Hotel (Shanghai) Co.,Ltd. ■ 5. Accor ■ 6. Marriott International Inc.

Figure 9 - 1 Top international hotel companies in Chinese Mainland, 2013

(Data source: *China Tourism News*, 2014)

Majority of the top 30 foreign brands published jointly by CHA and Inntie in January 2015 belong to the above six companies. The top 30 foreign hotel brands in China are presented in Table 9 - 1.

Table 9 - 1 Top 30 foreign brands in Chinese Mainland, 2015

Rank	Brand	Parent group	Number of rooms	hotels
1	Super 8	Wyndham Hotel Group	53,838	706
2	Crowne Plaza	InterContinental Hotel Group	25,552	70
3	Sheraton	Starwood Hotels and Resort International Group	23,573	63
4	Holiday Inn	InterContinental Hotel Group	21,815	71
5	Shangri-La	Shangri-La Hotel Group	16,139	35
6	Ramada	Wyndham Hotel Group	15,218	58

续　表

排名	品牌名称	所属集团	客房数	门店数
7	豪生大酒店	温德姆酒店管理集团	14630	44
8	智选假日	洲际酒店集团	13166	52
9	洲际酒店	洲际酒店集团	12944	31
10	宜必思	雅高酒店集团	11566	74
11	希尔顿	希尔顿酒店集团公司	10812	25
12	戴斯酒店	温德姆酒店管理集团	9960	55
14	希尔顿逸林	希尔顿酒店集团公司	7692	21
15	最佳西方	最佳西方酒店	7446	29
16	威斯汀酒店	喜达屋全球酒店及度假村集团	7125	20
17	铂尔曼酒店	雅高酒店集团	7089	22
18	万丽酒店	万豪国际酒店集团	6872	17
19	福朋酒店	喜达屋全球酒店及度假村集团	6640	22
20	索菲特酒店	雅高酒店集团	5790	18
21	凯悦酒店	凯悦酒店集团	4573	12
22	君悦酒店	凯悦酒店集团	4311	9
23	美爵酒店	雅高酒店集团	4078	14
24	温德姆至尊豪庭	温德姆酒店管理集团	3880	10
25	JW 万豪酒店	万豪国际酒店集团	3788	9
26	诺富特酒店	雅高酒店集团	3734	12
27	丽笙酒店	卡尔森环球酒店公司	3425	11
28	丽思卡尔顿	万豪国际酒店集团	3152	9
29	日航饭店	日航酒店集团	3121	7
30	万怡酒店	万豪国际酒店集团	3087	10

（资料来源：盈蝶咨询,2015）

● **洲际酒店集团**

目前在中国内地最大的国际酒店公司当属洲际酒店集团。这个总部在

Continued

Rank	Brand	Parent group	Number of rooms	hotels
7	Howard Johnson	Wyndham Hotel Group	14,630	44
8	Holiday Inn Express	InterContinental Hotel Group	13,166	52
9	InterContinental	InterContinental Hotel Group	12,944	31
10	Ibis	Accor Hotel Group	11,566	74
11	Hilton	Hilton Hotel Management（Shanghai）Co., Ltd.	10,812	25
12	Days Inn	Wyndham Hotel Group	9,960	55
13	Marriot	Marriott International Inc.	7,729	18
14	Double Tree by Hilton	Hilton Hotel Management（Shanghai）Co., Ltd.	7,692	21
15	Best Western	Best Western International	7,446	29
16	Westin	Starwood Hotels and Resort International Group	7,125	20
17	Pullman	Accor Hotel Group	7,089	22
18	Renaissance	Marriott International Inc.	6,872	17
19	Four Point	Starwood Hotels and Resort International Group	6,640	22
20	Sofitel	Accor Hotel Group	5,790	18
21	Hyatt	Hyatt Hotel Group	4,573	12
22	Grand Hyatt	Hyatt Hotel Group	4,311	9
23	Mercure	Accor Hotel Group	4,078	14
24	Wyndham Plaza	Wyndham Hotel Group	3,880	10
25	JWMarriot	Marriott International Inc.	3,788	9
26	Novitel	Accor Hotel Group	3,734	12
27	Raddison	Carlson Rezidor Hotel Group	3,425	11
28	Ritz-Carlton	Marriott International Inc.	3,152	9
29	Nikko Hotels	JAL Hotels Company Ltd	3,121	7
30	Courtyard	Marriott International Inc.	3,087	10

（Data source：Inntie，2015）

● InterContinental Hotel Group

The biggest international hotel player in Chinese Mainland seems to be the

英国的酒店公司被认为是全球最大的酒店公司。该公司遍布于 100 个国家和地区,拥有 35 万名员工。在全球范围内,洲际酒店集团目前拥有 9 个品牌:洲际、皇冠假日、英迪格、假日酒店、智选假日系列、Staybridge Suites,Candlewood Suites,EVEN™ 以及华邑酒店及度假村(见图 9 - 2)。

图 9 - 2　洲际酒店集团的品牌系列(洲际酒店集团官网,2014)

如图 9 - 2 所示,截至 2013 年 9 月,洲际酒店集团在全球共有 4653 家酒店、679050 间客房,更有 1102 家在建酒店。所有品牌中,假日酒店和智选假日系列的酒店数和客房数最多,在建酒店中也属这两个品牌的酒店数量最多。该公司的豪华品牌 —— 洲际、皇冠假日及其精品酒店英迪格也有激进的扩张计划和项目。

表 9 - 2　洲际酒店集团品牌明细

品　　牌	已开业酒店(家)	已开业酒店房间数(间)	筹建(酒店)(家)
洲际	174	59136	50
皇冠假日	388	107936	96
英迪格	53	5969	48
假日酒店	1168	211996	234
智选假日	2235	210793	471
假日酒店度假村	34	7904	17
Holiday Inn Club Vacations	10	3701	1
Staybridge Suites	193	21088	78
Candlewood Suites	309	29482	80
华邑酒店及度假村	—	—	21
EVEN	—	—	4
其他	89	21018	2
总　计	4653	679050	1102

(资料来源:洲际酒店集团官网,2014)

洲际是最早进入中国内地的国际酒店公司之一。早在 1984 年假日酒店

InterContinental Hotel Group. The UK based company, InterContinental Hotels Group is recognized as the largest hotel operator in the world, operating hotels in 100 countries and regions, employing more than 350,000 staff. Worldwide, IHG currently operates nine hotel brands—InterContinental, Crowne Plaza, Hotel Indigo, Holiday Inn, Holiday Inn Express, Staybridge Suites, Candlewood Suites, EVEN™ Hotels and HUALUXE™ Hotels and Resorts (see Figure 9 – 2).

Figure 9 – 2   IHG brands worldwide (IHG official website,2014)

As Figure 9 – 2 shows that IHG operates a total of 4,653 hotels with 679,050 rooms worldwide as of September 2013. And there are 1,102 hotels in its pipeline. Among all the brands, Holiday Inn and Holiday Inn Express have the largest number of hotels and rooms, and have more projects in its pipeline. Its luxury brands of InterContinental and Crowne Plaza, as well as its boutique brand—Hotel Indigo also have ambitious expanding plans and projects.

Table 9 – 2   Brand specifics of InterContinental Hotel Group

Brands	Number of opened hotels	Number of rooms of opened hotels	Number of hotels in pipeline
InterContinental	174	59,136	50
Crowne Plaza	388	107,936	96
Hotel Indigo	53	5,969	48
Holiday Inn	1,168	211,996	234
Holiday Inn Express	2,235	210,793	471
Holiday Inn Resort	34	7,904	17
Holiday Inn Club Vacations	10	3,701	1
Staybridge Suites	193	21,088	78
Candlewood Suites	309	29,482	80
HUALUXE	—	—	21
EVEN	—	—	4
Other	89	21,018	2
Total	4,653	679,050	1,102

(Data source: IHG official website,2014)

IHG is one of the first international hotel companies to enter into Chinese Mainland

便在中国落户,截至今日,洲际酒店集团是中国内地最大的酒店运营者。

洲际酒店集团旗下的九大品牌中,有六大品牌已经进入中国内地。从豪华品牌的洲际、到中档品牌的假日酒店、到经济型酒店智选假日品牌。该公司的精品酒店品牌——英迪格也已进入中国内地(见图9-3和表9-3)。

图 9-3　入驻中国内地的洲际酒店品牌

表 9-3　入驻中国内地的洲际酒店品牌

品牌	开业酒店数(家)	房间数(间)	筹建中酒店数(家)
洲际	26	11048	22
皇冠假日	64	22991	50
英迪格	5	613	6
假日酒店	61	19836	38
智选假日	39	9858	38
假日酒店度假村	3	893	4
华邑	—	—	21
总计	198	65239	179

(资料来源:洲际酒店集团官网,2014)

在不同市场开发不同品牌的理念下,洲际在中国内地市场开发了华邑酒店品牌。该酒店品牌完全为中国客户量身定做。该品牌属于高档品牌,号称亲近自然,却也不失豪华的个性化的服务,主要目标人群是中国内地日益壮大的中产阶级。

(图片来源:洲际酒店集团官网,2014)

● **温德姆酒店管理集团**

在中国内地的第二大国际酒店公司是美国的温德姆酒店管理集团。酒店集团是温德姆公司的三大业务之一。就酒店数量而论,温德姆位列全球榜首。

three decades ago. The history dates back to 1984 when Holiday Inn entered Chinese Mainland and started to manage the Holiday Inn. IHG is now the largest international hotel operator in Chinese Mainland.

Of all the brands under IHG, six of them have entered the mass market of Chinese Mainland, ranging from luxury brand of InterContinental to mid-scale brand of Holiday Inn which boasts the first mid-scale international brand in Chinese Mainland, to its budget hotel brand of Holiday Inn Express. Its boutique hotel brand—Hotel Indigo has also entered Chinese Mainland (See Figure 9 - 3 and Table 9 - 3).

Figure 9 - 3　IHG brands in Chinese Mainland

Table 9 - 3　IHG brands in Chinese Mainland

Brands	Number of opened hotels	Number of rooms	Number of hotels in pipeline
InterContinental	26	11,048	22
Crowne Plaza	64	22,991	50
Hotel Indigo	5	613	6
Holiday Inn	61	19,836	38
Holiday Inn Express	39	9,858	38
Holiday Inn Resort	3	893	4
HUALUXE	—	—	21
Total	198	65,239	179

(Data source: IHG official website, 2014)

Guided by the principle of having right brands in the right market, IHG has made one step further in creating a localized brand— HUALUXE (HUALUXE Hotels and Resorts) which is a tailor-made brand for the customers in Chinese Mainland. It is an upscale hotel brand, boasting pro-nature concepts, with luxurious and attentive services, to capitalize on the burgeoning middle class in China.

(Picture from IHG official website, 2014)

● **Wyndham Hotel Group**

The second biggest international hotel player in Chinese Mainland is Wyndham Hotel Group from the USA. Wyndham Hotel Group (Wyndham) is one of the three

目前该公司拥有 7673 家酒店、667362 间客房,在 70 个国家运营。表 9－4 罗列了这些品牌的明细。

表 9－4　温德姆品牌信息

品　牌	酒店(家)	客房(间)	市场定位
贝蒙特酒店及套房	373	30012	中档
戴斯酒店	1,784	144231	北美、中东及拉丁非洲:经济型 亚太:中高档
Dolce 酒店及度假村	24	5530	高档
山楂套房	99	9825	中档
豪生	419	45588	北美、中东及拉丁非洲:经济型/中档 亚太:高档
骑士客栈	392	24476	经济型
Microtel 酒店及套房	325	23302	经济型
华美达	840	116409	中高档
速 8	2519	161538	经济型
Travelodge	422	31025	经济型
TRYP	122	17455	中高档
温盖特	153	13929	中档
温德姆酒店及度假村	201	44042	高档
总计	7673	667362	

(资料来源:温德姆酒店集团官网,2015)

从图 9－4 中可以看出,温德姆旗下目前有 13 个酒店品牌,包括贝蒙特酒店及套房、戴斯酒店、Dolce 酒店及度假村、山楂酒店套房、豪生、骑士酒店、Microtel 酒店及套房、华美达、速 8、Travelodge、TRYP、温盖特以及温德姆酒店及度假村(温德姆,2015)。

图 9－4　温德姆旗下品牌

businesses under Wyndham Worldwide Corporation. In terms of number of hotels, Wyndham is probably the largest in the world. The company has now 7,673 hotels with over 667,362 rooms in 70 countries (see Table 9 - 4).

Table 9 - 4 **Wyndham hotel brands information**

Brands	Number of hotels	Number of rooms	Market positioning
Baymont Inn & Suites	373	30,012	Midscale
Days Inn	1,784	144,231	Economy in N. America, EMEA and Latin America, but Upper-Midscale in Asia Pacific
Dolce Hotels and Resorts	24	5,530	Upper-Upscale
Hawthorn Suites by Wyndham	99	9,825	Midscale
Howard Johnson	419	45,588	Midscale/Economy in N. America, EMEA, and Latin America, but Upscale in Asia Pacific
Knights Inn	392	24,476	Economy
Microtel Inn & Suites by Wyndham	325	23,302	Economy
Ramada	840	116,409	Mid-and Upper-Midscale
Super 8	2,519	161,538	Economy
Travelodge	422	31,025	Economy
TRYP by Wyndham	122	17,455	Upper-Midscale
Wingate by Wyndham	153	13,929	Midscale
Wyndham Hotels and Resorts	201	44,042	Upper-Upscale
Total	7,673	667,362	

(Source: Wyndham official website, 2015)

As shown in Figure 9 - 4, there are currently 13 hotel brands under Wyndham, including Baymont Inn & Suites, Days Inn, Dolce Hotels and Resorts, Hawthorn Suites by Wyndham, Howard Johnson, Knights Inn, Microtel Inn & Suites by Wyndham, Ramada, Super 8, Travelodge, TRYP by Wyndham, Wingate by Wyndham, and Wyndham Hotels and Resorts (Wyndham, 2015).

Figure 9 - 4 Hotel brands under Wyndham Hotel Group

这些品牌当中许多都拥有子品牌。比如温德姆酒店及度假村品牌又细分为三个子品牌：温德姆酒店及度假村、温德姆至尊酒店精选和温德姆花园酒店。另外华美达品牌下有六个子品牌，以满足各类市场，具体如下：

（1）华美达大酒店；

（2）华美达；

（3）华美达有限服务酒店；

（4）华美达酒店及套房；

（5）华美达度假村/华美达酒店及度假村（美国以外）；

（6）华美达安可（美国以外）。

温德姆酒店管理集团目前在中国内地有 695 家酒店，数量最多的是速 8 酒店，共 706 家酒店、53838 间客房；华美达酒店，共 58 家酒店、15218 间客房；豪生酒店共 44 家酒店、14630 间客房；戴斯酒店，共 55 家酒店、9960 间客房；温德姆大酒店，共 10 家酒店、3880 间客房。在这些品牌中，温德姆大酒店和豪生品牌属于高档及豪华类型，速 8、华美达和戴斯酒店属于经济型到中档酒店范畴。图 9-5 列示了温德姆在中国内地的品牌。

图 9-5 在中国内地的温德姆酒店品牌

● **喜达屋全球酒店及度假村集团**[①]

根据喜达屋年度报告，截至 2014 年年底，喜达屋全球酒店及度假村集团共有 1222 家酒店、约 354000 间客房。该集团在 100 个国家运行，拥有员工 180400 名（喜达屋，2015）。

喜达屋从 2006 年开始实行轻资产发展战略（喜达屋，2015）。在它的 1222 家全球酒店中，583 家（193900 间客房）是在委托管理和松散型合资企业的商业模式下运营的，588 家（139200 间客房）在特许加盟模式下，只有 36

---

① 在本书写作时喜达屋还未被并入万豪集团。

Many of the above brands have their respective brand portfolios. For example, Wyndham Hotels and Resorts is further tiered into three sub-brands of Wyndham Hotels and Resorts, Wyndham Grand Hotels and Resorts, and Wyndham Garden Hotels. For another example, Ramada has 6 different sub-brands, catering for different market segments, shown as below:

(1) Ramada Plaza.

(2) Ramada.

(3) Ramada Limited.

(4) Ramada Hotel & Suites.

(5) Ramada Resort / Ramada Hotel & Resort (Outside the US).

(6) Ramada Encore (Outside the US).

Wyndham Hotel Group currently has 695 hotels in Chinese Mainland. The best performing brands under Wyndham in Chinese Mainland include Super 8 Hotel (706 hotels, 53,838 rooms), Ramada Hotel (58 hotels, 15,218 rooms), Howard Johnson Hotel (44 hotels, 14,630 rooms), Days Inn (55 hotels, 9,960 rooms), and Wyndham Plaza (10 hotels, 3,880 rooms). Among these brands, Wyndham Plaza and Howard Johnson belong to the up-scale and luxury categories, while Super 8, Ramada, and Days Inn are more toward the mid-scale and economy hotel categories. The figure below presents the brands under Wyndham, which have presence in the Chinese Mainland market of Chinese Mainland.

Figure 9-5　Hotel brands under Wyndham in Chinese Mainland

● **Starwood Hotels & Resorts Worldwide, Inc**[①].

According to the annual report produced by Starwood, by the end of 2014, there were 1,222 properties with about 354,000 rooms in 100 counties, employing 180,400 staff members (Starwood, 2015).

Same as other hotel giants, Starwood has embarked on asset-light business strategies since 2006 (Starwood, 2015). Among its 1,222 hotels worldwide, 583 hotels (193,900 rooms) are under the business format of "Managed and unconsolidated joint venture hotels", 588 hotels (139,200 rooms) are under franchising, while only 36 hotels (13,500

---

① By the time this chapter was drafted, Starwood was not aquired by Marriot yet.

家(13500 间客房)酒店是公司直营酒店;另有 15 家酒店(7600 间客房)属于度假胜地和独立酒店(喜达屋,2015)。

根据喜达屋年度报告,自 2006 年起,该公司为了追求利润和现金流的最大化,卖掉了 87 家酒店,转为以委托管理和特许加盟为主的商业模式,尽管该公司传统的业务收入来源来自直营,或者租赁和紧密合资酒店。

喜达屋更注重豪华及超高档酒店。目前该公司有 9 大主要品牌,包括:圣瑞吉(豪华完全服务型酒店、度假村及公寓)、豪华精选(豪华完全服务型酒店及度假村)、W 酒店(豪华、超高档完全服务型酒店、疗养及公寓)、威斯汀(豪华、超高档完全服务型酒店、度假村及公寓)、艾美(豪华、超高档完全服务型酒店、度假村及公寓)、喜来登(豪华、超高档完全服务型酒店、度假村及公寓)、福朋(选择服务型酒店)、雅乐轩(选择服务型酒店)和元素(延长住宿酒店)。这九大品牌中,前六大品牌以豪华和超高档酒店为主,后三大品牌以选择服务型酒店为主,但是目标市场迥异:福朋——商务首选;雅乐轩——因设计而异;元素——延长住宿新概念(喜达屋,2015)。表9-5列出了这九大品牌的详细信息。

表 9 - 5 喜达屋品牌信息

喜达屋全球九大品牌				
圣瑞吉 ST REGIS	33 家酒店 7300 间客房	豪华精选 THE LUXURY COLLECTION	92 家酒店 18100 间客房	W 酒店 W HOTELS WORLDWIDE	46 家酒店 13100 间客房
威斯汀酒店 WESTIN HOTELS & RESORTS	203 家酒店 76600 间客房	喜来登酒店 Sheraton	436 家酒店 15340 间客房	艾美 LE MERIDIEN	98 家酒店 26100 间客房
雅乐轩 aloft HOTELS	91 家酒店 15400 间客房	福朋 FOUR POINTS BY SHERATON	193 家酒店 34300 间客房	元素 element BY WESTIN	14 家酒店 2200 间客房

(资料来源:喜达屋酒店集团官网,2015)

在众多喜达屋品牌中,属喜来登和威斯汀的运营历史最久。喜达屋已经

rooms) are directly owned by the company, and the rest 15 hotels (7,600 rooms) are under "Vacation ownership resorts and stand-alone properties" (Starwood, 2015).

According to the Starwood's 2014 annual report, the company has sold 87 hotels since 2006 to pursue the objective of maximizing earnings and cash flow by increasing management contracts and franchise agreements, although, historically, the company derived their major income through their owned, leased and consolidated joint venture hotels.

Starwood focuses more on the luxury and upper upscale segments. So far there are nine brands under Starwood, including St. Regis (luxury full-service hotels, resorts and residences), The Luxury Collection (luxury full-service hotels and resorts), W (luxury and upper upscale full-service hotels, retreats and residence), Westin (luxury and upper upscale full-service hotels, resorts and residents), Le Méridien (luxury and upper upscale full-service hotels, resorts and residences), Sheraton (luxury and upper upscale full-service hotels, resorts and residence), Four Points (select-service hotels), Aloft (select-service hotels), and Element (extended stay hotels). The first six of the brand series are more toward the luxury end, while the last three select-service hotels with distinct features—Four Points is Best for Business; Aloft is Different By Design; Element is Extended Stay Reimagined (Starwood, 2015). Table 9 – 5 provides the number of hotels under the nine different brands worldwide.

Table 9 – 5   Brand specifics of Starwood

Nine Distinct, Global Lifestyle Brands					
ST REGIS	33 hotels 7,300 rooms	THE LUXURY COLLECTION	92 hotels 18,100 rooms	W HOTELS WORLDWIDE	46 hotels 13,100 rooms
WESTIN HOTELS & RESORTS	203 hotels 76,600 rooms	**Sheraton**	436 hotels 15,340 rooms	LE MERIDIEN	98 hotels 26,100 rooms
aloft HOTELS	91 hotels 15,400 rooms	FOUR POINTS BY SHERATON	193 hotels 34,300 rooms	element BY WESTIN	14 hotels 2,200 rooms

(Source: Starwood official website, 2015)

As the above table shows, Sheraton and Westin are the two biggest and oldest brands under Starwood. Sheraton has served the world since 75 years ago, while Westin has been in existence since 60 years ago.

The three select-service brands are relative new to the Starwood brands family, but they have been expanding quickly. For example, Four Points have already 193 hotels and

有 75 年的运营历史,而威斯汀也已经有 60 年。

以上选择的三个服务品牌虽然历史尚短,但是发展迅速。比如福朋已经有 193 家酒店,而雅乐轩也已经有 91 家酒店。

和其他酒店巨头一样,快速在国际市场上拓展是该公司的首要策略。中国自然也是其首要目标市场。

在大中华区域,喜达屋一般采用两种商业模式 —— 委托管理和特许加盟,前者是其主要模式。在中国内地的 146 家酒店中,有 140 家在委托管理模式下运行,只有 6 家以特许加盟的模式运行。所有的品牌中,喜来登是第一个进入中国内地的品牌,也是目前最为人们熟知的品牌,它在中国内地的酒店及房间数量最多。福朋虽然起步很晚,然而,随着市场趋势向以价值为中心的方向转变,该品牌得以快速扩张(见图 9-6 和表 9-6)。

图 9-6　喜达屋在大中华区域的品牌

表 9-6　在大中华区域的喜达屋品牌分布

品　牌	管理合同		特许加盟	
	酒店(家)	客房(间)	酒店(家)	客房(间)
威斯汀	20	7047	1	288
喜来登	64	27524	3	1836
W 酒店	4	1465	—	—
艾美	9	3131	1	160
圣瑞吉	6	1657	—	—
豪华精选	6	1306	—	—
雅乐轩	9	2101	—	—
福朋	22	6527	1	126
元素	—	—	—	—
总计	140	50758	6	2410

(资料来源:喜达屋酒店集团官网,2015)

● **雅高酒店集团**

雅高酒店集团是又一家在中国内地酒店市场扮演重要角色的酒店集团。

Aloft 91 hotels.

Same as other international hotel giants, fast expansion to the international markets is one of the top priorities of the company. Chinese Mainland is certainly their No. 1 target market.

In Greater China, Starwood only pursues two types of business format—management contracts and franchising, with the former the dominant format. Among the 146 hotels in the market of Chinese Mainland, 140 hotels are under management contracts, while only 6 hotels under franchising. Among all the brands, Sheraton was the first brand entering the market of Chinese Mainland, and now is the most well established brand, with the most hotels and rooms in the country. Four Points started late. However, as the market trends change toward a value centered status, this brand gained fast expansion (see Figure 9 – 6 and Table 9 – 6).

Figure 9 – 6   Hotel brands under Starwood Hotel Group in Chinese Mainland

Table 9 – 6   Starwood brands in Greater China

Brands	Management contract		Franchising	
	Hotels	Rooms	Hotels	Rooms
Westin	20	7,047	1	288
Sheraton	64	27,524	3	1,836
W Hotel	4	1,465	—	—
Le Meridien	9	3,131	1	160
St. Regis	6	1,657	—	—
Luxury Collection	6	1,306	—	—
Aloft	9	2,101	—	—
Four Points	22	6,527	1	126
Elements	—	—	—	—
Total	140	50,758	6	2,410

(Source: Starwood official website, 2015)

● **Accor**

Accor is another world leading hotel group that plays important role in Chinese

截至 2014 年年底,该公司在 92 个国家拥有 3700 家酒店,共计 480000 间客房,180000 名员工(雅高年度报告,2014)。该公司有着激进的扩张计划,声称每两天新开一家酒店。如今共有 156000 间客房在建。其中,29% 在法国,31% 在法国以外的欧洲,24% 在亚太,另 10% 在北美、拉丁美洲及加勒比海地区,剩余 6% 在非洲及中东。

雅高把其业务归为两大类——酒店营运者和业主/投资者。在所有酒店中,1354 家是雅高直接拥有或者租赁的,剩下的酒店采取轻资产模式——委托管理或者特许加盟。作为酒店运营者,该公司管理 2211 家酒店,包括 1354 家直接拥有或者租赁的酒店,剩余 1506 家属特许加盟(Accor,2015)。

截至 2014 年年底,雅高共有 17 个不同档次的酒店品牌。表 9-7 和图 9-7罗列了该集团详细的品牌信息。

表 9-7　雅高品牌信息

品　　牌	市场定位	酒店数(家)	客房数(间)
索菲特传奇	豪华	5	873
索菲特	豪华	121	30941
索菲特特色	豪华(特色)	3	463
美憬阁	高档	71	7082
铂尔曼	高档	93	25953
美爵	高档	43	8164
赛贝尔	高档公寓	21	1309
诺富特	中档	414	79220
诺富特套房	诺富特旗下	31	3853
美居	中档	711	89203
阿德吉奥公寓酒店(阿德吉奥,阿德吉奥阿克瑟斯,阿德吉奥特级)	中档	96	10441
宜必思	经济型	1,031	129009
宜必思尚品	经济型	277	25100
宜必思快捷	经济型	537	51022
F1 酒店	经济型	238	17906

(资料来源:Accor,2015)

以上品牌中,经济型或者有限服务型品牌在发展计划中占了一半的位置,可以满足全球不断增长的经济型旅客。比如说,宜必思在全球平均每三

Mainland. The company ran around 3,700 hotels with 480,000 rooms in 92 countries, employing 180,000 staff by the end of 2014 (Accor Annual Report, 2014). The company has ambitious expansion progress, boasting opening one hotel in every two days.It has now 156, 000 rooms in pipeline. Of all the hotels, 29% of them are within France, 31% in the rest of Europe, 24 % in Asia-Pacific, 10% in North America, Latin America, and Caribbean, and the rest 6% in Africa and Middle East.

Accor has two major modes of business: "hotel operator" and "owner/investor". Among all hotels, 1,354 of them are under owned and leased mode, while the rest of the hotels adopting asset light mode—either management contract or franchising. As a hotel operator, the company operated 2, 211 hotels under management, including the aforementioned 1,354 owned and leased hotels, while the rest 1,506 hotels were under franchise, by the end of 2014 (Accor, 2015).

By the end of 2014, Accor offered 17 brands of all tiers to meet the needs of different segments. Table 9 – 7 and Figure 9 – 7 below provide the details.

Table 9 – 7   Accor brand specifics

Brands	Market positioning	Number of hotels	Number of rooms
Sofitel Legend	Luxury	5	873
Sofitel	Luxury	121	30,941
Sofitel So	Luxury (lifestyle)	3	463
MGallery	Upscale	71	7,082
Pullman	Upscale	93	25,953
Grand Mercure	Upscale	43	8,164
The Sebel	Upscale apartments	21	1,309
Novotel	Midscale	414	79,220
Suite Novotel	Under Novotel	31	3,853
Mercure	Midscale	711	89,203
Apart hotels Adogio(Adagio, Adagio access, Adagio Premium)	Midscale	96	10,441
Ibis	Economy	1,031	129,009
Ibis Styles	Economy	277	25,100
Ibis Budget	Economy	537	51,022
Hotel F1	Economy	238	17,906

(Data source: Accor, 2015)

Among the above brands, economy hotels (or limited-service) represent 50% of expansion, catering for the budget conscious travelers worldwide. For example, there is

天新开一家。雅高的豪华及高档品牌也有激进的扩展计划,大概占计划中酒店的22%。中档酒店如美居和诺富特正在更新产品,以更好地服务市场。

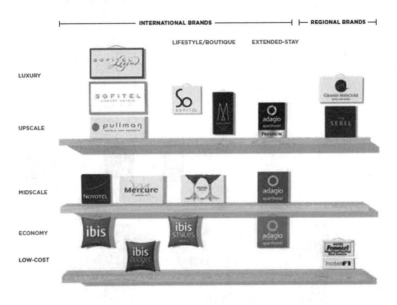

图 9-7 雅高品牌结构
(资料来源:Accor,2015)

雅高1985年进入中国内地,签了第一个管理合同。这么多年来,雅高已经在中国内地市场站稳脚跟,和中国内地当地集团如首都旅游集团、锦江集团及万达集团等建立了牢固的合作关系(谷惠敏和秦宇,2010)。"把重心放在中国"是雅高写在2014年年度报告里的战略。目前,雅高有144家酒店在中国内地(见图9-8),共8个品牌,具体如下:

(1)豪华型/高档:索菲特、铂尔曼、美憬阁、美爵;

(2)中档:诺富特、美居;

(3)经济型:宜必思、宜必思尚品。

图 9-8 雅高在中国内地的品牌
(资料来源:Accor,2015)

one new Ibis opening every three days around the world. The luxury and upscale segment also has ambitious expansion plans, accounting for 22% of planned openings. The midscale brands such as Mercure and Novotel are undergoing revitalization to better serve the market.

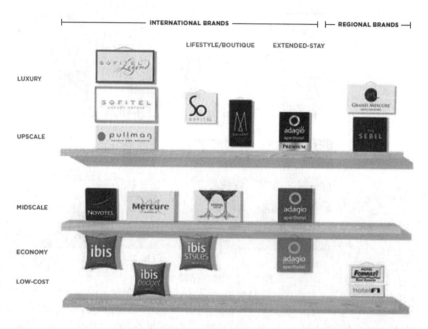

Figure 9 - 7　Accor Brand Tiers

(Data source:Accor, 2015)

Accor entered Chinese Mainland as early as 1985, when the first management contract was signed. Over the years, Accor has well rooted in the market of Chinese Mainland, establishing solid relationship with big local groups such as Beijing Tourism Group, Jinjiang Group, and Wanda Group (Gu and Qin, 2010). "Focus on China" is a stated strategy in Accor Annual Report 2014. Currently, the company has 144 hotels in Chinese Mainland (see Figure 9 - 8), across eight brands shown as below:

(1) Luxury / upscale: Sofitel, Pullman, Mgallery, Grand Mercure

(2) Midscale: Novotel, Mercure;

(3) Economy: ibis, ibis Styles.

Figure 9 - 8　Accor brands in Chinese Mainland

(Date source: Accor,2015)

● 万豪国际酒店集团

万豪于 1997 年在 Delaware 建立集团,并于 1998 年上市。截至 2014 年年底,该公司在全球有 4175 家酒店,714756 间客房,横跨 80 个国家,雇有 360000 名员工(万豪酒店集团官网,2015)。万豪旗下共有 19 个品牌:丽思卡尔顿、宝格丽、艾迪逊酒店、JW 万豪、傲途格精选品牌系列、万丽酒店、万豪酒店、Delta 酒店及度假酒店、万豪行政公寓、万豪假日俱乐部、盖洛德酒店、AC 万豪酒店、万怡酒店、旅居套房酒店、春季山丘套房酒店、弗农商务旅游酒店、长住酒店、Protea 酒店、Moxy 酒店(万豪酒店集团官网,2015)。

万豪的主要商业模式也是委托管理和特许加盟。根据 2015 年发布的万豪年度报告,截至 2014 年年底,该公司共有 1102 家酒店(291840 间客房)在委托管理模式下运行,42 家酒店(9419 间客房)在长期租赁模式下运营,另外直接拥有和管理 9 家酒店(2082 间客房);同时,该公司有 2882 家酒店(388687 间客房)在特许加盟模式下运行,另有 82 家(9879 间客房)酒店在松散合资模式下运行,58 家挂牌分时度假酒店及其他类型的酒店。截至 2014 年年底,万豪在中国内地已经有 76 家酒店,28256 间客房(见图 9-9)。

图 9-9 在中国内地的万豪品牌
(资料来源:万豪酒店集团官网,2015)

● 希尔顿国际酒店集团

拥有百年历史的希尔顿是世界又一酒店巨头。截至 2014 年年底,希尔顿在 94 个国家共有 4322 家酒店、度假村及分时度假酒店,715062 间客房,雇有 157000 名员工(Hilton Worldwide,2015)。该公司共有 12 个品牌,包括它的旗舰品牌 —— 希尔顿酒店及度假村;它的高端品牌系列及奢华生活品位酒店品牌 —— 华尔道夫酒店及度假村、康拉德酒店及度假村、Canopy 品牌;完全服务型酒店 —— Curio 品牌、希尔顿逸林及尊盛酒店;专注服务型(有限服务)品牌—— 希尔顿花园酒店、欢朋酒店、欣庭酒店、惠庭酒店;以及及

● **Marriott International, INC. (Marriot)**

Marriott was organized as a corporation in Delaware in 1997, and became a public company in 1998. The company has 4,175 hotels worldwide, with 714,756 rooms by the end of 2014, operating in 80 countries, employing over 360,000 employees (Marriot official website, 2015). Marriott boasts a broad portfolio of 19 brands listed as below: The Ritz-Carlton, BVLGARI, EDITION, JW Marriott, Autograph Collection Hotels, Renaissance Hotels, Marriott Hotels, Delta Hotels and Resorts, Marriott Executive Apartments, Marriott Vacation Club, Gaylord Hotels, AC Hotels by Marriott, Courtyard, Residence Inn, SpringHill Suites, Fairfield Inn & Suites, TownePlace Suites, Protea Hotels and Moxy Hotels (Marriott official website, 2015).

The main business modes of Marriott are management contract and franchising. According to the annual report of Marriott in 2015, by the end of 2014, the company operated 1,102 hotels (291,840 rooms) under long-term management agreements, 42 hotels (9,419 rooms) under long-term lease agreements with owners (management and lease agreements together), and directly owned and managed 9 hotels (2,082 rooms); moreover, there were 2,882 hotels (388,687 rooms) under franchising, and 82 hotels (9,879 rooms) under the format of unconsolidated joint venture properties, 58 licensed timeshare, and other types of hotels. Up till the end of 2014, Marriott operated 76 hotels with 28,256 rooms in Chinese Mainland (see Figure 9 – 9).

Figure 9 – 9   Marriott brands in China
(Source: Marriott official website, 2015)

● **Hilton Worldwide (Hilton)**

Having almost 100 years of history, Hilton Worldwide (Hilton) is another hotel giant in the world. By the end of 2014, Hilton had 4,322 hotels, resorts and timeshare properties with 715,062 rooms operating in 94 countries, employing 157,000 staff members (Hilton Worldwide, 2015). The company has established 12 brands so far, including its flagship full—service Hilton Hotels & Resorts brand; its premier brand portfolio / luxury and lifestyle hotel brands—Waldorf Astoria Hotels & Resorts, Conrad Hotels & Resorts and Canopy by Hilton; its full-service hotel brands, Curio-A Collection by Hilton, Double Tree by Hilton and Embassy Suites Hotels; its focused-service (limited service) hotel brands—Hilton Garden Inn, Hampton Hotels, Homewood Suites by

分时度假品牌——希尔顿度假俱乐部（见表9-8）。

希尔顿把自己的业务分成三大块：（1）委托管理和特许加盟；（2）直接拥有（所有权）；（3）分时度假（Hilton Worldwide,2015,2015）。第一块最为主要，截至2014年年底，共有4134家酒店（649314间客房）；所有权板块有144家酒店（58954间客房），分时度假44家酒店（6794间客房）。

表9-8 希尔顿品牌明细

品 牌		市场定位	酒店（家）	客房（间）
WALDORF ASTORIA HOTELS & RESORTS / CONRAD HOTELS & RESORTS / Hilton HOTELS & RESORTS / CURIO A COLLECTION BY HILTON / DOUBLETREE BY HILTON / E EMBASSY SUITES HOTELS / Hilton Garden Inn / Hampton / HOMEWOOD SUITES BY HILTON / HOME2 SUITES BY HILTON / Hilton Grand Vacations	华尔道夫酒店及度假村	豪华	26	10653
	康拉德酒店及度假村	豪华	24	8091
	希尔顿酒店及度假村	超高档	560	201045
	Curio——希尔顿精选	超高档	5	3170
	希尔顿逸林	高档	410	100879
	尊盛酒店	超高档	219	52140
	希尔顿花园酒店	高档	618	86095
	欢朋酒店	中高档	2,005	198914
	希尔顿欣挺	高档	359	40056
	希尔顿惠庭	中高档	45	4726
	希尔顿分时度假俱乐部	分时度假	44	6794
	希尔顿Canopy	豪华	2家在建,13家已签	

（资料来源：Hilton Worldwide,2015）

图9-10所示是希尔顿在中国内地的品牌。

图9-10 希尔顿在中国内地的品牌

Hilton and Home2 Suites by Hilton and its timeshare brand—Hilton Grand Vacations (see Table 9 – 8).

Hilton divides its business into three segments: (1) management and franchise; (2) ownership; (3) timeshare (Hilton Worldwide, 2015). The first segment-management and franchise comprises the biggest segment—4,134 hotels with 649,314 rooms by the end of 2014. The ownership segment is consisted of 144 hotels with 58,954 rooms, and its timeshare segment 44 properties with 6,794 rooms by the end of 2014.

Table 9 – 8   Hilton brands specifics

Brands		Market positioning	Number of hotels	Number of rooms
	Waldorf Astoria Hotels & Resorts	Luxury	26	10,653
	Conrad Hotels & Resorts	Luxury	24	8,091
	Hilton Hotels & Resorts	Upper upscale	560	201,045
	Curio—A Collection by Hilton	Upper upscale	5	3,170
	DoubleTree By Hilton	Upscale	410	100,879
	Embassy Suites Hotels	Upper upscale	219	52,140
	Hilton Garden Inn	Upscale	618	86,095
	Hampton Hotels	Upper midscale	2,005	198,914
	Homewood Suites by Hilton	Upscale	359	40,056
	Home2 Suites by Hilton	Upper midscale	45	4,726
	Hilton Grand Vacation	Timeshare	44	6,794
	Canopy by Hilton	Luxury	2 in pipeline, 13 signed	

(Data source: Hilton Worldwide, 2015)

Figure 9 – 10 shows Hilton brands in Chinese Mainland.

Figure 9 – 10   Hilton brands in Chinese Mainland

经济型酒店
Budget Hotels

第 10 章 经济型酒店在中国内地的发展

学习目标

- 了解经济型酒店在中国内地的发展史
- 了解中国内地经济型酒店的现状

有人曾说,中国内地的酒店市场将多半是经济型酒店的天下。这样的酒店发展趋势与国内经济的持续增长和大众旅游时代的到来是息息相关的。统计数据显示,2012 年中国国内游游客达到了 31.3 亿人次,这已将中国推上了全球最大国内游市场的位置(Shen, 2013)。自 2003 年以来,中国内地的经济型酒店的数量年增长平均保持在 70% 左右的幅度。据中国内地经济型酒店著名品牌——华住酒店集团的创始人季琦先生说,中国内地的经济型酒店业的良好发展势头至少会持续 10~20 年(季琦,2014)。

经济型酒店在国外也被称为有限服务型酒店。此类酒店的主要特点是:只提供核心服务,比如客房＋早餐,价格低廉,但是性价比高,酒店规模比较小。李志平在《中国经济型酒店成功之道》一书中对于经济型酒店的定义为:"经济型酒店是一种投入较少,成本较低的酒店,只提供最基本的住宿设施,如客房、早餐服务;有些经济型酒店只提供客房而另一些则提供客房和早餐。

Chapter 10　The Development of Budget Hotels in Chinese Mainland

 Learning Outcomes

- Understanding the development history of budget hotel in Chinese Mainland
- Understanding the current situation of the budget hotel sector in Chinese Mainland

There is a commonly held view that budget hotel is going to dominate hotel development in Chinese Mainland in near future. This trend has a close relationship with the fast and continuous growth of economy in Chinese Mainland and the arrival of mass tourism. Statistics show that domestic tourism has reached 3.13 billion in 2012, which has made Chinese Mainland the biggest domestic tourism market (Shen, 2013). The annual growth rate of budget hotels in Chinese Mainland has been around 70%. According to Mr. Ji, who is the founder of a famous domestic budget hotel company in Chinese Mainland—China Lodge, the momentum of budget hotel development in Chinese Mainland will last for at least 10~20 years' time (Ji, 2014).

Budget hotel is also called limited service hotel in foreign counties. The main features include providing only core product, such as guestroom and breakfast, inexpensive, but cost effective, and the scale of the hotel is usually small. According to Li (2009), budget hotel is a type of hotel with low investment, low cost, providing only basic facilities such as guestroom, breakfast; some budget hotels provide guestroom only, while others provide both guestrooms and breakfast. The price is lower than full service counterparts, normally less than 350 RMB. Majority of budget hotels in Chinese Mainland belongs to

它的房价相对高星级酒店而言,较低廉,目前一般最高不超过 350 元。"(李志平,2009)除以上定义外,经济型连锁酒店的主要特色有:广阔的地域覆盖、容易到达、中央预定系统、品牌产品、标准的单位建筑和客房设计、房价基本统一、有限服务以及高性价比等（Brothernton,2004）。这样的酒店产品特点对于如今的中国内地消费大众来说是最适合不过了。

从全球范围来看,经济型酒店比完善服务型酒店发展历史短。根据 Gilbert 和 Lockwood（1990）的文献,经济型酒店于 1963 年在美国加利福尼亚州起步,最早的经济型酒店叫 Motel 6（类似于汽车旅馆,只提供房间,一个晚上只需 6 美元）。经过几十年的时间,全球经济型酒店均得到快速发展。例如,至 2010 年为止,经济型酒店占英国总客房数的 14%,在美国是 25%,法国为 23%（Ruetz 和 Marvel,2011）。此类酒店的快速发展应归因于消费者的消费态度、生活方式以及价值观的变化。国内旅行的快速增长、各国经济的增长以及酒店行业的日趋成熟也是促使经济型酒店快速发展的重要原因。投资商和业主对于经济型酒店也颇为青睐,其原因和该酒店模式的高投资回报率是分不开的（Harris,2000）。

经济型酒店在中国内地的发展时间尚短。如果说 1997 年在上海徐家汇开的第一家锦江之星标志着经济型酒店在中国的开端的话,至今也不过是 20 年的时间。然而在短短的 20 年内,经济型酒店在中国内地的发展如雨后春笋,其增长速度备受全世界瞩目。经济型酒店也是唯一一块国际品牌多年以来难以竞争的一个酒店领域。据最近 Hotel 杂志酒店集团排行榜公布的信息,在数量上,中国有两家集团位列前十,更有另三家跻身前二十:锦江排名第 9、如家排名第 10、7 天排名第 14、华住酒店集团排名第 16、格林豪泰第 18（Hotel,2014）。论品牌排名,中国内地的经济型酒店集团也毫不逊色:如家排名第 8、7 天排名第 13、锦江之星排名第 19、莫泰 168（如家旗下）排名第 39（Hotel,2014）。这样的排名在 10 年前是难以想象的。这也足够说明经济型酒店在中国内地获得了巨大的成功。

在众多经济型酒店品牌中,属如家、7 天、锦江之星以及汉庭等连锁型酒店集团在数量和规模上的增长最为快速。以如家为例,至本书写作之际,如家酒店

budget hotel chains, which have the features of wide geographic coverage, easy accessibility, central reservation system, branded product, standard unit construction and guestroom design, consistent room rate, limited service, and value for money (Brothernton, 2004). This type of hotel product suits the mass tourists in Chinese Mainland best at the moment.

Internationally, budget hotel enjoys shorter development history compared with its full service counterpart. According to Gilbert and Lockwood (1990), budget hotel started in California, the USA, with the first Motel 6 in 1963, which offers a guestroom at the rate of 6 dollars only per night. After decades of development, budget hotels have gained fast development internationally. For example, up till 2010, budget hotels accounted for 14% of total hotel rooms in the UK, while 25% in the USA, and 23% in France (Ruetz & Marvel, 2011). The fast development of budget hotel can be attributed to a change in consumer attitude, life style, and values. The fast development of domestic tourism, economic development, and the maturity of hotel industry are also important factors contributing to the development of budget hotels. Moreover, budget hotel is also favored by investors and owners, due to its high return on investment (Harris, 2000).

Budget hotel has a shorter development history in Chinese Mainland. It has been only about 20 years' time if the first Jinjiang Inn opened in Shanghai in 1997 was the start of budget hotels in Chinese Mainland. However, within the 20 years, the rapidity of its development has attracted attention from worldwide. Budget hotel sector in Chinese Mainland is the only hotel sector that has been dominated by domestic companies. Foreign hotel companies have not been able to compete in terms of growth rate in this hotel sector. According to the rankings of hotel companies in *Hotel* magazine based on hotel numbers, there are two Chinese hotel companies being ranked among the top 10, and another 3 companies listed among the top 20: Jinjiang was listed as No. 9, Home Inns No. 10, 7 Days Inn No. 14, China Lodge No. 16, and Green Tree No. 18 (*Hotel*, 2014). Within the realm of budget hotels, Home Inns was listed as No. 8, 7 Days Inns No. 13, Jinjiang Inn No. 19, Motel 168 (a brand under Home Inns) No. 39 (*Hotel*, 2014). The above rankings have demonstrated the huge success of budget hotels in Chinese Mainland, considering the short development history.

Among all the budget hotel companies in Chinese Mainland, Home Inns, 7 Days Inn, Jinjiang Inn, and China Lodge, are among the fastest growing companies in terms of hotel numbers. Taking Home Inns as an example, up till 2014, the company has

集团已经遍布全国 270 多座城市,拥有连锁酒店 1900 多家(如家酒店集团官网,2015),并且其目前仍然处于快速增长的状态。除了如家,汉庭、7 天、锦江之星也发展势头良好。以上四大经济型连锁酒店的发展路径将在本章具体描述,以供借鉴。

10.1　中国内地经济型酒店发展简史

1997 年前在中国内地市场上也出现过零星的经济型酒店,但却由于各种原因没有得到持续发展。真正意义上的经济型酒店被普遍认为是第一家在上海徐家汇开业的锦江之星。国内经济型酒店真正开始发展是在 2003 年之后,于 2005—2007 年之间得到快速发展,甚至在 2008—2009 年的金融危机期间,经济型酒店的增长率依旧保持在 30%～40%。图 10 - 1 展示了从 2001 年到 2012 年间中国内地经济型酒店在酒店数和客房数方面的增长情况。值得注意的是,国内经济型酒店多半属于连锁酒店集团。目前排在前四位的是:如家、7 天、华住(汉庭)以及锦江之星。这四个集团的酒店数量加起来已经超过国内经济型酒店总数的 50%。这四个集团均为中国民族企业。与此同时,国际酒店集团的经济型酒店品牌也在 2004 年之后开始进入中国内地,比较知名的例子是美国圣达特酒店集团下的速 8(Super 8)、法国雅高旗下的宜必思(Ibis)、美国著名品牌天天客栈(Days Inn)、英国洲际集团的假日智选(Holiday Inn Express)以及国际青年旅舍等。虽然其扩张速度不及国内四大品牌,但不少品牌已经赢得了市场的部分份额。

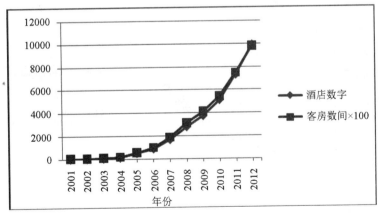

图 10 - 1　中国经济型酒店增长情况
(资料来源:盈蝶咨询,2013)

表 10 - 1 罗列了经济型酒店在中国内地发展的主要历程。

covered 270 cities in Chinese Mainland with more than 1,900 hotels (Home Inns official website, 2015), and the expansion is still going on. The rest three companies are also maintaining tremendous development momentum. The development route of these four companies will be elaborated later.

10.1 Brief History of Budget Hotel Development in Chinese Mainland

Prior to 1997, there were a few small scale budget hotel companies in Chinese Mainland. But due to various reasons, these budget hotel companies did not gain continuous development. The start of budget hotel is commonly believed to be the first Jinjiang Inn in Shanghai. Fast development took place after 2003, and gained tremendous expansion during the years from 2005 to 2007. The growth rate remained 30% ~ 40% even during the financial crisis in 2008 and 2009. Figure 10 - 1 demonstrates the growth of budget hotels in Chinese Mainland in terms of hotel numbers and room numbers. Noticeably, majority of the budget hotels in Chinese Mainland belong to budget hotel chains. Currently, Home Inns, 7 Days Inn, China Lodge, and Jinjiang Inn are in the dominating positions. The numbers of hotels under these four budget hotel chains adding up together account for more than 50% of the total budget hotel numbers in Chinese Mainland. These four companies are all domestic. Meanwhile, international companies started entering the market of Chinese Mainland since 2004. Examples include Super 8 under Cendant from the USA, Ibis under Accor from France, Days Inn from the USA, Holiday Inn Express under Intercontinental from the UK, and International Youth Hostel, etc. These international hotel companies have enjoyed slower growth rate, but many of them have won their respective market share already.

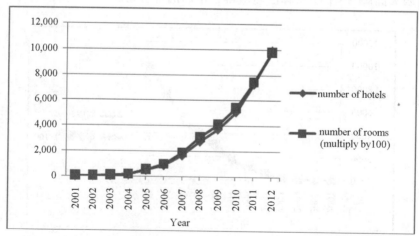

Figure 10 - 1   Growth of budget hotels in Chinese Mainland
(Data source: Inntie, 2013)

Table 10 - 1 below shows the milestones of budget hotel development in Chinese Mainland.

表 10 - 1　经济型酒店在中国内地发展大事记

时间	发展历程
1997 年 2 月	锦江之星上海锦江乐园店开业,中国内地第一家经济型酒店诞生
2002 年 7 月	第一家如家酒店在北京开业
2003 年 5 月	第一家莫泰 168 酒店营业
2004 年 1 月	中国内地第一家宜必思在天津开业,标志着外资经济型酒店在中国内地的开端
2004 年 6 月	美国速 8 在中国内地的第一家酒店在北京开业,成为第二个外资品牌
2004 年 11 月	中国内地的第一家格林豪泰酒店于上海开始起步,并迅速扩张
2005 年 1 月	第一家 7 天分店在广州成立
2005 年 8 月	莫泰 168 在上海正式营业,开启了经济型酒店产品结构细分的先河
2005 年 8 月	第一家汉庭酒店在江苏开业
2005 年 12 月	摩根士丹利以 2000 万美元购入莫泰约 20% 股权,标志着经济型酒店资本大战拉开序幕
2006 年 10 月	如家成功登陆纳斯达克,融资 1.09 亿美元,成为中国内地第一家海外上市的经济型连锁酒店
2007 年 7 月	丽星邮轮在杭州开出了首家"我的客栈",并打出了 99 元的震撼低价
2007 年 10 月	如家并购七斗星经济型酒店,掀起酒店业以资本直接并购浪潮的第一幕
2008 年 9 月	汉庭酒店集团第三个品牌——汉庭客栈的第一家店在杭州开业。行业内低端市场竞争日益激烈。
2008 年年底	7 天连锁酒店逆市获得国际金融机构 6500 万美元的融资
2009 年 5 月	如家酒店集团与携程正式签订 5000 万美元融资协议
2009 年 11 月	7 天连锁酒店在美国纽约证券交易所成功上市
2010 年 3 月	汉庭酒店在纳斯达克上市
2010 年 9 月	锦江之星收购金广快捷 70% 股权
2011 年 5 月	如家酒店集团以 4.7 亿美元收购莫泰 168 全部股权

Table 10 – 1   Selected milestones of budget hotel development in Chinese Mainland

Time	Milestones
Feb. 1997	The first Jinjiang Inn opened in Shanghai, which marked the beginning of budget hotel sector in Chinese Mainland.
July, 2002	The first Home Inn opened in Beijing.
May, 2003	The first Motel 168 was put into operation.
Jan, 2004	The first Ibis got established in Tianjin, China, which was the beginning of foreign branded budget hotels in Chinese Mainland.
June, 2004	The first Super 8 from the USA got opened in Beijing, which was the second foreign budget hotel brand.
Nov., 2004	Green Tree started its first hotel in Shanghai, and got expanded quickly since.
Jan., 2005	7 Days Inn had its first branch in Guangzhou.
Aug., 2005	Motel 168 got established in Shanghai, which marked the beginning of market and product segmentation in the budget hotel sector in Chinese Mainland.
Aug., 2005	The first Hanting Inn (China Lodge) opened in Jiangsu.
Dec., 2005	Morgan Stanley purchased 20% of share from Motel with 20 million US Dollars, which marked the beginning of capital war in the budget hotel sector.
Oct., 2006	Home Inns got successfully listed in NASDAQ, raising 209 million US Dollars. It is the first Chinese budget hotel company which got listed in overseas stock market.
July, 2007	Star Cruises started "My Inn" in Hangzhou, with historical low price of 99 RMB.
Oct., 2007	Home Inns acquired Top Star Hotel Group, which was the first capital acquisition wave.
Sep., 2008	The third brand under China Lodge—Hanting Inn started in Hangzhou, which made the competition in lower end market more intensive.
The end of 2008	7 Days Inn successfully raised capital of 65 million USD from international financial companies.
May, 2009	Home Inns entered into a capital raising agreement at the amount of 50 million USD with Ctrip.
Nov., 2009	7 Days Inn got successfully listed in New York Stock Exchange.
Mar., 2010	Hanting (China Lodge) got listed in NASDAQ.
Sep., 2010	Jinjiang Inn acquired 70% stock ownership of Goldmet Inn.
May, 2011	Home Inns acquired 100% stock ownership of Motel 168 with 470 million USD.

续　表

时间	发展历程
2011 年 7 月	7 天连锁酒店以 1.36 亿元人民币现金收购华天之星全部股权
2011 年 9 月	锦江之星与菲律宾的上好佳签约,以品牌输出的方式跨出国门
2011 年 12 月	锦江之星与法国卢浮酒店集团在上海举行签约仪式,将以品牌联盟形式亮相法国
2012 年 6 月	汉庭集团宣布入股中档连锁酒店星程,成为其控股股东
2012 年 7 月	如家完成收购安徽"e 家快捷"
2012 年 7 月	凯雷投资集团宣布已投资橘子酒店,获 49% 控股权
2012 年 11 月	汉庭酒店集团正式更名为"华住酒店集团"

（资料来源：盈蝶咨询,2013）

经济型酒店在中国内地的发展历史虽然短暂,但是发展历程却是跌宕起伏,其竞争态势从开始的蓝海战役逐渐演变成红海战役,在短短的十几年内见证了多次大型的兼并、并购,各类资本运作,上市、海外联合等。除了扩张、融资、并购、联盟等措施以外,各大经济型酒店在产品市场细分方面也下足了功夫。从开始的单一品牌,到从低价品牌到中高端品牌的品牌尝试,这其中有成功也有失败。值得庆贺的是,中国内地的经济型酒店民族品牌在整个发展以及竞争过程中一直占据主导地位,甚至发展到能够以品牌输出和品牌联盟方式走出国门。

10.2　中国内地经济型酒店发展现状

据盈蝶咨询 2013 年的统计数据,截至 2012 年年底,中国内地市场上共有经济型酒店 9924 家,约占国内酒店总数的 18%。虽然这个数字比起美国的 70% 来说显得很小,然而对于发展起步晚的中国市场,这个比例已经显得举足轻重了。中国内地经济型酒店大多数属于连锁酒店集团。据盈蝶咨询(2013)数据统计,中国内地市场上目前有 488 个品牌的连锁经济型酒店集团。这 488 个品牌中,超过 70% 以上的经济型酒店来自于 10 个酒店集团。这其中,前四个集团酒店数量总和超过了所有经济型酒店数量的一半以上。图 10-2 反映了 2012 年年底这 10 个经济型酒店集团在客房数量和门店数量上的排名和市场份额数据。

Continued

Time	Milestones
July, 2011	7 Days Inn acquired 100% stock ownership of Huatianzhixing Hotel Chain with 136 million RMB.
Sep., 2011	Jinjiang Inn signed agreement with Oishi from the Philippines, which started brand exporting to other countries.
Dec., 2011	Jinjiang Inn signed agreement with Hotel Du Louvre from France, and will start its presence in France in the form of brand alliance.
July, 2012	Hanting announced that it will become the controlling shareholder of the mid-scale chain hoter—Starway Hotel.
July, 2012	Home Inns completed its acquisition of "e Home Inns" in Anhui Province.
July, 2012	The Carlyle Group announced its investment in Orange Hotel, and obtained 49% of stock ownership.
Nov., 2012	Hanting Hotel Group officially changed its name into "China Lodge".

(Data source: Inntie, 2013)

The above milestones of development in the budget hotel sector which enjoyed only short history show that this hotel sector has experienced many ups and downs, turning its blue ocean battle field gradually into red ocean battle field. In about 20 years' time, this hotel sector has witnessed multiple merges, acquisitions, capital operation of many kinds, getting listed in stock exchange, foreign alliances formation, and so on. The competition is getting ever more intensive. Apart from the above actions, the budget hotel companies have invested their efforts in market segmentation as well. From single brand to multiple brands, from low-price brands to mid-and-upper level brand, the journey is full of successes and failures. It is notice worthy that the Chinese domestic budget hotel brands have been playing a dominant role in its development history. The companies of Chinese Mainland are now starting to step outside of Chinese Mainland via brand exporting and strategic alliance.

10.2 Current Situation of Budget Hotel in Chinese Mainland

According to statistics from Inntie (2013), up till the end of 2012, there were 9,924 budget hotels in Chinese Mainland, accounting for 18 % of the total hotel number in Chinese Mainland. While this figure is far less than the "70%" in America, it is already a big number considering the short development time in market of Chinese Mainland. Majority of budget hotels in Chinese Mainland belong to budget hotel chains. According to Inntie (2013), there are 488 brands in the budget hotel sector in Chinese Mainland. Among all these hotels, 70% of them belong to the top 10 hotel groups. Figure 10 - 2 shows the ranking of the ten budget hotel groups in terms of room number and hotel

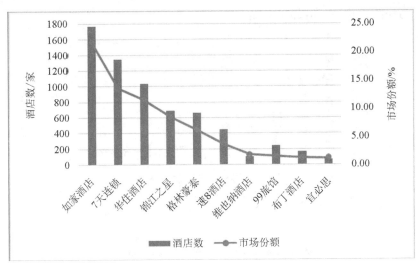

图 10-2　中国内地十大经济型酒店集团

（资料来源：盈蝶咨询,2013）

如图 10-2 所示,截至 2012 年年底,占中国内地经济型酒店市场前三位的经济型酒店集团是如家酒店、7 天连锁和华住酒店。锦江之星位列第四,虽然其所占市场份额远远小于前三大集团,然而其在市场上所扮演的引领角色,使得锦江之星通常和前三大集团一起被列为中国内地经济型酒店市场上的四大巨头。被人们津津乐道的是,这四家经济型酒店集团均属民族企业。虽然国际巨头对中国内地经济型酒店市场垂涎已久,但其业绩始终无法和这四家企业相比。而在豪华酒店市场中,中国内地民族企业能够和国际集团竞争的并不多见。

盈蝶咨询将中国内地经济型连锁酒店又划分为中档连锁酒店、快捷连锁酒店以及平价酒店,该划分以品牌为基准（见图 10-3 到图 10-5）。

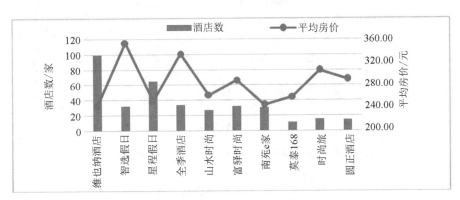

图 10-3　2012 年中档连锁酒店品牌排行榜（10 强）

（注：以上数据不含筹建酒店；资料来源：盈蝶咨询,2013）

number, as well as their market share.

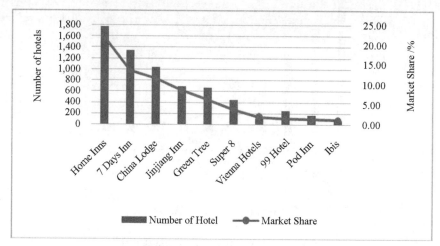

Figure 10 - 2　Top 10 budget hotel chains in Chinese Mainland

（Data source：Inntie，2013）

As Figure 10 - 2 shows, up till the end of 2012, the biggest three market players are Home Inns, 7 Days Inn, and China Lodge. Although Jinjiang Inn is ranked the fourth, its market share falls far behind. However, considering its unique position and contribution in the budget hotel sector, it is usually listed as one of the four giants in budget hotel market in Chinese Mainland together with the three other companies. The above four companies are all domestic. International budget hotel companies have attempted to catch up, but so far not competitive enough. However, everyone knows that international hotel groups dominate the luxury hotel sector in Chinese Mainland.

Inntie has categorized budget hotels in Chinese Mainland into mid-scale budget hotels, fast chain hotel, and inexpensive hotels, which is done according to brands （Figures 10 - 3 to 10 - 5）.

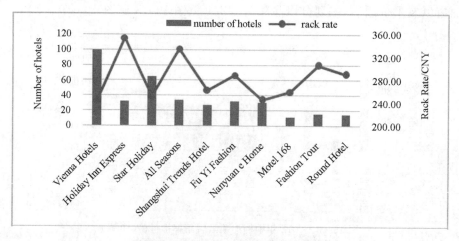

Figure 10 - 3　Top 10 mid-scale budget hotels，2012

（Note：Hotels in piles are not included；Data source：Inntie，2013）

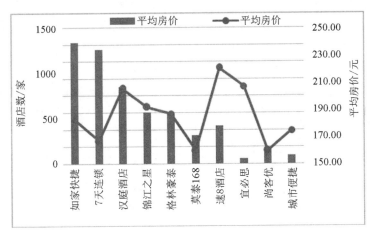

图 10 - 4　2012 年中国内地快捷连锁酒店品牌排行榜（10 强）
（注：以上数据不含筹建酒店；资料来源：盈蝶咨询，2013）

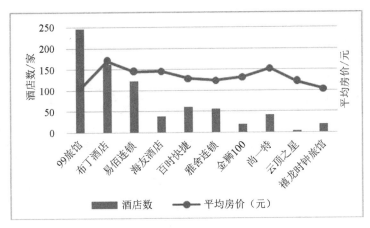

图 10 - 5　2012 年中国内地平价酒店品牌排行榜（10 强）
（注：以上数据不含筹建酒店；资料来源：盈蝶咨询，2013）

图 10 - 3 到图 10 - 5 显示，中国内地的经济型酒店市场目前还是以快捷酒店为主，中档酒店及平价酒店的客房数和门店数远不及快捷酒店的数量。

10.3　中国内地经济型酒店商业及运营模式

中国内地经济型连锁酒店集团的商业模式与中国传统的酒店业截然不同。中国内地的经济型连锁酒店多数采用租赁＋改造运营的商业模式进行运作。它们向第三方租赁物业，并将旧物业改造成经济型酒店。这个过程平均需要 3～6 个月时间，开业后一般需要 6 个月达到 80% 以上的入住率。相比中国内地传统酒店业重资产的商业模式，中国内地经济连锁酒店轻资产的模式允许酒店集团在短时间内进行快速扩张。该模式投资小，风险也相对

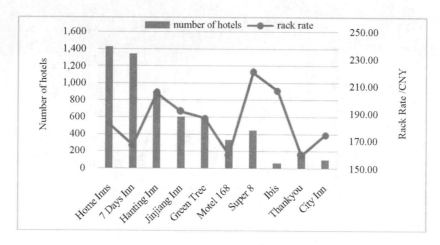

Figure 10 - 4　Top 10 fast chain hotel，2012

（Note：Hotels in piles are not included；Data source：Inntie，2013）

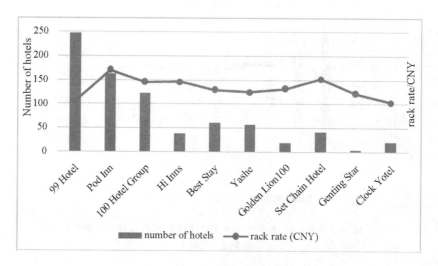

Figure 10 - 5　Top 10 low price budget hotels in Chinese Mainland，2012

（Note：Hotels in piles are not included；Data source：Inntie，2013）

Figure 10 - 3 to 10 - 5 show that fast budget hotels are dominating the market in Chinese Mainland，while the number of mid-scale and low price hotels is far less.

10.3　Business Mode of Budget Hotels in Chinese Mainland

The business mode of budget hotels in Chinese Mainland differs from traditional hotels in Chinese Mainland greatly. Budget hotels in Chinese Mainland usually adopt the business mode of lease plus operation. The hotel companies lease old properties from a third party，and renovate the properties into hotels. On average，this takes three to six months，and the occupancy rate can reach 80% within 6 months after the hotel is

小,投资回报快。

除了租赁＋改造运营的商业模式,中国内地的主流经济型连锁酒店集团也倾向采用加盟＋管理的模式。这种模式投入更少,在资金有限的情况下,开发商更加青睐该模式,它可使集团能够更加快速地扩张以快速占有市场份额。这种方式可以为连锁酒店集团增加收入和利润,虽然所产生的利润少些,但是品牌的品质基本上可以得到保证。很多集团更看重的是在整个市场中所占的份额。

除以上商业模式以外,各经济型酒店集团也会有少量纯特许加盟的酒店,全部交给加盟商自己经营。这种商业模式虽然面临品牌被稀释的风险,但是为了实现快速增长,部分酒店集团也愿意冒险。

相比传统酒店的大规模(通常五星级酒店有 350 以上的房间数,4 星级酒店有 200 以上的房间数),一家典型的中国内地经济型酒店客房数为100～120 间。这些经济型酒店不参与全国星级评定,但是其客房质量可以与二、三星级酒店客房质量相比。这些酒店主要经营产品为客房,部分酒店自带小型餐厅,有些则连餐厅都没有。它们提供便利、简单、统一且具备基本舒适度的住宿产品。酒店选址一般具有较便捷性、可到达性,或者临近主要的商业区,或者靠近主要的交通枢纽。每晚价格一般在 100～300 元。这样的价位最贴近中国消费大众能够负担得起的区间。

opened. Compared to the traditional heavy equity hotel business mode in Chinese Mainland, the light equity mode of budget hotels in Chinese Mainland allows fast expansion, and is low investment, low risk, and quick return on investment.

Apart from the business mode of lease plus operation, most budget hotel companies prefer the operation mode of franchise plus management. This mode allows lower investment, and is thus favored by developers when there is limited capital. It also allows fast expansion by occupying the main markets. The profit margin under this mode might be lower, but the quality of the brands can be ensured. Most budget hotel companies focus more on their market occupation.

In addition, pure franchising is a supplement for the budget hotel companies for expansion. This mode leaves the operation completely at the hand of the franchisees. This may make the brands face risk of brand dilution. However, for the purpose of fast expansion, some budget hotels companies are willing to take this risk.

The main features of the budget hotels in Chinese Mainland include the following: first, compared to their full service counterparts (in Chinese Mainland, five star hotels usually have 350 rooms or above, and four star hotel above 200), budget hotels normally have 100~120 rooms. These hotels do not participate in star rating, but the quality of the hotel rooms are comparable to most 2~3 star hotels. Secondly, these budget hotels focus on the core product of guestroom. Some may have small restaurants, others do not. The hotels provide convenient, simple, and consistent product with minimum level of comfort. Thirdly, the locations of the budget hotels feature easy accessibility, being close to the CBD areas or major transportation hubs. Fourthly, budget hotels in Chinese Mainland target the mass tourists, and thus offer affordable prices at around 100~300 RMB per night.

第 11 章　中国内地主要连锁经济型酒店品牌简介

 学习目标

■ 了解中国内地经济型连锁酒店的主要品牌

　　如上所述,中国内地经济型酒店市场目前在引领位置的有如家酒店集团、7 天连锁、华住酒店集团以及锦江集团旗下的锦江之星。以下篇幅将具体介绍这四大巨头,并讨论这四大巨头的主要特点。

11.1　如家酒店集团

　　如家酒店集团创立于 2002 年,2006 年 10 月在美国纳斯达克上市(股票代码:HMIN)。如家酒店集团旗下拥有如家酒店、和颐酒店、莫泰酒店三大品牌,至本书写作之际已在全国 270 多座城市拥有连锁酒店 1900 多家,是目前国内最大的经济型连锁酒店。在其旗下三个品牌中,如家酒店(又称如家快捷)数量最多,知名度最广。该品牌的宗旨是提供标准化、干净、温馨、简洁、贴心的酒店住宿产品,提供安心、便捷的旅行住宿服务,传递着适度生活的简约生活理念。该酒店房价在 150～250 元人民币,根据区域和需求淡旺季,价格会有适度浮动。客户可以通过如家酒店集团官网、电话系统、携程及其他网络预订房间,非常便利。酒店的地理位置通常也比较便利(如家酒店集团官网,2015)。

Chapter 11   Major Budget Hotel Chains in Chinese Mainland

Learning Outcomes

■ Understanding the major budget hotel chains in Chinese Mainland

It is shown earlier that Home Inns, 7 Days Inn, China Lodge, and Jinjiang Inn are the four leading budget hotel chains in Chinese Mainland. This Chapter provides elaboration of these companies, with a discussion of the main features of their products.

11.1   Home Inns Hotel Group

Home Inn Hotel Group (Home Inns) was established in 2002, and got listed in NASDAQ in October, 2006. Currently, there are three brands under this hotel group—Home Inn, Yitel, and Motel (two other brands are to be developed). Home Inns now cover 270 cities across the country, with more than 1900 hotels, which makes Home Inns the biggest budget hotel chain in Chinese Mainland. Among the three brands,

Home Inn (also Home Inn Express) has largest number of hotels, and is more firmly established in the market. This brand boasts standard, clean, homey, simple, and sweet hotel product, which also features safe and convenience, conveying simple life concept. The price range is between 150~250 Yuan RMB depending on the location and seasons. Customers could book the hotel rooms via Home Inns' official website, telephone reservation system, Ctrip, and other intermediaries, which is very convenient. The locations of the hotels under Home Inns are usually convenient (Home Inn official website, 2015).

11.2　华住酒店集团

　　华住酒店集团创立于 2005 年。建立初期名为"汉庭酒店集团"。集团创始人季琦也是如家酒店创始人之一。在他的带领下,该集团于 2010 年在美国的纳斯达克成功上市。该集团主要以长三角、环渤海湾、珠三角和中西部发达城市为主,形成了密布的酒店网络。截至 2013 年,华住在中国超过 200 个城市里已经拥有 1400 多家酒店和 30000 多名员工,旗下拥有 6 个酒店品牌,包括商旅品牌——禧玥酒店、全季酒店、星程酒店、汉庭酒店、海友酒店,以及度假品牌——漫心度假酒店。这一系列品牌覆盖了从高端到平价、商务差旅到休闲度假的酒店类型(华住酒店集团官网,2014)。

11.3　7 天连锁

　　7 天连锁酒店(7 Days Inn)创立于 2005 年,2009 年 11 月 20 日在美国纽约证券交易所上市。2013 年 7 月 17 日,7 天连锁酒店被铂涛酒店集团成功私有化收购,成为该集团旗下的全资子品牌。截至 2013 年 11 月 30 日,7 天连锁酒店已拥有分店超 2000 家,覆盖全国超过 300 个主要城市。7 天连锁酒店建立的"7 天会"拥有会员达 7000 万,是中国内地经济型酒店中规模最大的会员体系。7 天连锁在被铂涛集团收购之前一直坚持单一酒店品牌的建设和运营,这也是 7 天连锁能够快速复制的主要原因之一。7 天品牌核心价值主张"年轻的选择"——在实现住宿功能需求的同时,追求简约品质旅途生活。在这个核心价值下,7 天最近在广州宣布,除现有 7 天酒店以外,另增加两个新的品牌——7 天优品和 7 天阳光。

华住酒店集团旗下七大品牌

11.2   China Lodge

China Lodge / Huazhu Hotel Group (formerly known as Hanting) was established in 2005. The founder of China Lodge, Mr. Ji Qi, was also the founding member of Home Inns. Under his leadership, China Lodge was listed in NASDAQ in 2010. The hotel group centers on the Yangtse River Delta, Bohai Bay, Pearl River Delta, and the developed areas in Mid and West areas in Chinese Mainland. Dense hotel network is formed. Up till 2013, China Lodge has over 1400 hotels in more than 200 cities, with over 30,000 staff members. There are six brands under China Lodge—Joya Hotel, All Seasons, Starway Hotel, Hanting Inn, Hi Inn, and Manxin Resort Hotel, covering hotel ranges from high end to low price hotels, and from business hotels to resort hotels (Huazhu official website, 2014).

11.3   7 Days Inn

7 Days Inn was established in 2005. It got successfully listed in New York Stock Exchange in November 2009. In July 2013, 7 Days Inn was acquired by Plateno Hotel Group and became one of the affiliating brands under the company. Up till November 2013, 7 Days Inn had over 2000 hotels in the country, covering 300 major cities. What 7 Days Inn is most proud of is that it has over 70 million of members, which is the largest membership system in budget hotels in Chinese Mainland. Before it was acquired by Plateno, 7 Days Inn persisted in single brand development and operation, which was one of the reasons that 7 Days Inn could replicate in a tremendous speed. The core value of 7 Days Inn is: choice of the young, achieving simple travel life while fulfilling the need of accommodation. Under this core value, 7 Days Inn recently announced in Guangzhou that it is going to have two new brands——7 Days Premium and 7 Days Sunshine.

Brands under China Lodge

7 天优品为一、二、三线城市市场提供更有品质、更为舒适的酒店产品；7 天阳光面向四、五线城市的县镇市场，在满足消费人群核心住宿需求的基础上，增强酒店的设计时尚感，提升酒店档次，适当增加会友聚客的功能（7 天连锁酒店官网，2014）。

11.4　锦江之星

锦江之星旅馆有限公司（简称锦江之星）是锦江国际集团旗下一家经营管理经济型连锁酒店的专业公司。作为中国内地首家经济型酒店，锦江之星自 1996 年创立至今，现已有 1000 家，连锁酒店网络广泛分布于全国 31 个省市自治区的 200 多个大中型城市，客房总数近 10 万间，已然成为中国内地最具影响力的经济型酒店品牌之一。锦江之星旗下的各品牌包括锦江之星酒店、金广快捷酒店、白玉兰酒店、百时快捷酒店（锦江之星官网，2015）。锦江之星在中国内地市场上的创立具有划时代的意义。在品牌产品的设计上也与中国内地传统酒店产品迥异。锦江之星因其清新洋气却又简约的风格而深得人心，快速赢得市场。

除以上简要描述，笔者通过对中国内地四大经济型连锁酒店集团的研究得出以下结论：首先，经济型酒店集团的发展速度快，快速占领市场份额是这四家经济型酒店集团共有的发展战略。其次，各经济型酒店集团地域覆盖广，四大经济型酒店集团均已覆盖中国内地大多数省份；再次，各大经济型酒店纷纷实行品牌多样化，以追求大市场下各细分市场份额最大化。尽管各集团的主打品牌依然是中低档的经济型酒店，但各集团已开始尝试中高端酒店品牌，比如如家的和颐和华住的全季。这些尝试虽然有成功也有失败，但是至少说明众酒店集团已经意识到中国的酒店市场在中档酒店方面的空缺。另外，各大经济型酒店均以便利的酒店预订平台为战略竞争优势，这也说明信息技术的发展对于经济型酒店的快速发展起到较大的影响作用。

11.5　经济型酒店客户

中国内地的经济型酒店发展至今，已经渐渐脱离了其发展初期对于西方经济型酒店设计和运行管理理念的依赖，并渐渐开创出适合中国内地大众消费者需求的经济型酒店产品。酒店集团及相关研究机构对中国内地大众消费者关于经济型酒店的消费行为及满意度的研究显示，经济型酒店客户的消

7 Days Premium provides better quality and more comfortable hotel products in first, second and third tier markets; while 7 Days Sunshine is targeted at fourth and fifth tier markets where smaller towns are located. The latter also attempts to provide a sense of fashion in design, upgrade the standard of the hotel, and add a party function to the hotels, apart from simply fulfilling the need for accommodation (7 Days Inn official website, 2014).

11.4   Jinjiang Inn

Jinjiang Inn is a budget hotel company under Jinjiang International. As the first budget hotel company in Chinese Mainland, it has now over 1000 hotels across the country covering over 200 cities in 31 provinces and autonomous regions in Chinese Mainland, with almost 100,000 rooms. It is now one of the most influential budget hotel companies, under with there are brands such as Jinjiang Inn, Golden Met Hotel, Magnotel, and Bestay (Jinjiang official website, 2015). The founding of Jinjiang Inn is the mark of era in the budget hotel sector in Chinese Mainland. The design of the product is very different from Chinese traditional hotels, and it has won the market with its fresh but simple style.

The following analysis is made based on the above brief introduction of the four leading budget hotel chains in Chinese Mainland. First of all, the growth rate of the budget hotel chains has been tremendous, and it is the common strategy of the four chains to occupy the market as fast as they could. Secondly, the geographic coverage of the four budget hotel chains is wide, covering most provinces and major cities in Chinese Mainland. Thirdly, the four budget hotel chains have started to achieve their product diversity, catering for different market segments. While their main focus of the four chains have been low price hotel products, they have started to engage in the mid and upper-mid markets. The examples include Yitel under Home Inns and All Seasons under China Lodge. These attempts have led to successes as well as failures. In addition, gauging convenient reservations systems for the customers has been a main strategy for the four companies, which proves the importance of information and communication technology in the development of budget hotel chains in Chinese Mainland.

11.5   Budget Hotel Customers in Chinese Mainland

Up till this moment, budget hotels in Chinese Mainland are no longer relying on the design and operation concept of those in western countries. Instead, they gradually root their development upon the needs of the customers of Chinese Mainland. Budget hotel

费者行为正在发生很大的变化。德勤(Deloitte，2009)对于经济型酒店客户的调查报告显示，此类型酒店的客户满意度为 80%，这说明总体来说经济型酒店在中国内地享有较高的受欢迎程度。报告显示，价格、地理位置、干净程度和服务质量是中国内地消费者选择经济型酒店最重要的因素。其中较年轻者更为关注价格，而较年长者更为关注酒店的地理位置。商务旅行者更关注经济型酒店的品牌。复旦大学在 2012 年的调查研究(Shen，2013)显示：中国内地经济型酒店顾客喜欢中等大小的房间(15～25 平方米)，他们选择经济型酒店的重要影响因素包括床、卫生情况、客房隔音、交通便利、早餐质量和分店数量。50%以上客户使用会员卡、优惠和积分卡，90%以上的客户通过电话或者网络预订。

以上对于经济型酒店客户的研究给经济型酒店管理和投资者们所带来的启示如下：首先，经济型酒店的开发和管理者需要着眼于酒店的核心要素——地理位置、便利因素、性价比、客房质量和服务质量。其次，酒店覆盖网络和品牌连锁酒店的质量与服务的一致性渐渐在发挥越来越重要的作用，并最终影响品牌的形象及集团的发展。再次，传统的酒店预订方式已经不再适用，网上预订平台及电话预订平台是经济型连锁酒店必备的条件。

companies and other research institutes have conducted surveys among the customers and found their consuming behavior is gradually changing. Deloitte's (2009) research among budget hotel customers in Chinese Mainland leads to the finding that the overall customer satisfaction is 80%, which is to say that this type of hotel product is welcomed by the mass tourists in Chinese Mainland. The research also shows that, for the customers of Chinese Mainland, price, location, cleanliness, and service quality are the most important factors when they select budget hotels. Among them, young travelers care more about the price, while the senior groups care more about the location of the hotel. For business people, branding is more important. Another survey conducted by Fudan University (Shen, 2013) shows that the Chinese budget hotel customers favor medium sized rooms(15 ～ 25 square meters). The survey also shows that factors including the comfort of the bed, hygiene situation, sound insulation, transportation convenience, the quality of the breakfast, and the number of hotels under the same hotel chain, are important for the customers. 50% of the customers have various types of membership or credit cards, while 90% of the customers book the rooms via internet or telephone.

The lessons learned from the above studies on budget hotel customers in Chinese Mainland are of significant reference for budget hotel managers and developers. Firstly, the developers and managers should focus on the core elements of the budget hotel product—location, convenience, value for money, quality of the room, and service quality are the landing points for the budget hotel businesses. Secondly, the geographic coverage and the concept of branding, as well as the consistency of quality product and service are getting more and more important, which will eventually influence the image and the development of the hotel companies. Moreover, traditional reservation approach is no longer popular among the customers, instead, internet and telephone reservation is a critical condition for the budget hotels.

第 12 章 中国经济型酒店发展趋势及战略研究

 学习目标

- 了解中国内地经济型酒店行业的发展趋势
- 了解中国内地经济型酒店行业的发展战略

12.1 高增长潜力

据统计,目前中国内地经济型酒店在整个中国内地酒店市场中所占比重仅为 18%,远远少于美国的 70%。因此,中国内地的经济型酒店增长空间较大。据专家估计,未来的 5~10 年将是中国内地经济型酒店持续增长的阶段。汉庭创始人季琦先生在最近的发言中谈论到中国内地经济型酒店的大规模市场。信息的流通和度假市场的兴起直接推动了经济型酒店的发展。中国内地的城市化进程计划间接暗示了经济型酒店增长的巨大空间。如果按照人口数量或者按照能够消费经济型酒店的人口数量来算,中国内地的人口和经济型酒店数量还不成正比,由此可见,中国内地经济型酒店在未来的几年内将继续保持高增长势头。

12.2 中低档为主、品牌多样化的发展路线

据盈蝶咨询 2012 年的中国经济型酒店行业报告,就全国而言,对于经济型酒店的价格接受度,依然在 151~200 元。有 27.25% 的客户可接受范围在 201~300 元。这个数据主要来自京、沪、杭等一线城市的品牌商务连锁酒店。对于经济型酒店的主要客源来说,301 元以上的价格,接受度最低,仅占 4.63%,这主要取决于个别酒店在城市中所占据的绝佳地理位置。而针对 300 元以上

Chapter 12   Developing Trends and Strategies of the Budget Hotels in Chinese Mainland

 Learning Outcomes

■ Understanding the development trend of the budget hotel industry in Chinese Mainland
■ Understanding the development strategies of the budget hotel industry in Chinese Mainland

12.1   High Growth Potential

It is estimated that budget hotels only accounted for 18% of total number of hotels in Chinese Mainland, which is far less than the 70% in the USA. Therefore, there is still huge development space in this area in Chinese Mainland. Experts predict that this hotel sector will continue to grow in the next five to ten years (Ji, 2014). Mr. Ji from China Lodge contends that the information flow and the emergence of the holiday market directly drive the growth budget hotels in Chinese Mainland (Ji, 2014). Moreover, the progress of urbanization in Chinese Mainland also indicates the huge developing potential for budget hotels. Calculating the numbers of budget hotels in Chinese Mainland against the population which could afford the consumption of budget hotel products, the percentage is still small. Based on the above, it can be concluded that the budget hotel sector is going to continue its growth in the years to come.

12.2   Focusing on Mid and Low Level Budget Hotels, while Achieving Multi-branding

According to Inntie (2012) report on budget hotel industry, the most acceptable price range among the customers nationwide is still between 151 and 200 Yuan RMB. For the 27.25% of customers who can accept the price range of 201~300 Yuan RMB is mostly from the first tier cities of Beijing, Shanghai, and Hangzhou, and the customers mostly stay in business type budget hotels. Only 4.63% of the customers can accept prices over 301 Yuan RMB, which depends much on the location of the hotels. For the market that is beyond 300 RMB, customers care more about the differentiation and functions of the hotels. Based on the above results, it is evident that budget hotels in near future will

的市场,可能更多地要考虑酒店产品的差异化和功能性。由此可见,未来 5～10 年甚至 20 年内中国内地的经济型酒店市场还是以中低档为主线、中档及中高档为辅。与此同时,品牌多样化将是各经济型酒店集团追求的趋势。

12.3　未来核心战略

然而,随着这个市场的逐渐成熟,市场竞争已经从蓝海战役转为红海战役。未来的经济型酒店战略核心显然将发生巨大的转变。以下未来战略核心是笔者总结各专家和市场研究而得出的。

1. 品牌战略

中国内地经济型酒店的发展已经进入品牌竞争时代,而且这种竞争将日趋激烈。当顾客可以选择的空间变大的时候,品牌就变得很重要了。中国内地消费者越来越重视品牌,这在很多报告中都有所提及。比如德勤的报告提到,对于商务客人来讲,经济型酒店品牌很重要(Deloitte,2009)。季琦先生在最近的言论中也提到"中国更需要品牌"。人们需要通过品牌来区分产品的种类、档次、风格以及品质。随着中国内地消费大众对品牌的重视度日渐增加,经济型酒店也避免不了品牌战。

目前,尽管多数经济型连锁酒店集团采用多品牌战略,但是除少数集团外,多数经济型酒店还处于初始发展阶段,因此品牌战略对它们来说还很新鲜。尽管如此,品牌的建设和维护将不可避免地成为未来经济型酒店市场的主要竞争优势之一。

2. 信息技术

信息技术对大型经济型连锁酒店集团的经营和管理,以及市场营销来说起着关键性的作用。其所覆盖内容包括日常运行和管理、财务管理、预订以及会员管理等。信息技术在经济型连锁酒店的地位将越来越重要。以预订为例,盈蝶咨询 2009 年的经济型酒店住客调查资料显示,67% 的商旅住客喜欢在网上直接预订客房,另有 70% 以上的住客直接从网络上获取酒店相关信息。华住酒店集团把自己定位成一个带有网络基因的酒店集团(华住酒店集团官网,2014),并且认为

still focus on the mid-lower end of the market, supplemented by mid-upper end product. At the same time, multi-branding is going to be the trend and strategy of the budget hotel companies.

12.3　Future Competitive Strategies

Nevertheless, as the budget hotel sector in Chinese Mainland gradually gets mature, the market has turned to red sea battlefield from a blue sea battlefield. The competitive strategies of the budget hotel companies are changing too. The following are a few noticeable competitive strategies based on various studies.

1. Branding Strategy

The development of budget hotels in Chinese Mainland has entered an era of branding competition, and this trend is going to be ever more intensive. When the customers have more choices nowadays, the concept of branding becomes more important. The customers of Chinese Mainland emphasize brands, and this is well known. For example, Deloitte (2009) mentioned that branding is important for business customers. Mr. Ji Qi has similar assertion in recent speech that "Chinese people see more in branding". People infer category, level, style, and quality of the products according to brands. Therefore, it is unavoidable for the budget hotel sector to adopt branding as its main competitive strategy as the mass travelers attach more importance to branding.

Currently, brand development for many budget hotels companies are still in the initial stage, although the leading chains have successfully developed its multi-branding strategy. The concept of the branding for many companies is still novel. Nevertheless, the brand construction and maintenance are going to be the focus of future budget hotel sector.

2. Information Technology

Information technology (IT) is key to the operation, management, and marketing of budget hotel chains. The application of information technology covers daily operation and management, financial management, reservation, membership management, and so on. The importance of IT is going to be ever greater. Taking reservation for example, as early as 2009, Inntie (2009) has identified that 67% of business and tourism customers like to reserve hotel rooms on internet, while over 70% of the customers obtain information of the hotels via websites. China Lodge has positioned itself as a hotel group with the gene of internet (Huazhu official website, 2014). In addition, social media nowadays has profound impact on the development of hotels. Taking Home

除了以上功能之外,社交网络媒介对于酒店集团的发展起到很大的影响作用。对于如家来说,信息技术在管理中的应用是如家取得快速拓展的关键因素之一(Zhang 等,2013)。7 天更是如此,7 天的创业团队本身就是 IT 精英,他们深谙信息技术能够在连锁酒店中发挥的巨大作用,因此整个集团的运作从一开始便是以 IT 为竞争砝码的。

3. 会员制

截至 2013 年年底,华住会员数量为 1500 万,并且 90% 的客房预订来源于华住会员(华住酒店集团官网,2014)。7 天目前拥有 7000 万会员,这无疑是 7 天以及 7 天目前所属的铂涛集团在未来的酒店市场竞争中最大的优势。据估计,会员对 7 天收入的贡献率高达 98%。庞大的会员体系大大减少了对第三方代理的依赖,节省了中介代理费用,并将更多的利益回馈给顾客。

4. 服务质量

如果提倡会员制的目的是增加回头客、提高顾客忠诚度的话,那么在当今中国经济型酒店市场中,服务质量将对此发挥很大的影响作用。对于经济型酒店客户,转换成本很低,且很多会员同时是多家经济型酒店集团的会员,因此选择哪家酒店将会很大程度上受服务质量的影响。这就又回到了之前的话题——品牌的建立和维护。

Inns for example, studies have found that the application of IT is one of the critical success factors of the company (Zhang, et al., 2013). 7 Days Inn is even more so. The company itself is comprised of a team of IT elites, who firmly understands the important role of IT in budget hotels, and therefore 7 Days Inn adopts IT as its competitive advantage from Day One.

3. Membership

Up till the end of 2013, Huazhu has 15 million members, and 90% of reservation comes from its members (Huazhu official website, 2014). 7 Days Inn now has over 70 million members, which is the biggest competitive advantage that 7 Days Inn brings to Plateno. According to estimation, membership contributes 98% of business to 7 Days Inn. Such large membership system greatly reduces the companies' reliance to third party distributors, saving intermediary cost, and can therefore benefit the customers more with the cost saved.

4. Service quality

If the membership system retains customer loyalty by attracting repeat customers, service quality plays equally important role in the budget hotel market. For budget hotel customers, the switching cost is low. At the same time, many customers may hold multiple membership cards to many budget hotel chains. Therefore, eventually service quality is the factor that influences customers' choice. This brings back the topic to the construction and maintenance of brands.

参考文献
References

Accor（2015）. *Accor Annual Report* 2014. Retrieved from http://www. accorhotels-group. com/en/finance/financial-library/regulated-information/annual-financial-report.html May 2015.

Aledo，A.，&Mazon，T.（2004）. Impact of residential tourism and the destination life cycle theory. In F.D. Pineda，C.A. Brebbia，& M. Mugica（Eds.），*Sustainable Tourism*（pp. 25 – 36）. Southampton：WIT Press.

Allen，L.R.，Hafer，H.R.，Long，P.T.，et al.（1993）. Rural residents' attitudes toward recreation and tourism development. *Journal of Travel Research*，31(4)，27 – 33.

Boley，B.B.，& McGehee，N.G.（2014）. Measuring empowerment：Developing and validating the Resident Empowerment through Tourism Scale（RETS）. *Tourism Management*，45，85 – 94.

Brotherton，B.（2004）. Critical success factors in UK budget hotel operations. *International Journal of Operations & Production Management*，24(9)，944 – 969.

CEIC China Database（2016）. *CEIC data*.［Online］. Retrieved on April 20，2016 from http://ceicdata.securities.com/cdmWeb/data Manager.html? languageCode＝zh［Authorized access］.

Chen，M-H.，& Kim，W. G.（2010）. Hotel Valuation in China：A Case Study of a State-Owned Hotel. *Cornell Hospitality Quarterly*，51：429 – 445.

Choi，H. C.，& Sirakaya，E.（2005）. Measuring residents' attitude toward sustainable tourism：Development of sustainable tourism attitude scale. *Journal of Travel Research*，43(4)，380 – 394.

Chow，V.（2012）. Anger at mainland visitors escalates with "Locust" Ad. *South China Morning Post*，February 1，City 1.

CHTA（China Tourism Hotel Association）.（2011）. *The Year Book of China*

Hotel. Beijing: China Tourism Press.

China Hospitality Association（CHA）&Inntie（2018）.*Chinese Hotel Chain Development and Investment Report 2017*.Retrieved from: http://www.chinahotel. org.cn/on 07/04/2018.

Deloitte.（2009）. *Survey on business travelers*. Retrieved on August 31, 2012 from www.deloitte.com.

Diedrich，A.，& Garcia-Buades，E.（2009）. Local perceptions of tourism as indicators of destination decline. *Tourism Management*，30(4)，512 – 521.

Eyster，J.，& de Roos，J（2009）. *The Negotatiation and Administration of Hotel Management Contracts*. 4th edition. London: Pearson Custom Publishing.

Euromonitor International（2012）. *Tourism Outbound Flows of China*. London: Euromonitor International.

Dev，C.S.，Thomas，J. H.，Buschman，J.，et al.（2010）. Brand rights and hotel management agreements. *Cornell Hospitality Quarterly*，51(2):215 – 230.

Enz，C. A.（2010）. *Hospitality strategic management: concepts and cases*.2nd edition. New Jersey: John Wiley & Sons，Inc.

Gilbert，D.，& Lockwood，A.（1990）. Budget hotels—the USA，France and UK compared. *EIU Travel & Tourism Analyst*，No. 3. —Hotels / Accommodations.

Gross，M. J.，& Huang，S.（2011）. Exploring the internationalization prospects of a Chinese domestic hotel firm. *International Journal of Contemporary Hospitality Management*，23(2):261 – 274.

Guillet，B. D.，Zhang，H. Q.，& Gao，B. W.（2011）. Interpreting the mind of multinational hotel investors: Future trends and implications in China. *International Journal of Hospitality Management*，30(2)，222 – 232.

Harris，S.（2000）. Comments: The future of the European branded budget hotel sector.*Journal of Leisure Property*，1(2):113 – 118.

Hilton Worldwide.（2015）. *Hilton Worldwide Annual Report* 2014. Retrieved from http://ir.hiltonworldwide.com/financial-reporting/annual-reports May 2015.

HNN（Hotel News Now）（2015）. *Hotel News Now Special Report — The* 2015 *Big Brands Report*. Retrieved from http://www. hotelnewsnow. com/media/File/PDFs/ Misc/BIG%20BRANDS% 20REPORT%202015_compressed.pdf. May 2015.

Homeinns Offical Website（2015）. http://english.homeinns.com/phoenix.zhtml? c＝203641&p

=irol-IRHome (Accessed in April，2015)

Hong Kong Census & Statistics Department （2012）. 2011 *Population Census*. Retrieved on September 15，2105，from http://www. statistics. gov. hk/pub/ B11200552011XXXXB0100.pdf.

Hong Kong SAR （2014）. *Hong Kong Monthly Digest of Statistics—November*. Hong Kong：The Author.

Hong Kong Tourism Board （2014）. *Visitor Arrival Statistics—December* 2014. Hong Kong：The Author.

Hotel （2014）. *Hotel* 325 *Special Report* 2013. Retrieved from http://www. marketingandtechnology. com/repository/webFeatures/hotels/023 _ h1207 _ Special _ Report_325_iPad.pdf May 2015.

Hsueh，C.T. （2013）. *The Effects of Psychographics on Behavioral Intention—A Study of Mainland Chinese Leisure Tourists to Taiwan*. The Hong Kong Polytechnic University DHTM thesis.

Huazhu Official Website （2014）. http://www.huazhu.com/.（Accessed in March 2014）

IHG （2014）. *IHG Annual Report* 2014. Retrieved from http://www.ihgplc.com/ files/reports/ar2014/ May 2015.

Inntie. （2009）.*Survey on future needs of budget hotel customers，2009*. Retrieved from：www.inn.net.cn （retrieved on 31-08-2012）

Jinjiang Official Website （2015）. http://www. jinjianghotels. com. cn/En/. （Accessed in April，2015）

Lankford，S.V.，& Howard，D.R. （1994）. Developing a tourism impact attitude scale. *Annals of Tourism Research*，21(1)，121–139.

Latkova，P.，& Vogt，C.A. （2012）. Residents' attitudes toward existing and future tourism development in rural communities. *Journal of Travel Research*，51(1)，50–67.

Liu，A.，&McKercher，B. （2014）. The impact of visa liberalization on tourist behaviors—The case of China outbound market visiting Hong Kong. *Journal of Travel Research*，55(5)，603–611.

Lynch，K. （1960）.*The Image of The City*. Cambridge，MA：MIT Press.

Marriot （2015）. *Marriot International Annual Report* 2014. Retrieved from http://investor.shareholder.com/mar/marriottAR14/index.html May 2015.

Pearce，P.L.（1977）. Mental souvenirs: A study of tourists and their city maps. *Australian Journal of Psychology*，29（3），203－210.

Pearce，P.L.（1982）. Tourists and their hosts: Some social and psychological effects of inter-cultural contact. In S.Bochner（ed.）. *Cultures in contact: Studies in cross-cultural interaction*（p. 199）. New York,: Pergamon Press.

Perdue，R.R.，Long，P.T.，& Allen，L.（1990）. Resident support for tourism development. *Annals of Tourism Research*，17（4），586－599.

Pine，R.（2002）. China's hotel industry: serving a massive market. *Cornell Hotel and Restaurant Administration Quarterly*，43：61－70

Robinson，G.，&Nemetz，L.（1988）. *Cross-Cultural Understanding*. Harlow: Prentice Hall.

Ruetz，D.，& Marvel，M.（2011）. Budget Hotels: Low Cost Concepts in the US，Europe and Asia. In R. Conrady，& M. Buck（eds），*Trends and Issues in Global Tourism 2011*. Heidelberg: Springer Verlag.

Shen，H（2013）. The Development of Economy Hotels in China. *J. of Hotel Bus Manage*. 2: e104. doi:10.4172/2169-0286.1000e104.

Starwood（2015）. *Starwood Annual Report* 2014. Retrieved from http://www. starwoodhotels. com/corporate/about/investor/reports. html? language ＝ en ＿ US May 2015.

STR（Smith Travel Research）.（2015）. 2015 *STR Global Chain Scales*. Retrieved on March 2017，from http://www. cheiorg. com/Uploads/Editor/2017-04-19/58f6f67abf98b.pdf.

The Hong Kong Polytechnic University（2016）. *Toward Sustainability: Exploring the Social and Economic Dimensions of Travel to Hong Kong by Mainland Chinese*. Hong Kong: The Author.

Triandis，H.C.（1977）. Subjective culture and interpersonal relations across cultures. Issues in Cross-Cultural Research. *Annals of New York Academy of Sciences*，285，418－434.

United Nations World Tourism Organization.（2001）. *Tourism* 2020 *vision*. Madrid: Author.

United Nations World Tourism Organization（2006）. *China—The Asia and the Pacific Intra-regional Outbound Series*. Madrid: Author.

United Nations World Tourism Organization（2012）. *The Chinese Outbound*

Travel Market. Madrid: Author.

United Nations World Tourism Organization (2015). *Tourism Highlights* 2015. Madrid: Author.

United Nations World Tourism Organization (2016). *Yearbook of tourism statistics*. Madrid: Author.

Wen Wei Po. (2010).Mainland mothers giving birth in Hong Kong do not regret. *Wen Wei Po*, August 2 p. A02.

Woosnam, K.M. (2012). Using emotional solidarity to explain residents' attitudes about tourism and tourism development. *Journal of Travel Research*, 51(3), 315 - 327.

Wyndham (2015). *Company Backgrounder*. Retrieved from www.wynham.com May 2015.

Yang, J., Ryan, C., & Zhang, L. (2014). Sustaining culture and seeking a Just Destination: Governments, power and tension—A life-cycle approach to analysing tourism development in an ethnic-inhabited scenic area in Xinjiang, China. *Journal of Sustainable Tourism*, 22(8), 1151 - 1174.

Ye, B. H., Zhang, H. Q., & Yuen, P. P. (2013). Cultural conflicts or cultural cushion?. *Annals of Tourism Research*, 43, 321 - 349.

Ye, B.H., Zhang, H.Q., & Yuen, P.P. (2011). Motivations and experiences of Mainland Chinese medical tourists in Hong Kong. *Tourism Management*, 32(5), 1125 - 1127.

Ye, B. H., Zhang, H. Q., & Yuen, P.P. (2012). An empirical study of anticipated and perceived discrimination of Mainland Chinese tourists in Hong Kong: The role of intercultural competence. *Journal of China Tourism Research*, 8(4), 417 - 430.

Yu, L. (1992).Seeing stars: China's hotel-rating system. *The Cornell H.R.A. Quarterly*, 24 - 27.

Yu, L., & Gu, H. (2005). Hotel reform in China: A SWOT analysis. *Cornell Hotel and Restaurant Administration Quarterly*, 46: 153 - 169.

Zhang, G. R., Pine, R., & Zhang, Q. H. (2000). China's international tourism development: The present and future. *International Journal of Contemporary Hospitality Management*, 12(5): 282 - 290.

Zhang, H. Q., Ren, L, Shen, H., et al.(2013).What contribntes to the success of Home Inns in China? *International Journal of Hospitality Management*, 33,425 - 434.

7 Days Inn Official Website. (2014). http://www.7daysinn.cn/about.html. (accessed in March 2014)

谷慧敏，秦宇.（2010）.中国旅游企业年度报告 2010.北京：旅游教育出版社.

国家旅游局监督管理司、中国旅游研究院.（2011）.中国产业发展报告——饭店集团篇.北京：中国旅游出版社.

季琦.（2014）.中国经济型酒店仍将持续"牛市".中国旅游报，2014-03-05.Retrieved from http://info.meadin.com/IndustryReport/98207_1.shtml.

科尔尼.（2013）.中国酒店业的未来发展. Retrieved on April 2015，from www.atkearney.cn.

李志平.（2009）.中国经济型酒店成功之道.上海：上海交通大学出版社.

马勇，陈雪钧.（2008）.饭店集团品牌建设与创新管理].北京：中国旅游出版社.

迈点旅游研究院（Meadin Tourism Institute）.（2014）.2013 年中国酒店业品牌发展报告. Retrieved on April 2015，from http://res.meadin.com.

邱汉琴.（2014）.港澳中年轻上班族赴中国内地旅游研究报告.香港：香港理工大学.

邱汉琴.（2015）.港澳中老年人赴中国内地旅游研究报告.香港：香港理工大学.

盈蝶咨询.（2015）.2015 中国酒店连锁发展与投资报告. Retrieved on 30th，April，2015，from Http://www.inn.net.cn/a/baogao/yanjiu/2015/0422/1478.html.

盈蝶咨询.（2013）.2013 中国酒店连锁发展与投资报告. Retrieved on 30th，April，2015，from Http://www.inn.net.cn/a/baogao/yanjiu/2013/0422/1478.html.

袁宗堂.（2001）.中国旅游饭店发展之路.北京：中国旅游出版社.

中国国家旅游局（CNTA）.（2016）.2015 年中国旅游统计年鉴.北京：中国旅游出版社.

中国国家旅游局（CNTA）.（2014）.2013 年中国旅游统计年鉴.北京：中国旅游出版社.

中国酒店采购报.（2015）. China Hotel Purchase News.中国酒店采购报，2015-01-15 .

中国旅游报（2014）.2013 年度中国饭店集团 60 强名单. Retrieved on April 2015，from http://www.ctnews.com.cn/zglyb/html/2014-07/02/content_92315.htm? div=-1&WebShieldDRSessionVerify = Xw7bu5lff9CxcyOjNlYa&WebShieldSessionVerify = Xw7bu5lff9CxcyOjNlYa.